DATE DUE

5 00186955	
May 5/97	

CREATIVITY AND WORK

EMOTIONS AND BEHAVIOR
MONOGRAPHS
Monograph No. 9

edited by
George H. Pollock, M.D., Ph.D.
Chicago Institute for Psychoanalysis

Creativity and Work

by
ELLIOTT JAQUES
M.A., M.D., Ph.D., F.R.C.P.

INTERNATIONAL UNIVERSITIES PRESS, INC.
Madison   Connecticut

Library of Congress Cataloging-in-Publication Data

Jaques, Elliott.
  Creativity and work / by Elliott Jaques.
    p. cm.—(Emotions and behavior monographs; monograph no. 9)
  Reprinted from various sources.
  Includes bibliographies and index.
  ISBN 0-8236-1088-8
    1. Work—Psychological aspects. 2. Creative ability. I. Title.
  II. Series: Emotions and behavior monographs; no. 9.
    [DNLM: 1. Creativeness—collected works. 2. Work—collected works.
  W1 EM673 no. 9 / BF 481 J36c]
  HF5548.8.J27 1990
  158.7—dc19
  DNLM/DLC
  for Library of Congress
                                                              88-13641
                                                              CIP

Manufactured in the United States of America

Contents

Introduction

The theme around which I have chosen to select these essays is contained in the title. It is about the conditions under which people can work effectively and creatively—on their own and together with others. By conditions, I refer not simply to the psychological state of individuals, nor to the social or institutional circumstances within which they work, but to both. Creativity emerges from individuals finding or being given opportunities to work at their full level of capability.

In the above sense, then, all work is creative in principle. Goal-directed behavior requires the continuous play of thought, imagination, judgment, and decision making. Computers will never be able to do it. Work becomes uncreative when people are underemployed; that is to say, when the level of work they are doing is beneath that which they could do. And unfortunately in our industrial society, far too many people are either unemployed, or if employed, then underutilized.

What then is work? It may be noted that all human behavior falls into two main categories, goal-directed and non-goal-directed behavior. The latter, non-goal-directed behavior, comprises musing, reverie, dreaming, free-floating fantasy. The former or goal-directed behavior is, simply, work.

By work I refer to *all* goal-directed behavior. I do not

hold with the common or vulgar definition of work as being something we do because we have to do it, or do just for money. Work thus includes not only the work we do for a living, but also "creative" work, recreational work (goal-directed play activities), house- and homework, parental work, and so on. Work in this broad sense is necessary for sustaining psychological integration and life itself.

Creativity, in the sense in which it is used as referring to artistic or intellectual creativity, I take as simply one particular kind of work. It is work whose direction and goals arise almost exclusively from the inner world of the individual rather than from external injunction or for external purposes. But just because it arises internally does not mean for me that there are particular unconscious fantasy systems which can explain outstanding creativity. Fantasy enters into all work—and creative genius in its artistic sense arises from the same cognitive sources of outstanding capability as is the case for all work—except that the artist focuses upon getting internally generated thoughts out onto canvas or manuscript. The contents arise from unconscious fantasy and working-through of unconscious conflicts, but the greatness, I believe, arises as for all kinds of work, from the scale of complexity of the individual and the corresponding scale of the world which he or she can pattern and live in.

The essays in this book thus range from those mainly focused upon social institutions to those which are more focused upon individual functioning. The first two essays argue for a true science of society as the basis for developing a truly human society with industrialization. There then follow three essays written specially for this book, which treat of: the interplay between complexity as it exists in tasks in the social world; levels of complexity of cognitive processes in the individual and their iso-morphism with levels of task complexity; and the ma-turation of cognitive complexity and working capability in individuals.

The next four essays deal with connections between the psychological experience of uncertainty which is cen-tral to work, and the balance between intensity of un-certainty, felt level of work, and the sense of fair reward. These essays lead into three others which pursue the theme of level of work and how this can be measured by reference to time-spans of discretion, and a study of the nature of the experience of time.

"Death and the Midlife Crisis" stands on its own as a study of creativity which led to my formulation of the concept of the midlife crisis. And the book ends with four essays on some of the unconscious sources of social be-havior, social relationships, and social justice, and of psy-chopathology in work.

About half the essays were printed previously in *Work, Creativity and Social Justice* (1970). The present book might be thought of as a completely revised edition of that work.

Acknowledgments

A number of these papers have been printed or read before, and some of them appear here in an amended form. My thanks are due to the publishers for their permission to reprint:

"The Science of Society": Inaugural address on becoming Professor and Head of the School of Social Sciences, Brunel University; published in *Human Relations*, Vol. 19, No. 2, 1966.

"The Human Consequences of Industrialization": *Work, Creativity and Social Justice*, Heinemann Educational Books Ltd., London, 1970.

"Notes on the Psychological Meaning of Work": *Measurement of Responsibility*, Heinemann Educational Books Ltd., London, 1956.

"Learning for Uncertainty": *Work, Creativity and Social Justice*, Heinemann Educational Books Ltd., London, 1970.

"Theses on Work and Creativity": *Work, Creativity and Social Justice*, Heinemann Educational Books Ltd., London, 1970.

"The Work–Payment–Capacity Nexus": *Equitable Payment*, Heinemann Educational Books Ltd., London, 1961.

"The Conscious, Preconscious, and Unconscious Experience Called Time": *The Form of Time*, New York, Crane Russak, 1982.

"Time and the Measurement of Human Attributes": *Work, Creativity and Social Justice*, Heinemann Educational Books Ltd., London, 1970.

"Quantification in the Human Sciences": *The Form of Time*, New York, Crane Russak, 1982.

"Death and the Midlife Crisis": *International Journal of Psycho-Analysis*, Vol. 46, Part 4, 1965.

"Disturbances in the Capacity to Work": *International Journal of Psycho-Analysis*, Vol. 41, Parts 4–5, 1960.

"A Contribution to a Discussion of Freud's *Group Psychology and the Analysis of the Ego*": *Work, Creativity and Social Justice*, Heinemann Educational Books Ltd., London, 1970.

"Psychotic Anxieties and the Sense of Justice": *Work, Creativity and Social Justice*, Heinemann Educational Books Ltd., London, 1970.

"Guilt, Conscience, and Social Behavior": *Work, Creativity and Social Justice*, Heinemann Educational Books Ltd., London, 1970.

Chapter 1

The Science of Society

I

Although, in this scientific age, after 300 years of technical advance, we have come to recognize the revolutionary difference that a scientific approach can make in solving apparently intractable problems, we must yet ask why there is so little development in the use of scientific method in the government, in administration, and in the management of society and its institutions.

By government, administration, and management of society and its institutions, I am referring not to vague generalities, but specifically to the institutions that we ourselves take part in, or that affect us: our educational system and modes of teaching in schools; the structure and location of our cities and towns; our health service and administration of hospitals; how authority and responsibility are distributed in the relationship between government and nationalized industries; the organization and running of civil service departments, trade unions, and universities; the structure of responsibility for decisions in the management of industrial and commercial enterprises. In short, I refer to all types of institution in our society.

Our current mode of administering and managing our institutions is mainly by custom and practice built upon unchecked assumptions and conventions. We modify, adapt, and develop these methods by means of intuitive judgment, opinion, guesswork, and rule-of-thumb, or by debating and arguing with each other within a framework of various types of political philosophy.

This empirical, rule-of-thumb approach works not badly up to a point, so long as there is not too much disagreement about objectives and methods. But even at its best, modern social life cannot be said to be so satisfactorily arranged that the introduction of disciplined scientific thinking could not help to improve matters. Why, then, do we move so slowly and reluctantly in this direction? If we had at least a strong desire for a disciplined approach to the problems, there would be apparent in each of us the signs of resolute endeavor to forward research and thus increase our knowledge. It is the existence of the resolve and desire that I would question.

For let us make no mistake—it simply cannot be taken for granted that scientific knowledge, and its use to advance the satisfaction and well-being of mankind, are unreservedly accepted in our society. I do not, of course, refer to verbal acceptance. Nearly everyone will say he is in favor of science. It is like saying one is in favor of racial equality. There's no hardship in that! But being verbally in favor of science is a far cry from accepting the personal implications of the use of disciplined description of our own institutions and behavior as a practical everyday guide to our own decisions and actions.

For now we must seek to understand not only the inanimate world around us, but also the social world of which we form a part. We must have the courage to seek disciplined descriptions and adequate models of ourselves, individually and in relation to each other; of the social institutions in which we take up roles—at work, at home, and at leisure; of the larger social environment of the nation and of the world, in which we cooperate and survive, or fight and die.

Disciplined description meets resistance, for it seems to challenge the freedom of the human spirit—the freedom of ideas. What in fact is challenged is a spurious freedom, one not worth preserving. It is the freedom to believe that, because we think something, then it must be so—a kind of *cogito ergo est!* We resent losing the freedom to have our own personal models: prejudices about the effects of the death penalty; stereotypes about workers and business tycoons; fantasies about the best way to overcome the problems of the adolescent; opinions about whether comprehensive schools are best; illusions about the existence of absolute principles and policies—not to mention our anxiety about the possibility of losing relative position and privilege.

Francis Bacon (1620) described this resistance as "the rejection of difficult things from impatience of research; sober things because they narrow hope; the deeper things of nature from superstition; the light of experience from arrogance and pride . . ." (p. 134).

Freud explained it as the unconscious impulse in each one of us to seek the primitive state in which everything is magically pleasurable, in preference to the pain and limitation, albeit the maturity, of living under the constraint of the reality principle.

II

The anxiety about freedom shows in countless ways. One of these ways—and a most important one, widespread in its manifestations—is the cultivation of vagueness and confusion in our own organizations. The slogan is: "Let us leave it vague so that individual creativeness can have a greater chance!" Even some social scientists favor this

outlook, and express it in the concept of informal organization; that is to say, in purposely leaving unspecified
the responsibility in certain areas of organization, in
which individual endeavor is allowed to express itself in
personal networks, idiosyncratic to the persons who happen to be in the organization at a given time. Perhaps
the best illustration is provided by so-called old-boy networks.

Many readers will be familiar with an expression of
the reliance upon vagueness in the sections in the Robbins report (Ministry of Education, 1963) dealing with
the government of universities. I choose this example
because it is such an immediate issue to those connected
with universities and it may thereby help to illustrate
one of my main themes, which is that the point of social
science is its application to our own institutions, so that
it touches our own personal lives.

"Universities," the report states in discussing where
ultimate authority lies, "are no exception to the general
rule that a great gulf lies between constitutions on paper
and government in practice. A description of the function
and composition of the statutory bodies is not necessarily
an analysis of the real sources of initiative and power;
these depend partly on the imponderables of specific circumstances and individual personalities, and are almost
impossible to determine" (p. 87). Later, in regard to major
policy issues such as decisions about the size of the university and of the individual faculties, it says: "Such policy-making is thus essentially in the hands of the senior
academic staff" (p. 112), although it recognizes that this
arrogated power of the senior professors often frustrates
the reasonable expectations of the governors and the
other members of staff to take a greater part in policy-
making.

As a result of vaguely formulated constitutions of this

kind, some of the most crucial issues for the development of university policy are left vague and unresolved. Through confusion of the question of de jure authority, which can be identified, with that of de facto power, which must always be a dynamic field of changing forces, the major question of where the nation can locate accountability for the policy of the individual university is left vague and unsettled. And we are all aware what stress and tension and pain can be engendered by this vagueness. There is accepted by default what the report recognizes as "a system of government . . . which is based on an elaborate committee structure" (p. 114)—a structure which leaves the question of final accountability no clearer.

That this vagueness is something more than just an accident or oversight is demonstrated in a more explicit statement in the report on the role of the Vice-Chancellor. Here it is stated: "His is a role which, probably fortunately, is seldom precisely spelt out in written constitutions. Yet it would be difficult to overstate its importance, particularly in a period of expansion, which calls for imagination and continuous initiative" (p. 168). What the report fails to note in this praise of vagueness is its inconsistency with the statement further down the same paragraph that "governing bodies should give serious attention to improving their organization" (p. 168) with regard to the variety and burden of work of the Vice-Chancellor. Such improvement cannot be achieved for a role which is imprecisely defined.

I have quoted at some length from the Robbins report, not for the purpose of singling it out for criticism, but merely to illustrate how readily we accept the hope that issues of great moment will sort themselves out if only they are left sufficiently vague. Even in such a scholarly report, with its generally meticulous concern for fact, the emphasis is certainly not on the urgent need for a practical and systematic attack upon the problems mentioned. Nor is there even any evidence of regret that a more comprehensive and systematic solution was not available. No, somehow the interests of freedom—in this case academic freedom—are felt to be better served by lack of clarity.

III

We may ask, however, if our hanging on to descriptions we know intuitively to be inaccurate or incomplete really matters. Is this anxiety about what would happen if we tried to describe ourselves and our social environment more clearly of any great significance? Do we need, after all, to have such clarity and precision in our descriptions and our statements of policy, of organization, of principle, of authority and responsibility, of individual behavior? Are we not in danger of becoming too formal about these things? I do not believe that we are in such a danger. The danger lies in leaving things too informal, too vague.

These questions all have the same general implication: Are we not in danger of carrying accurate description too far? Where is it all to lead? We will be subjecting ethics, religion, everything, to scientific scrutiny—is nothing in all humanity to be left sacrosanct? It can only be said in reply that the healthy progress of humanity depends on our getting away from any and all unrealistic mental images of the world in which we live. For the alternative to having concepts and mental models based upon careful and minute description is not that of having no models at all; it is that of having formulations that are based upon biased conventions and unchecked assumptions. The resulting distorted models are important.

Once thought of and expressed, they influence our own outlook and actions, and the outlook and actions of others.

In the ordering of our social affairs, we are weighed down by countless such distorting formulations. They impede our actions, or, worse, cause us to act in ways which preclude the resolution of the problems we wish to settle. For instance, in trade-union/management negotiations it is held that union leaders are accountable for representing management's views to the workers. Strikes are often alleged to occur, and to persist intractably, because of distorted or false representation of these views. I believe that this description is often correct. But to castigate the union leaders causes resentment and heightens tension, and will not overcome the difficulty. The solution to the problem depends upon both management and unions recognizing that it is in fact the responsibility of managements to convey their own views directly to their workers. It is not the job of union representatives to do so, since they are accountable to the workers who elected them and not to management.

Examples of false and misleading formulations, tailor-made for trouble, abound in their hundreds and thousands: judging the performance of individuals on the basis of a few simple quantifiable aspects of what they do, like judging a teacher on the number of students he has who pass examinations, or a chief executive on the profit for the year; the assumption that there is one single cause for every problem; the assumption that if all students pass their examinations, then standards must be dropping, or that if there is a high failure rate, then the quality of the intake must be low; the assumption that those who do mental work should have shorter hours than those who do manual work. Ideas like these are to be found in every area of our social life, imprisoning our thoughts and actions and leading into muddle, argument, and unnecessary strife. They are a prime and dangerous enemy of freedom.

IV

Another explanation might be offered for the comparatively retarded development of the social sciences and psychology. Perhaps, it might be argued, scientific method cannot be applied to the study of really important social issues; they are too complex and we are too emotionally involved; moreover, one cannot experiment with serious issues concerning real people and institutions. This view is based upon a too narrow definition of scientific method with its picture of a cold, impartial, dry-as-dust scientist carrying out controlled, repeatable, and quantified experiments in an utterly detached impersonal manner. Such a definition is a definition of only a small part of science. Even in the natural sciences, as, for example, in astronomy with its massive achievements, experimentation is not always the keystone of scientific method. It is often necessary to wait for nature itself to produce the circumstances for observation and recording, to wait for what is sometimes termed an experiment of nature or an experiment of opportunity, such as an eclipse of the sun.

The problem of the social sciences and psychology is not that they cannot be scientific in the sense of using a disciplined scientific approach, but that they try to achieve academic respectability either by aping too rigidly the experimental sciences or by remaining theoretical and bookish. Neither being forced into a narrow scientific mold nor proliferating great theoretical systems will take the social sciences far. They are in their early stages and are in need of detailed teasing-out, observation, and description of our social institutions and behavior. Indeed, it is one of the current central tasks in these sciences to encourage a proper attitude toward the value of simple observation of great matters, and to overcome the belittling and devaluation of work that is not either experimental or based on intellectual theorizing.

Just think for a moment of the rate at which discoveries were made in mechanics and astronomy, in chemistry, in anatomy and physiology, and of the rapid advances in technology and medicine that became possible when men learned to give up being seduced by the intellectual grandeur of sweeping theories and came down from their academic towers to look at the world around them as it actually was; learned that enlightenment and true authority were to be gained from observing and describing the real natural environment.

For me, the most dramatic moment in the opening of this more humble road was when Vesalius, the father of anatomy, eschewed the niceness and the comfort of metaphysical theorizing about the structure of man himself, and set about the hard and practical task of dissecting the human corpse to see and minutely describe, at first hand, what there really was inside.

Bagehot (1867) described the need in his classic work, *The English Constitution,* in the following terms:

> The literature which has accumulated upon it [the English Constitution] is huge. But an observer who looks at the living reality will wonder at the contrast to the paper description. He will see in the life much which is not in the books; and he will not find in the rough practice many refinements of the literary theory [p. 3].

In so writing he was following in the tradition of Machiavelli, perhaps the first man to try to look in depth at social processes as they really were, to describe them, and to draw practical conclusions therefrom, untainted by political or religious ideology.

This step—the systematic observation of important issues—is a very difficult one in the social sciences. We are often too close ourselves to the material, too emotionally committed and involved. Yet, if we become too detached and uninvolved, the problems we study become unimportant and insignificant. The great issues are waiting to be tackled—freedom, the optimum forms of government, academic liberty, the nature of authority and accountability in management and administration, the nature of learning and the educational process, the problems of ethics in relations among men, the use of punishment and the nature of discipline, the relationship between law and morality.

Systematic observation of these issues calls for a special attitude, an attitude of detached involvement, to be achieved only with intense mental toil. By mental toil I mean that creative act in which our conscious beliefs, principles, and concepts are held not as perfect and immutable, as hard-and-fast currency, but as flexible counters, always uncertain and incomplete, and always under scrutiny for modification in the light of the reality of experience—concepts, ideas, principles, models, constantly subjected to the modifying influence of common perception.

Systematic observation does not arise spontaneously. It comes from directed and enduring curiosity which is an essential part of a disciplined scientific approach. Inherent in this curiosity are ideas about what one is looking for or might find. It is these ideas that give direction to our interest and attention. Sometimes we have merely an intuitive and inexpressible feeling about something, sometimes perhaps a roughly formulated hunch; sometimes, if we are working in a well-developed field, we start with comprehensively stated hypotheses derived from previous work or from a system of theories and laws.

Our concepts influence our observations, and our observations lead to changes in our concepts.

The objective of systematic observation is to perceive facts, so that we may group them into logically consistent concepts, which we can then use in communicating with each other. This process of concept formation is one of the central features of scientific advance. By concepts I mean verbalized and communicable ideas which define a particular collection of percepts. In the natural environment, concepts refer to what we ordinarily think of as things—chair, electron, plant cell. In the social environment, they refer to what we may equally refer to as things, though they are less tangible than physical things—like the concept of university, or role in a social system, or marriage. What makes the difference is that in the natural environment we build up our concepts from perceptions of tangible things, whereas in the social environment we are perceiving not the tangible bodies, but the social relationships among people. And determining the nature of social relationships is not always so easy. It starts at a more abstract level than that of observation in the natural environment.

In forming concepts, what we do is to draw boundaries (for this is what definition means), saying that our concept includes this percept and that one, but not those others. I can illustrate this process of boundary definition of concepts by the concept of scientific method that I am using. The boundary encloses enduring curiosity, systematic observation, and described and published perceptions. It excludes random observation, unrecorded perceptions, uncommunicated work, and artistic creativeness.

We can draw these boundaries rather loosely and widely, or very tightly and precisely, depending upon the extent of our knowledge at any given time. Scientific endeavor takes great strides forward as its concepts take on the formal and organized quality given to precise boundary definition. We have only to think of the tremendous progress that became possible with the fixing of the boundaries and the naming of concepts like electron, blood circulation, vitamin, genes. The organized and bounded perception makes it possible for us to speak together with the assurance that we are referring to perceptions that we already share—things that we have each seen or heard or otherwise perceived; or that we can go out and seek to perceive in order to build up a shared perception. In the opposite vein, we have only to think of the confused and fruitless discussion, the source of endless conflict, that arises when one says that the social sciences can never be scientific, while another argues that they can be and are—but each is subsuming a different set of perceptions under the same name.

The tricky thing about concepts is that they can be made up out of imagination and used as though they have perceptual content. For example, the concept of industrial democracy can be shown not to have any perceptual content. It is a hollow concept. It refers to no agreed percepts in the real social world which can be observed and shared. The constant testing of concepts against real perception is necessary if muddle is to be avoided.

What we observe, of course, is not the concept, but perceptual qualities of things—length, color, weight, sound—and qualities of relationships, like authority, love, power, jealousy, ambition. To define these qualities accurately requires the act of measurement, as Bridgman, adapted by Brown (1963), has shown: for example, the quality of length is defined by the steps involved in the construction and use of a yardstick.

Once we achieve the boundary definition of concepts and an operational definition of qualities, our scientific endeavor becomes objective. For the objectivity of science lies not in its experiments, nor in the impartiality of the observer. It lies in the communicability of its observed facts. As Karl Popper (1945) has said: "What we call 'scientific objectivity' is not a product of the individual scientist's impartiality, but a product of the social or public character of scientific method; and the individual scientist's impartiality is, so far as it exists, not the source but rather the result of this socially or institutionally organized objectivity of science" (p. 317).

The objectivity of science, therefore, depends upon the art of using language. As part of the very process of becoming conscious, our concepts attach themselves to words. Here, then, is an art that scientists must at least aspire to cultivate. It requires first of all a protective attitude toward words, an attitude of concern for the precise and careful use of language, so that the currency of words is not debased by lazy usage. There is required a sense of when new words are necessary to fit new concepts, and when a tighter definition of existing language is more proper to the aim of expressing increasing conceptual precision and the clarity derived from measurement.

V

With our concepts we can construct conceptual models. They are mental models with which we try to describe the natural or social environment. For example, a mentally constructed model of the organizational structure of a university, a factory, a civil service department, a trade union, a political party; showing the authority and accountability in each position, how decisions are arrived at, how the work actually goes on, the standards of performance, and setting out the required relationships between positions; or a system of factors presumed to be operating inside the individual, such as, for example, various unconscious factors, which are used to explain behavior.

Models of the real situation can be examined for their internal consistency, and inconsistencies in the real situation may thereby be discovered—for example, inconsistencies between the accountability in a particular position and the authority allocated to it. Moreover, developments in cybernetics, computers, and applied mathematics give promise of expressing these models in more rigorously mathematical terms.

We can modify these models in our minds, and think up new models, in accord with changing perceptions. We can hypothesize what would happen if these changes were actually implemented in the situation modeled. It is at this point that experiment—if it is possible—is so useful, for the hypotheses, and the models on which they are based, can be systematically tested ad lib.

In the social sciences we cannot, of course, experiment with new institutions as we like, trying this and trying that, and rejecting what does not work. Our institutions are part of our ongoing social life, and changes in them affect the lives of people. Every failure constitutes a social jolt. Nor can we make and remake individual human beings, merely casting aside our failures, for every one of us is entitled to endure.

But sometimes, when the moment is opportune, we may have the chance to test the new model and hypotheses in practice, either because we happen to be the responsible administrator or the person concerned, or because we have the opportunity to communicate with that administrator or person. Social science and psychology will find their major avenue of advance in applied and professional work, which provides a piecemeal testing in practice of hypotheses and models as the exigencies of real life allow, reinforced by such experiments as may be possible. But at no stage do we assume control over our personal and social environment in the same absolute sense in which we strive to dominate our physical environment. We must seek rather to gain systematic experience and knowledge, to provide a framework for our behavior, to express our laws as legislation, and wisely to regulate our personal and our social lives.

I can exemplify my meaning by returning to the passages I quoted from the Robbins report: "The real sources of initiative and power . . . depend partly upon the imponderables of specific circumstances and individual personalities and are almost impossible to determine" (p. 87). No! We cannot accept this outlook. Systematic observation, perception, and description of what actually happens in each situation—who takes initiative, who decides what, who gets credit for good decisions or is called to account for bad ones—these are the processes that can give us the shareable information necessary for assembling accurate models of what goes on even in universities, and for constructing new models where necessary in order to create the conditions needed for greater definition or responsibility.

In the case of universities, some conceptual clarification would be required before adequate model-building could be achieved. For example: What are the main operational tasks of the university? Who is accountable for teaching programs and to whom? What does "academic freedom" mean? Who appoints whom and who assesses whose performance? As these concepts and relationships are clarified and defined in boundary terms so that we know what shared percepts are involved and can assume with some assurance that we understand each other, model-building and modification can take place in terms of structure and relationships—including the authority and responsibilities of councils and senates, various types of committee, heads of departments, members of departments and students, and the nature of the required relationships among them. Upon the model chosen depend such significant decisions as whether we appoint figureheads for rubber-stamping councils, or working members of councils with authority.

Such a process of perception, concept formation, and model-building is not dramatic. It moves step by step as new perceptions are recorded. But it denies the existence of the imponderable and undefinable, so long as we have the will to ponder and describe in connection with our own organizations and behavior.

VI

We may rightfully conclude that a true science of society and its institutions, and of human behavior, is achievable. The fact that measurement is very little developed, and that the testing of predictions may have to rely rather more upon model-building and experiments of nature than upon controlled laboratory experiment, is no cause for pessimism or despair. Rigorous and disciplined scientific observation and description of ourselves and our social environment, with the construction and testing of models, and the development of a sound technology of society and the individual, ought to be capable of infinite elaboration.

There is, however, one difficulty that needs to be recognized. It is the difficulty of gaining access in depth to the data to be observed. By access in depth I do not mean statistical surveys of attitude or of population movements. I mean firsthand observation by means of work in situ with teachers and pupils, boards of directors, prisoners and prison staff, families, and tenants' associations, so that the details can be dissected and teased out of the structure of the situation: how relationships are mediated, how attitudes are influenced and changed, how policies are argued and fixed, in a live and telling manner. Unformulated and even unrecognized activities, policies, and motives can be identified and conceptualized, and accurate and comprehensive models constructed which do not suffer from the omission of the things that really count.

In the natural sciences, the route of access of deeper-lying or more distant data is through instrumentation —microscopes, spectroscopes, radioactive isotopes, and flights into space. But one does not have to ask the permission of the materials one is observing, and it does not matter if a certain amount of material is destroyed and thrown away in the process.

In the social sciences and psychology, because we are dealing with human beings, systematic study cannot even begin without some cooperation from the people involved. What is needed is a particular attitude in each of us, an attitude favorable not to vagueness but to knowledge, to discovery and clarification rather than to hidebound custom, practice, and tradition. It contains the resolution to understand oneself and one's own institutions. To the extent that any given society seeks enlightenment about its institutions will the science of society grow, and only to that extent.

Access to data in the social sciences should be sought only with the constructive aim of advancing social technology. Such an aim entails a professional collaborative relationship between the scientist and people who are determined to undertake the difficult task of doing what they are doing and understanding what they are doing at the same time. At its simplest level, the relationship involves discussion with subjects of the significance for them of their performance in a new test. At a more complex level, it is a full-scale collaborative relationship that may extend through long periods of time between a professional consultant and those—be it an individual, a marital couple, a trade union, a school, or other institution—who are seeking the insight and understanding they hope he will help them to acquire.

Within a professional working relationship of this kind between social scientists and people in roles collaborating to dispel vagueness, access to data and opportunity for observation not only are possible, they are demanded by the individual or by the organization. They are a part of the process of analysis whereby progress is expected. Unlike the natural scientist, therefore, the social scientist must have at least some competence in carrying a professional role. It is one of the prime working tools enabling him to carry out the fundamental scientific process of observation. And if it might be thought that scientific objectivity is lost because of this collaborative relationship, then that is only to say that the social sciences share this problem with modern physics which, with the discovery of the principles of relativity and uncertainty, is also affected by the relationship between the observer and his field.

Given a proper relationship with those of us who take part in their field of study, the social scientist and the psychologist can report their perceptions directly to us, and get some verification then and there, on the spot, of the soundness of their observation. This reporting and checking of results are constant characteristics, for example, of work in psychotherapy, and of social consulting work. In both cases, the client judges and responds to every interpretation or report. Although there may be technical difficulties involved in assessing the validity of these judgments, at least the judgments are available, in contrast to the field of study of the physicist which cannot speak to him at all.

It is in this possible collaboration between the social scientist or psychologist and people who seek a more disciplined approach to overcoming social problems that the social sciences have a potential advantage over the natural sciences. For, while the observation of the physicist cannot withdraw, crying "Leave me vague," neither can it engage with him in a collaborative attack upon the problem to be studied.

REFERENCES

Bacon, F. (1620), *The New Organum.* New York: Liberal Arts Press, 1960.

Bagehot, W. (1867), *The English Constitution.* Oxford: World's Classics, 1928.

Brown, W. (1963), Organisation and science. In: *Glacier Project Papers,* ed. W. Brown & E. Jaques. London: Heinemann Educational Books Ltd.

Ministry of Education (1963), *Higher Education.* Report of the Committee on Higher Education (Chairman: Lord Robbins). Cmnd 2154. London: HM Stationery Office.

Popper, K. R. (1945), *The Open Society and Its Enemies,* 2 vols., 4th rev. ed. London: Routledge & Kegan Paul, 1962.

Chapter 2

The Human Consequences of Industrialization

A massive change is taking place in the world, that is one of the outstanding features of the twentieth century. It is a change to a situation in which 90 percent or more of the working population of industrialized nations are employed for a wage or salary in work organizations. This change, of the order of that from slavery to feudalism, is the accompaniment of industrialization. Max Weber might have called it the bureaucratization of society; Karl Marx, the process of proletarianization.

Up until the nineteenth and twentieth centuries the majority of the working population were in one form or another self-employed or in service: either in one-family agricultural holdings; in small family businesses; on genuine piecework; as itinerant or seasonal labor; or in that special part-of-the-family called being in service. Only very few people, perhaps no more than 10 or 20 percent, were employed for a wage or salary in employment organizations—mainly in government, or in the army, or in the Church.

With worldwide industrialization, however, the whole situation is dramatically changing. There is a wholesale movement from the situation of self-employment to that of being employed in employment organizations for a

wage or salary; and the organizations themselves are rapidly becoming more and more vast; great industrial com-
plexes, commercial organizations, industrialized
agriculture, local authorities, social services, the health
service, educational organizations. This process of change
has been completed in the so-called industrially advanced
nations. But it is to be seen still taking place all over the
rest of the world. It is a social process best described as
herding everyone into a vast employment complex that
constitutes a new zone of society—the zone lying between
the nation and the state on the one hand and the family
and the individual on the other. I propose to call this the
intermediate zone.

The impact of this change on the individual and on
family life has been studied and vividly portrayed by
Miller and Swanson (1958). They have been able to show
that much of the self-reliance and family cohesiveness
that goes with possession of a small family holding or
business is undermined. Family ties are weakened, values alter in the direction of a lessening of social concern.
The changes are profound.

Despite the fact that this change is shaking the whole
foundation of society, little is known about the properties
of the employment organizations which make up the intermediate zone in which nearly everyone now works. In
particular, no standards have been established as to the
limits within which these employment organizations
must be managed if they are to contribute to a socially
healthy society, rather than contributing, as they do now,
to great disturbances of our society.

One of the difficulties is that too narrow an approach
is adopted in considering these organizations. Instead of
recognizing that together they constitute an immensely
significant intermediate zone influencing the whole of

society, we tend to consider each organization separately in terms only of its economic efficiency.

This approach, however, merely scratches the surface of the problem. It comes from those inside the organizations who are trying to make them run better in the sense of their giving less trouble, or of being more efficient or productive.

Within this limited frame of reference—the world of personnel work, business economics, management consultancy, and work study—all kinds of ad hoc procedures have the appearance of being reasonable and realistic: piecework, bonus schemes, and productivity bargains that supposedly reward people for working harder, but which in fact are spurious and hollow methods; Whitley Councils,[1] joint consultation, advisory committees, and similar institutions and procedures that are supposed to give more or less opportunity for participation, but which turn out to be empty procedures as far as any substantial influence on policy-making is concerned; procedures for assessing performance and for deciding progression and promotion, which are mostly inadequate even when systematically provided for, and which can never be effectively carried through because the relationships between superiors and subordinates are obscured and confused; and even arguments in favor of maintaining a state of moderate unemployment in society in order to avoid "overheating the economy," a metaphor whose crudeness conceals its denial of the realities of human needs.

This narrow approach, with its mere palliatives, will not do. We are not dealing with individual enterprises. We are dealing with a vast sector of society—a sector in which people have their most direct relationship with

---

[1] Whitley Councils are the bodies in the civil service in which "management" negotiates with "staff."

their society. How people are treated at work has a profound influence upon their attitude toward their society, and upon society itself. Criteria such as the productivity or the efficiency of the individual enterprise cannot be allowed to be of primary concern when the shape of society itself is at issue.

Nor will a sentimental approach based on the notion that men of goodwill ought somehow to be considerate toward each other be of any greater help; nor an egalitarian approach which says that all men ought to be equal and therefore ought to be paid equally; nor a power-bargaining approach which says that men ought to be able to combine to use their power to get whatever they want.

What is required today, and urgently required, is not endless preoccupation with so-called management studies, and payment schemes, and palliatives for trying to make work organizations run better, but a hard look at what these organizations in the intermediate zone are really like, and how they can be managed, if we are to be able to use them in a manner that will contribute to the good society.

It is at this point, however, that we encounter the major problem with which I am here concerned. If we are not to use efficiency as our criterion for assessing employment organizations, what criteria are we to use? We have had to rely on the brilliance of insight of philosophers, of religious and revolutionary leaders, of moralists, of political theorists, for our conceptions of the nature of the best forms of social, economic, and political organization. But all these theories suffer from two major drawbacks: first, they are based upon oversimplified and incomplete conceptions of the nature of the human beings for whom societies are being planned; and second, the conceptions of human behavior remain untested and untestable, so that the advantages of the various political ideologies remain a matter of opinion and political debate.

What is required is to find a more objective basis for our judgments. I am going to suggest that that basis may well be discovered in the findings of psychoanalysis. Instead of having to resort to general philosophical ideas of "the good," we can turn to more precise formulations of the nature of man based upon direct observation. By doing so we can inquire into the characteristics of our social organizations in terms of how much they may or may not reinforce and encourage the psychologically healthy parts of human personality and mitigate human destructiveness.

Such an approach implies two propositions: first, that generalizations about normal human behavior are possible; and second, that it is possible to describe social institutions in such a manner as to be able to display their psychological effects upon their members. I propose now to explore both these propositions. In doing so I shall assume a third, without being able to demonstrate it, namely, that if we construct our social institutions both in accord with the work to be done and in accord with the nature of human beings, then those institutions will function best. Such organization, paying due regard both to work and to human nature, may be termed *requisite* organization: requisite in the dictionary sense of "being required by the nature of things."

In pursuing my argument, let me first describe some features of the nature of employment organizations. Then I shall turn to consider the psychological implications of these organizations from the psychoanalytical point of view.

THE EXECUTIVE HIERARCHY

The type of the organization in which most of us are employed has not been identified sufficiently clearly to be named. It is variously referred to as a "family tree," or a "pyramid," or a "company," or most commonly simply as "the organization." These vague references will not suffice. They in no way satisfy our need for precision and clarity. In order to make it possible to consider the nature of these organizations in which people are employed, we shall need a name by which to refer to them. I propose to use the phrase "executive hierarchies"—executive in the sense of having been established in order to get things done and hierarchy because they are constructed in a manner which gives some people authority over others. Most people will be familiar with this kind of organization, since most of us are employed in them.[2]

Let me make it clear that I am considering only the organizations in which people are employed. I am not here considering the governing bodies of these organizations: variously referred to as Boards, or Boards of Directors, or Boards of Governors, acting on behalf of shareholders, or the government, or cooperators, or whichever association of people brought the organization into being in the first place.

Regardless of how or why these employment organizations are established, they all take on the same form of hierarchical structure. The larger they are, generally the more levels they have, ranging from two levels in very small shops or offices, to seven and eight levels in those very large organizations which employ tens or hundreds of thousands of people.

Clearly, there will be important differences between the large and the small executive hierarchies, differences, for example, in the content of work and in the degree of anonymity in relation to the total organization. But there are certain crucial common features of employment in

---

[2] I refer to them today as accountability hierarchies (AcH).

executive hierarchies, that is to say of employment in the intermediate zone of society, and it is some of these common features to which I shall turn.

Once the intermediate zone of society is established, practically the only way in which you can work to gain a livelihood is by finding employment in an executive organization. In order to work, in order to live, you have to get a job—and getting a job means taking up a position in an executive hierarchy. If you cannot find a job—that is, if you cannot find an organization that will employ you—then, by and large, you cannot work. For it is open to only a very few to be able to start a business of their own, or to get a small piece of land on which they can hope to live by growing their own food, raising chickens, and so on.

Second, once you get a job, you will find yourself in one of the most significant of modern human relationships—that obtaining between a superior and a subordinate. This relationship is variously called having an immediate manager, or a boss, or a supervisor, or a departmental head, or a foreman, or an administrator. Whatever the title, the relationship is the same, and it is a relationship with a highly charged emotional content.

In the first place, the superior has the authority to assign tasks to his subordinates, to determine what work they shall have to do. But at the same time, he himself remains accountable for the quality of the work that his subordinates do. He thus not only has authority over them, but he is also dependent upon them. Once he hands out work he must be able to rely upon his subordinates to carry it out.

Because the superior is held accountable for the work of his subordinates, he must have the authority to assess the quality of their work, and to influence the remuneration they receive and their progress. In the final analysis, if the superior is realistically to be held accountable, then he must be able to have subordinates who, though they might not be completely acceptable, are at least not unacceptable to him. Therefore, there must be provision for removal or transfer of subordinates who really prove to be unacceptable to a superior.

Here then is a situation of great psychological subtlety and complexity. There is the interplay and interaction of authority and accountability, of mutual dependence, of assessment of ability, of judgments about personal potentialities, of acceptability and dismissal, of recognition and award. The superior's career as well as the subordinate's career, their economic security, and their recognition and self-esteem are wrapped up in it.

Not only is the superior–subordinate relationship a psychologically complex one, it is both tremendously occupying and exceedingly widespread in industrial societies. It is occupying in that it takes up the largest part of the waking hours of those of us who are employed in executive hierarchies. It is exceedingly common in that each and every executive organization in the intermediate zone has only one superior–subordinate relationship less than the total number of people it employs; that is to say, if an organization employs ten thousand people, it brings into being 9,999 superior–subordinate relationships.

The third point I want to make is that the direction of each enterprise in the intermediate zone, and the policies by which it is run, are supposedly the responsibility of the board and not of the employees. Yet the reality is that there is a complex power situation involving the interests of the shareholders, the interests of the consumers, and the interests of the employees. Each of these groupings can close any enterprise down. The power of the shareholders is expressed through the board. The power of the consumer is expressed through sales representatives who visit them, or through public relations or market research institutions. By and large, however, there are no satisfactory institutions through which the power of employees can be exercised in a constitutional manner to influence policy. This fact is expressed in the political importance attaching to the urgency of developing means of so-called participation by employees.

The fourth point concerns remuneration. There is little need to do more than refer to the current situation with regard to the means of determining wages and salaries, to demonstrate what difficulties lie in this region. Note what happens.

The self-employed person earns what he can. He is independent and he must accept the risks as well as the advantages of this independence. His income level is dependent upon the public response to his own efforts.

For the employed person the situation is entirely different. His income level is determined by forces that seem to be entirely outside his own control or reckoning. What he does know is how his pay compares with others. That is what counts for most. Underlying these comparisons there is a demonstrable sense of fair pay that seems to tie in very accurately with the level of responsibility carried. People at the same level of responsibility feel fairly remunerated if they are receiving the same level of pay as others at the same level, more than those at lower levels, and less than those at higher levels.

Now consider what happens when under industrialization the intermediate zone of society is well established and encompasses 90 percent or more of all people at work. Cross-comparisons are made right across the board —teachers with factory workers, civil servants with bank staffs, social workers with secretaries, nurses with bookkeepers, mail carriers with bus drivers, engineers with

accountants, physicists with airline pilots, and so on. The
demand arises for equitable treatment for everyone working in the intermediate zone. And equitable treatment
means comparable treatment for all.

In short, with industrialization and the development
of the intermediate zone of society, first of all, whether
or not a person works is dependent upon his being able
to find a job; second, millions of superior–subordinate
relationships are formed, and the type of job a person has
depends upon how he is judged by his superior or potential
superior; third, employing organizations are not required
to establish institutions and procedures whereby employees can express their power in a constitutional manner and participate in making the policies within which
they are expected to work; and fourth, employees compare
their level of wages and salaries with other groups whom
they judge to be carrying equivalent levels of responsibility, regardless of differences in occupation. Thus, the
intermediate zone is treated as a single vast economic
field calling for equitable treatment for all.

PSYCHOLOGICAL IMPACT OF THE
INTERMEDIATE ZONE

Now what happens as a result of this way of living? It is
an understatement to say that uncertainty about a job,
having your future career influenced by being assessed
by someone else, being dependent upon the work of others
in order to discharge your own responsibilities, finding
the nature of your employment organization changing
without having a say, and not having any way of being
sure of equitable and fair reward, are each a source of
anxiety; in combination they are sources of chronic tension.

But it is not enough merely to say that anxiety is

generated. Such matters are not to be taken for granted. If people were different from what they are, they might thrive upon being able to leave everything in the hands of someone else. Indeed such an outlook characterizes the lotus-land fantasies of men—the only trouble with such fantasies being that they do not match the realities of the nature of man.

The disturbance that is stirred by this employment situation in the intermediate zone is twofold. First, there is the reality-based sense of uncertainty and insecurity; and second, the stirring of unconscious psychotic anxieties, the unresolved leftovers of the emotionally turbulent situation of early infancy.

Work in the intermediate zone is insecure, performance is never perfectly judged, reward is inequitable, opportunity to participate is minimal. These circumstances run counter to the normal nature of man, as I shall try to show in a moment. If we had sufficient constitutional and economic knowledge we could overcome these problems without too much difficulty. But we do not have that knowledge as yet—we are only beginning gradually to acquire it.

To make matters worse—and here lies the most difficult problem—the stirring of unconscious psychotic anxieties in the group situation sets up one of the most formidable barriers to learning and to change. I am not saying the *only* barrier; I am saying a very formidable barrier.

The employment situation I have described can arouse intense feelings of persecution, and in doing so stirs up an unconscious reliving of the unresolved persecutory anxieties first experienced in infancy. It is these stirrings of unconscious anxieties and their accompanying defense mechanisms that add peculiarly intractable difficulties because they become projected into the social situation where they produce incalculable complications.

We owe it to the insights of Melanie Klein into the unconscious mental life of children that we can follow through the complex processes of the very primitive anxieties which she termed *paranoid,* or *persecutory,* anxiety. What happens, briefly, is that to the extent that his primitive infant conflicts remain unresolved, a person is unable to control his unconscious loving and hating impulses. Two factors contribute to the primitive difficulties: first, the intensity of the impulses themselves; and second, the environmental situation—that is to say, inadequacies and inconsistencies in care and handling by the mother which arouse frustration and rage alternating with gratification and love. The resulting ambivalence is intolerable—it is emotionally traumatic to hate and to try to destroy what you love—it is equally traumatic to love your persecutors.

Ambivalence is resolved by splitting. The object is either perceived as a persecutor and hated; or it is perceived as good and loved. But there is no mixing. Of course the price to be paid for splitting is loss of reality by means of denial: denial of opposing feelings, so that hate and persecution cannot be mitigated by love.

Along with splitting of feelings, and denial, goes a third major feature of the paranoid–schizoid position, that of projection and projective identification. This unconscious mechanism supports splitting and denial by attributing the person's own hate to others, so that the sense of persecution is intensified. Similarly, love is projected, and the good part of the object thus gains in good qualities and becomes ideally good and loving. The end result is not difficult to envisage—intense idealization oscillating with intense persecution. This pattern firmly established is extraordinarily resistant to change.

Evidence that this unconscious persecutory situation is stimulated in people by the situation in the intermediate zone is not difficult to find. Splitting occurs in the taking of sides: all bosses are grasping and bad; all employees are greedy and irresponsible and lazy; everyone on your own side is good, everyone on the other side is bad. A particularly rigid and harsh black-and-white outlook dominates the intergroup relationships, despite the fact that the very same people may have a much more flexible attitude based on mutual respect when they meet each other as real individuals in the work situation as against the artificialities of the group situation where they must represent the views of others.

Along with this splitting and projective identification goes rampant denial, and evasion of reality. Gimmicks abound, reminiscent of the philosopher's stone and of alchemy. So-called productivity bargains are solemnly made, despite the fact that productivity cannot be measured, and even if it were possible to measure it, it would still not be possible to ascribe any increase to the activities of any particular work group. Bargaining procedures are used which require greed and selfishness as sources of power; and yet greed, selfishness, and the use of power are denied, at the same time that the dedicated and restrained are punished economically. The idea of management development has become the fashion, yet there is no generally agreed definition of what a manager is. Job evaluation is supposed to be a solution: but no one apparently notices that when you really look into it it is simply power bargaining in another guise.

These pseudosolutions and procedures are to be found everywhere. The point about them is not so much that they are ineffectual, but that they are believed to be realistic and are treated as if they were so. This uncritical approach is the product of unconscious denial on a mass

scale. It blocks all attempts to come to grips with reality.
Clarity of definition and conceptual precision are often
avoided. Everyone is entitled to mean what he wants to
mean. The turbulent social situation has come to serve
a widespread pathological function: that of acting as a
reservoir in which to pile up and store inner unconscious
psychological conflict and persecutory anxieties.

The mass unconscious collusion to deny reality and
enhance conflict combined with what is in any case an
intellectually difficult problem, almost precludes any rational solution to the management of the intermediate
zone of society. And yet if the problem is not resolved,
and resolved by the turn of the century, social chaos on
a massive scale will be the result.

THE NATURE OF MAN

The problem then is how to break through the unconscious anxieties about effective social institutions in the
intermediate zone. At least four rights must be firmly
established for the employed 90 percent of the working
population: the right to employment at full capacity; the
right of appeal against the judgments of superiors; the
right to participate in policy-making; and the right to
equitable reward.

It might be considered that these rights were self-evident. But self-evident truths are arguable. They are not
always evident to everyone. They are articles of faith.
They are therefore open to question. And in the world of
business and commerce, or government, or the provision
of social services, where financial resources are always
in short supply, self-evident truths are too easily set aside
if they threaten to add to the burden of expense. Arguments in favor of establishing fair and equitable condi-

tions are thus readily pushed aside as being unrealistic, or "soft," or at best as being totally uneconomic.

It occurred to me, however, that we might bring the argument on to much firmer ground if we could know what social conditions reinforce normal human behavior and diminish the projection of psychotic anxieties into society. Such knowledge requires that we should know what, if anything, is normal behavior—or even if there are general criteria of normality. Here is a difficult question that we might resolve by referring to certain findings implicit in psychoanalysis. For analysis does not deal only with psychopathology, it deals also with the normal personality—although this fact may be far less evident. Every time an analyst interprets his patient's behavior, the interpretation is made against a conception of what the patient would be like if he or she were not subject to the unconscious play of unresolved early conflict. As the analysis progresses and conflict is reduced, types of behavior are noted that are accepted as more normal. And finally, as the analysis reaches the point of possible termination, the so-called criteria of termination are used by the analyst in judging when a stopping point is appropriate.

We may note further that many of these criteria of termination are general; as, for example, sexual potency, the capacity to comprehend verbal communication, control of murderous impulses, capacity to love and to recognize the needs and abilities of others, capacity to utilize abilities to the full in work, and so on. Such criteria are accepted as applying to everyone, not on moral or ethical or any a priori grounds, but as a result of repeated observation that individuals have these characteristics when they are freed from unconscious unresolved primitive conflict.

From the point of view of establishing the nature of

requisite organization in the employment organizations
of the intermediate zone, I would like to pick out the
following features of personality consistent with the termination of an analysis—our so-called normal personality characteristics.

First, the normal person seeks not only to work, but
to work at a level of responsibility that taxes his capacity
to the full. Man is a problem-solving animal and must
make continuous use of his mental and physical apparatus.

Not to be able to work at full capacity is restrictive,
depressing, and finally persecuting. The avoidance of
work at full capacity, or the acceptance of underemployment, is symptomatic of emotional disturbance.

Second, the normal person is independent in several
important senses. He seeks to establish for himself the
goals for which he is working, or at least to take part in
establishing them if he is working in a group. He may
not always appear to be in that state of mind, since if the
objects of the nation, or the work group, or other associations in which he is involved, are sufficiently satisfactory to him, he does little. If, however, they are
unsatisfactory, he feels the demand in him to have the
right to try to alter those objects.

This independence is not inconsistent with a normal
capacity to be involved in group consensus, that is to say,
in taking part with others in arriving at a generally acceptable object and adhering to it, even though it may
not completely satisfy him.

Another way in which this independence shows itself
is in a rejection of subjecting himself to the final judgment
of any one individual alone. Under circumstances where
judgments are to be made—whether in the assessment
of his performance at work, or of entitlements in the community, or of his behavior in law—he does not accept the

judgment of one person, whether manager, or official, or judge. He demands recourse not only to a review of any such judgment if he is not satisfied with it, but to public review in a lawful setting.

In short, normal man is law-abiding and law-demanding in the sense of conforming to social consensus and due process of law, and in the sense of requiring independence from total control from any other individual acting privately.

The individual who gives himself up to the judgments of others and to the objects of others is observed to have the psychopathology of passivity and masochism. He is observed to attempt to relinquish his own personality to the analyst in the transference situation. Independence of view and of behavior is a sine qua non of successful treatment.

Third, normal man has a strong sense of equity and social justice. He is committed to achieving what he judges to be his proper place in society, and to taking part in a social arrangement which provides that proper place for himself and for everyone else. He is aware of the differences between himself and others, and can judge in what respects others may be more or less competent than himself.

In the absence of this sense of differences, of equity and of justice, what we see is the individual disturbed by omnipotence or by impotence and self-depreciation. Freed from such pathology, the individual seeks to participate in a society which provides appropriate differential treatment to individuals in accord with their normal makeup. In the employment work situation, this normal propensity shows up as a readily demonstrable set of norms of fair differential payment related to differentials in level of work carried and differentials in individual capacity.

This normal man would, of course, have his own strong

individuality—characteristics in which he would differ
from other people, such as in his interests, his ambitions,
his likes and dislikes, his capacities. But there are also
these positive qualities that each fully analyzed person
would possess. They may sound exceedingly virtuous. In
some respects they combine all the characteristics of the
godly man as perceived by the major religions, Christian,
Muslim, Jewish. They are the qualities of the Greek her-
oes, as well as those of the good and ethical men of the
philosophers—of Aristotle, Plato, Kant, and others concerned with ethics and morality. They are also the qualities of the reasonable man whom the lawyers use as the
yardstick against which to judge whether a particular act
was or was not culpable.

But what I would like to suggest is that what we find
in the religions, in ethics, in politics, in law, is not really
a description of a "good" man—it is nothing more than
an approximation to a description of what men are like
when they are undisturbed both from within and from
without. That is to say, the good man turns out to be
nothing more than man in his normal social and psychological state. There is really nothing either good or bad
about it. It is just what it is. With our strong deistic and
magical tendencies, however, we have been inclined to
attribute a form of godliness to our natural state.

Conversely, it is noteworthy that what is called sinful
in religion, unethical in philosophy, illegal in law, is also
behavior that would not occur in a society of normal men
and women living within social codes reinforcing that
normal behavior. Unethical, sinful, immoral, illegal, are
value-laden terms to describe deviations from normal individual behavior in a normal social setting.

REQUISITE ORGANIZATION

We may now pose our original problem more sharply.
Modern industrial society organizes its work in executive

employment hierarchies, built up from hundreds or thousands of dyadic superior–subordinate relationships. Nearly everyone who works is left no choice but to obtain work in these hierarchical systems. The executive hierarchy has thus come profoundly to affect the nature of society. Yet practically nothing has been known about these social systems—they have hardly yet been identified sufficiently to have come into the explicit awareness of society.

Our brief consideration of some aspects of the nature of man suggests that if executive hierarchies, with their built-in superior–subordinate accountability and authority, are to function in a socially constructive manner, they must provide for at least four major needs that are demonstrably features of any normally functioning human being. The four needs of the person are: utilization of his full capacity in problem solving at work; involvement in setting the objectives or policies of any group or institution in which he is joined; independence from control by any individual without recourse to public process of review of that control by others; possession of his appropriate differential position in the group and cohesive response to an all-round equitable distribution of status and reward.

These needs demand that our industrialized society must provide: abundant employment in society at large; opportunity for all employees to participate in setting the policies of the executive hierarchy in which they are working; the right of the subordinate to appeal against the judgment of his superiors; authority for the accountable superior to judge the performance of his subordinates and to cause this judgment to affect their progress; the right of everyone to equitable remuneration.

In fact, the situation in society is that marginal unemployment is endemic, so that it is difficult for anyone to find employment that fully stretches his capacities; opportunity for participation exists practically nowhere, nor do individual appeal systems; and systems of equitable remuneration not only do not exist, the very idea is almost universally held to be uneconomic and impractical.

The result is that work in industrial society, instead of strengthening normal mental processes, is in fact contributing to the strengthening of psychopathological processes and to the eruption of violence. Passivity is encouraged and omnipotence provoked. Unnecessary frustration and insecurity are to a greater or lesser extent continuously experienced. Greed and envy are stirred by manifest inequity. Autocratic and unjust treatment is inevitable, even with the best of goodwill, in the absence of provision for participation and appeal. All the conditions are present for the revival of the primitive paranoid-schizoid situation.

Society is suffering from these effects. Projection, with accompanying idealization and persecution, is widespread and accepted as ordinary. Splitting and fragmentation follow, and the split society is the result. It is from this splitting based upon paranoid–schizoid mechanisms that the violence stems.

The industrial-relations approach to overcoming these problems is grossly inadequate. The problem is wider than industry, or commerce, or the civil service. What is needed is a political science of the intermediate zone, with standards derived not from ethics or religion, but from the objective analysis of the nature of man. I have tried to illustrate the application of psychoanalysis to the discovery of these standards. These have been described elsewhere (Jaques, 1961; Brown, 1965; Brown and Jaques, 1965), the results of twenty years of work at the Glacier Metal Company. This work has, in my view, demonstrated how the analysis of the nature of work, of superior–subordinate relationships, of executive organization, of the role of elected representatives, can lead to the development of effective institutions for management and for participation, for appeals and for reward. The various institutions have so far been the subject of far too little attention by managers.

The difficulties in managing our executive hierarchies have led to their earning an increasingly bad name. They have in fact been autocratic, because of the absence of requisite organization. It is understandable, therefore, that students and those concerned with human welfare should adopt a rejective attitude.

But such negative attitudes are wide of the mark. The advantage of the executive hierarchy is that it has made large-scale technology possible. If we are to have this advantage, we must recognize that the executive employment hierarchy is not in itself a force either for good or for bad in society; it is neither a healthy nor an unhealthy form of institution. The issue is whether or not we can learn how to establish on a constitutional basis a modus operandi for these organizations that will demand and permit the application of normal human qualities and endeavor. Given the development of requisite institutions, the emergence of the intermediate zone could contribute both to the mental health of the individual and to the strengthening of a healthy society.

REFERENCES

Brown, W. (1965), *Exploration in Management*. London: Heinemann Educational Books Ltd.

—— Jaques, E. (1965), *Glacier Project Papers*. London: Heinemann Educational Books Ltd.

Jaques, E. (1961), *Equitable Payment*. London: Heinemann Educational Books Ltd.

Miller, D. R., & Swanson, E. (1958), *The Changing American Parent.*
New York: John Wiley.

Chapter 3

Task Complexity

In our construction of the world we live in we are faced by the complexity of the phenomena and the data and information flows which we encounter. This complexity comes in how information is patterned and in its sheer quantity. That the complexity exists "in reality" there can be little doubt. For we modify the complexity of the world in many ways: sometimes we simplify it by technological advances which enable us to improve our ability to process information and make problems easier to solve; and, equally, we may make it more complex by discoveries which increase the amount of information. Sometimes we may even strive to make the world more complex; for example, by means of deceptive information flows aimed at strengthening a competitive position.

Phenomena vary in complexity, from the ultrasimple (the so-called child's play) to the ultracomplex which are beyond any possible grasp of comprehension by human beings. So, too, do individuals vary in their ability to unravel the complexities which confront them and to handle the information which may confound them. This ability to deal with complexity is concerned largely with cognitive psychological processes, the means we have of organizing the information flows, both material and social, in which we live.

The issue of identifying the inherent complexity of

phenomena can be of considerable practical importance, as, for example, in organizing the work of large-scale hierarchical bureaucratic work systems. These systems are structured to handle complexity in a methodical way; the higher up the system, the greater is the complexity of the work to be done. To the extent that it became possible to define and to measure complexity, it would become possible to distribute tasks to an appropriate level in the hierarchy with all the advantages of conscious understanding in doing so—and to strengthen the possibility of having people at those levels with the cognitive capability to cope with the complexity.

It may be noted that I am distinguishing between two kinds of complexity. On the one hand, there is the complexity to be found in nature, in the external world of material and social processes in which we act; and since I am concerned with how we operate in this world of process, how we solve problems and carry out tasks, I shall refer to this complexity outside us as *task complexity*. On the other hand, there is the complexity we can muster internally in relating to our world of significant externals, our world of external information which we have to keep in order; and I shall refer to the quality of patterning of the cognitive psychological processes necessary in doing so as the *cognitive complexity* of those processes. I shall assume, in accord with the gestalt view of the world, that the structure of these cognitive processes must be isomorphic with the structure of the external world. Furthermore, I shall term the psychological capability in the person in mustering his or her full cognitive complexity and applying it to organizing the world in carrying out tasks and solving problems as that person's *cognitive power*.

It is my purpose in this chapter to consider task complexity, and to turn to cognitive complexity in the next chapter. I shall do so from a point of view that is not overly familiar in the social sciences; namely, that as information complexity increases there are qualitative changes in the nature of that complexity, so that we live in a world made up of a hierarchy of discrete states of task complexity. Equally, in order to relate to this hierarchy of tasks and of information of qualitatively different kinds of complexity, we have to organize our cognitive processes in an isomorphic hierarchy of different kinds of cognitive complexity, to which the concept of *levels of abstraction* may aptly be applied. This outlook may be familiar as the ordinarily accepted experience that things in the outside world do undergo sudden and discontinuous changes in quality or state.

SOME BACKGROUND

The argument to be pursued derives from research experience over the past thirty years in the development of concepts and principles for designing and structuring our social institutions in such a manner as to support constructive and effective human interaction and individual creativity and satisfaction. I shall not dwell upon this work, but shall cull only those findings which initiated the present lines of thought. (A full description will be found in such works as: Jaques, 1976, 1982a,b, 1986; Jaques, Gibson, and Isaac, 1978; Stamp, 1981, 1986; Jacobs and Jaques, 1986.) The first major finding concerns the structure of bureaucratic systems. These systems, when well regulated, have been observed to have a regular and universally occurring underlying structure of levels of organization, a universal pattern of stratification (McNeil, Jaques, and McNicol, 1969; Rowbottom and Billis, 1978; Jaques et al., 1978; Evans, 1979). This pattern shows up when you measure the time-span (T/S) at which those in roles at different levels in the systems are required to work. The T/Ss are measured by the tasks with the longest target times for completion which can be found in a given role.

The T/Ss of roles increase as you go higher in the hierarchy, just as complexity increases; the higher in the system the longer the timeframe in which work takes place. But the interesting thing is that those T/Ss also give a fix on what constitutes effective manager–subordinate relationships. For some reason or other (to be discussed below) no full-scale managerial roles are found with T/Ss below the three-month mark. That is to say, if you have a so-called manager in a two-month T/S role, with a "subordinate" working at, say, one week, then the subordinate will really look to whomever is next up in the hierarchy working above three months as his or her true, immediately accountable superior. In the same way it does not work for a manager in a role of less than twelve-month T/S—say nine months—to have subordinates in roles between three- and nine-month T/S. The manager will not operate as a fully accountable manager should because he/she will be too close; the manager will be felt to be breathing down the subordinates' necks, and felt to be neither setting context nor adding value.

Similar boundaries occur at two-, five-, ten-, twenty-, and fifty-year T/S, giving the optimum pattern of strata shown in Figure 3.1. This diagram is intended to illustrate the finding that lines of command A and B will be experienced as having the "right" number of managerial levels, whereas lines C and D will be experienced as having "too many" levels (the commonly found situation) wherever there are two or more roles compressed within one of these strata with its specific time-span band.

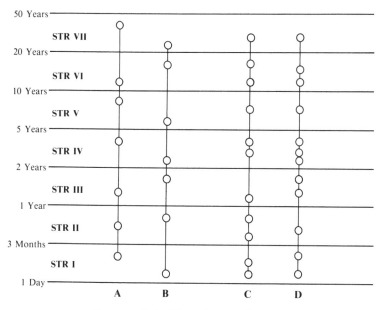

FIGURE 3.1. Time-Span Strata.

WHY THESE UNIVERSALLY OCCURRING
BOUNDARIES AND ORGANIZATIONAL STRATA?

These firm boundaries were first noticed in the late 1950s, some five or six years after time-span as an objective measure of level of work had been discovered (Jaques, 1961, 1964; Richardson, 1971). The existence of the boundaries was intriguing and called for explanation. What could there be about effective full-scale manager – subordinate relationships, which required the manager to be operating in one particular time-span range while the subordinate was operating in the next lower range? What was so magic about T/S three-months, one-year, two-years, and so on? It had something of the same quality as the peculiar significance of the 0°C and 100°C boundaries for changes in state of H_2O through crystal, liquid, and vaporous states at sea level pressure. There was some sort of equivalent change-of-state phenomenon, but change in state of what?

The only reasonable hypothesis which came to mind was that there must be changes in the nature of work and in the capability of individuals to do that work. And so initial hypotheses were constructed, based upon some observations of the nature of tasks at these various strata (Jaques, 1965). There was a concreteness to tasks at Str. I, II, and III, and a more general quality to Str. IV and V. So a first construction was formulated in terms of perceptual concrete work at Str. I, imaginal concrete at Str. II, and conceptual concrete at Str. III. Str. IV and V were formulated in terms of abstract modeling and theory construction respectively. This first attempt at hypothesis construction was a bit of a shot in the dark, based upon preliminary data about differences in the quality of work. But it was a start, and has been the subject of repeated reformulation since. It did, however, suffer from a major shortcoming which has dogged attempts at clarification until the present time; namely, it failed to make a clear distinction between task complexity and cognitive complexity, mixing them into one conceptual set in which tasks could be described in terms of their levels of abstraction, cognitive capability could be described in terms of tasks achieved, and vice versa. The latest of these developments was published in Jaques (1986) and Jacobs and Jaques (1986).

In this chapter, two entirely different sets of constructs will be put forward. The first set of constructs will describe the complexity of the external reality of tasks and information, and will do so in terms of the pathways which have to be traversed in order to reach a particular goal using available knowledge and technology. The second set of constructs will describe the complexity of the cognitive processes used to cope with external reality and its problems, and will do so in terms of the complexity of the mental sets or categories which individuals build as a means of ordering the external reality with which they choose to deal.

THE NATURE OF WORK

There are two major and all-inclusive categories of human activity. One is the category of purposeful activity, expressed in goal-directed behavior. The second is the category of free-floating musing, reverie, and dreaming, without immediate goals. Both activities are essential for reason and sanity. I shall focus upon the former, and shall refer to goal-directed activity as *work,* for it is in relation to working upon our environment, both internal and external, that we encounter both task complexity and cognitive complexity. It will be essential for our present purpose, therefore, that we should be clear and unequivocal about the meaning of *work.* I shall define it as the exercise of judgment (discretion) in order to reach a goal, always within limits and always with a maximum targeted completion time. The *task* is expressed in terms of the goal to be achieved, within the targeted completion time and resources. The *work* has to do with the effort connected with the use of judgment (discretion) in traversing a pathway to reach the goal, and in choosing that pathway (if it has not been provided). The *task complexity* lies in the complexity of the pathway to the goal. *Cognitive complexity* refers to the complexity of the categories created by the individual in exercising the judgment. The *limits* refer to the objective laws, policies, rules, regulations, and established custom and practice, as well as the resources, within which the individual is constrained in exercising judgment: adherence to limits is a matter of knowing what is required, and, other than at the boundaries, is not a matter of judgment. Computers can be programmed to stay within limits; they cannot (and never will) exercise judgment. Judgment is a prime human activity, and the processes by which choices are finally made are unconscious. Judgments result in decisions in the form of observable choices (Jaques [1982b, chapter 5]). In that cognitive processes are unconscious, cognitive complexity therefore has to do with the nature of the structure of unconscious purposeful mental activity. We can infer the processes and their complexity by observing the outcomes in choice patterns in moving along pathways toward articulated goals.

TASK COMPLEXITY IN BUREAUCRATIC HIERARCHIES

Tasks come in a vast range of degrees of complexity, from the very simplest (putting a lump of sugar into a cup) to the massively complex (putting a man on the moon). They also come in packages, or categories, they change in nature as they get more complex.

It is like H_2O; H_2O can come in a vast range of temperatures from $-273°C$ to many thousands of °C, but at the same time it also comes in packages or categories, changes in state, as it gets warmer, from solid ice, to liquid water, to vaporous steam. For H_2O, under normal conditions of pressure, these changes in state occur at predictable temperatures. For tasks, under normal conditions of task assignments (nonemergency multiplicity of tasks), the changes in form (i.e., changes in state) occur at predictable T/Ss.

Substances	Property	State	Measure
H_2O	Temperature	Ice/Liquid/Vapor	°C
Task	Complexity	Linear/Diagnostic/etc.	T/S

But it is critically important to note that *task complexity lies in the path to the goal, not in the goal.* Whether or not a particular goal is complex depends upon what you have to do in order to achieve it. For example, "Put a man on the moon" is very complex at present because of what you have to do; but it might become very much less complex in years to come, as knowledge and experience make it much easier to do. Thus, in order to get at the complexity of a task, you must analyze what the individual is required to do with the available knowledge and resources.

The following are descriptions of task complexity as found in the seven strata outlined above. Let me start with problems at the first level, namely Str. I, and build up to the nature of the higher-level corporate work at the end.

First-Order Complexity: Practical Judgment

At Str. I: First-line manual work and clerical work.

- *Main characteristics:* A task is assigned in terms of an output which can be concretely illustrated by a drawing or example of what is wanted. A path/method and resources are specified. Find ways of overcoming any obstacles as you hit them, and if you find you cannot do so, then see your manager (or your manager's surrogate, if there is one):
  - Type this memorandum, coping with words difficult to read or hear.

- Machine this batch (say, by turning or milling or drilling), sensing how to deal with unexpected characteristics of metals machined.
- Drill holes with this jackhammer, and by touch-and-feel get around big rocks in the ground in the way of the drill.
- Police this beat, sensing how best to deal on the spot with any suspicious signs.
- Get the answers to these questions from this family, feeling your way into getting round an uncooperative mother who won't answer questions.

In short, at Str. I an individual uses a touch-and-feel shaping approach to achieve the required output, proceeding along a given pathway to a goal, getting continual feedback, and overcoming immediate obstacles.

Second-Order Complexity: Diagnostic Accumulation

At Str. II: First-line managerial work, and what is ordinarily described as specialist work of the kind to be done by "graduates" (graduate engineers, graduate scientists, graduate therapists—but not graduate lawyers and doctors).

- *Main characteristics:* Task outputs cannot be completely specified, they need some interpretation. Touch-and-feel shaping is now encompassed in the need to accumulate data of significance which can in due course be put together in order to resolve a problem:
  - As her manager, get this new subordinate trained up in four months, judging how to proceed as you go, in the light of your accumulating judgment of her progress.

- Design a new jig for this machining process, working out the design as you go, accumulating data on how various parts are best likely to fit together so that the whole will work well.
- Use good detective procedures to accumulate the evidence necessary to find the hit-and-run driver.
- Diamond-drill a 3,000-foot-deep bore hole, accumulating judgments about the geological structures you cut through, in order to keep your drill straight and to assist the survey geologists in analyzing the underground structure.
- Carry out a case work-up on this family, using your judgment in gathering what you consider to be significant data to arrive at your diagnosis of how best to handle their problem.

In short, at Str. II an individual not only uses touch-and-feel shaping but also must *reflect on what he or she is doing,* so as to *accumulate the significant data necessary to be able to conclude what to do and how to go about doing it.*

Third-Order Complexity: Alternative Logical Tree Pathways

At Str. III: Managing mutual-recognition units employing up to a maximum of 250 to 300 people; and the kind of work done by senior or chief engineers, scientists, and so on, or graduate lawyers or doctors.

- *Main characteristics:* In order to get on with work, including both touch-and-feel shaping and diagnostic accumulation, the person must first consider the situation and work out alternative pathways or routes by which the problems might be resolved; and in particular, find a path which stands a chance of coping with short-run requirements (say, weeks or a few months) while at the same time providing the initial stages of a realistic path toward longer-term goals a year or more ahead. He must be able to change to alternative paths if his initial choice of path turns out to be unsatisfactory:

- A unit manager of a machining unit works out a number of possible ways of meeting a target of increasing output by 10 percent over eighteen months while holding his current output targets. He chooses one path from several which he has constructed, a path which makes it difficult to keep to his output targets for nearly six months, but then he will begin to catch up and get on top of his targets after a year.

- A project manager in a computer company heads a team of four programmers on a project to find a program which will make it possible to translate material from one computer language to another. He constructs three possible paths to the goal: one would be sure but would take much too long; one would be excellent if it worked but would lead to project failure if it did not; the third is relatively sound and could most likely be completed in the time available, although it might be slow and create uncertainty in the early stages. He opts for the third.

In short, at Str. III, in working you must not only use touch-and-feel shaping and do so reflectively and with diagnostic accumulation, but you must also be able to encompass the whole process within a plan and pathway which you have worked out in the first place—and have alternative paths to change to if need be. In thinking out various pathways, you have to envisage critical choice points which you are likely to encounter, and to assess those choice points as a series in relation to one another; that is to say, as a logic tree.

Fourth-Order Complexity: Parallel Processing of Multiple Pathways: PERT Charts

At Str. IV: Here we move across one of the key boundaries from direct management at Str. III to general management at Str. IV. It is the world of the product development GM, the production GM, and the sales GM, of senior project managers, researchers, or analysts.

- *Main characteristics:* It is no longer sufficient to pursue one pathway. You have to deal with a number of level 3 logic tree pathways all running at the same time and all interconnected with one another—either by yourself pursuing a number of different projects simultaneously and connecting them as you go, or by managing a number of subordinates each sailing energetically down his or her own pathway, and keeping them in synchrony with one another in resourcing and on schedule. You must not only be able to guide any of them into alternative paths, but you yourself must be able to contrast what they are doing, by paired comparison with other possible Str. III methods of getting the work done.

  The planning of projects of this kind can be carried out with PERT charts. It is like driving a chariot with five lively horses each on a separate set of reins, each fighting for its own head, and having to be pulled in and let out in relation to the other four, so that the chariot runs smoothly and rapidly as the horses gallop along in controlled unison:

- A factory general manager develops a PERT chart for a three-year program to reduce cost and increase volume of output, within which he agrees initial eighteen-month paths for each of his unit managers—in the foundry, rough machining, finished machining, works engineers, tool room, production engineering, scheduling, and personnel departments—as a part of that program. He then adjusts, and keeps in balance, the rate of progress in each of those departments, adding or withholding resource allocations as necessary; and reconstructing the PERT chart if required.
- A designer and developer of new venture products for a large corporation (who has four assistants to help him) has to construct and pursue simultaneously a number of development paths—a developing design of the product and product applications; an in-group analysis of potential international markets; the making and testing of models of the new product; and a sustained commercial analysis of potential value of business to the corporation. A balanced focusing of attention upon each of them in relation to the others is essential and difficult to achieve. The designer may require to change any of the pathways at any time, and in doing so he will have to adjust each of the others, all in relation to each other.

In short, at Str. IV you have to *parallel process numbers of interacting projects,* pacing them in relation to one another in resourcing and in time. You probably do it by *paired comparison*—taking one project at a time and comparing it with another, or comparing it with some other possible alternative which you might want to use.

*Fifth-Order Complexity: Unified Whole Systems
(Plerimorphs)*

At Str. V: Here we move into the most interesting and
important of all the orders of complexity. It is the level
at which you have to use practical judgment and sensing
to deal with whole systems. By unified whole system I
mean a true system as assumed in systems theory; that
is to say, an open system intact and complete in itself
and operating in an unbounded environment. It is of such
central importance to the analysis of complexity that I
shall coin a new term for it: the *plerimorph* (full form).

- *Main characteristics:* It is a quality of human nature
  to be able to organize complexity out to a five- to
  ten-year time-horizon and to retain the ability to
  predict or forecast with sufficient confidence to undertake budgeted plans and projects. Beyond that
  the crystal ball grows dim—and we shift from forecast planning to determining a so-called long-range
  vision beyond ten and twenty years forward—the
  envisionment of what we would like to see but cannot yet plan for in concrete resourcing.
      The complexity is that of being able to sense or
  to get an overall judgment of the likely impact of
  changes or events—either from outside the plerimorph or from inside it—on any and all parts of the
  system; to pick out those parts where the impact is
  likely to be severe or important; to trace the likely
  second- and third-order consequences of those im-
  pacts; and to sustain an active anticipation of what
  changes are likely to unfold:
    - A strategic business unit (SBU) president is driv-
      ing a group of a half-dozen critical tasks to achieve
      a seven-year plan, and has continually to pick up

the important areas of impact and the high-prior-
ity likely consequences of a never-ending kalei-
doscope of changes and events: on customer
attitudes; on competition and policies; on world
commodity prices; on legislation; on third world
countries; on tariffs; on technology; on his own
R&D programs; on interest and foreign exchange
rates; on availability and cost of capital; on cash
flow, and so on. In order to do all this, he main-
tains an ongoing "what-if" analysis of business
priorities to sharpen his judgments of what has
to be done at any given time. He steers his business in the surrounding environment to keep his
profits at a reasonable level while maintaining
customer goodwill, a high morale among his own
people, and the survival of his business in the ten-
year term.

In short, at Str. V you have to cope by means of touch-
and-feel judgment, with a constantly shifting kaleido-
scope of events and consequences with vastly too many
variables to map on a PERT chart, while steering your
way on course through an open environment.

*Sixth-Order Complexity: Worldwide Diagnostic
Accumulation: Asset Values*

At Str. VI: The shift from fifth-order to sixth-order complexity is the most significant shift of all; tasks of first-
order to fifth-order complexity can all take place inside
the boundary of a unified system. Tasks of sixth-order
(and higher) complexity can no longer be so readily contained. They constitute the work of corporate executives
at Str. VI, commonly titled executive vice-presidents
(EVPs) or senior VPs.

It is the shift from P&L accounting to the balance sheet; that is to say, from the SBU president's operation of a P&L business to the overseeing not only of that operation but of the overall *value* of the business as reflected in the balance sheet and in its being an object of increased or decreased investment or of possible divestment.

- *Main characteristics:* Work at Str. VI occurs in a setting of continual bombardment of political, economic, social, technological, and intellectual events from the whole wideworld environment—the PESTI-W^3E space in which you float. It calls for the understanding of that world and action to influence it in favorable ways. It is the world of the operations EVP overseeing groups of SBUs, the corporate treasurer, the corporate counsel, the EVP corporate strategic analysis, the EVP human resources.

    The focus of the work is on worldwide networking in any and all areas likely to be significant to the corporation in a given field of endeavor. You must accumulate significant data (as in second-order complexity but worldwide and unbounded) and screen out the less significant. And you must reflect relevant national and world situations back into the corporation and into subordinate Str. V plerimorphs (again, similar to the reflective working upon the first-order basic element at Str. II, but the reflective work is unbounded), thereby sustaining as friendly an environment as possible for the corporation and its plerimorphs:
    - An operational EVP, overseeing six full-scale P&L account SBUs, sustains a worldwide PESTI network and information sources and picks out changes which may constitute unexpected threats or opportunities for any of his SBUs. He applies

pressure to influence this environment, by such
means as sponsoring or encouraging particular
pieces of research in given universities or research
associations, seeing political and government
leaders and senior public servants, working with
trade associations, keeping contact with the top-
level executives of large customers. Against this
background, and within corporate capital expenditure policies, he decides whether and when to
seek changes in the major resourcing of a given
SBU, taking into account other corporate priority
demands.

• A corporate treasurer operates in similar fashion,
but concentrates on networking in the major
world capital markets in order to keep close to
events and to influence financial world leaders.

In short, at Str. VI you must move about in *PESTI W³E
space,* reacting to it and influencing it, helping to provide
a friendly environment, and judging corporate investment priorities so as to enhance the *value of corporate
assets* as reflected in the balance sheet and to ensure
corporate long-term success and survival.

Seventh-Order Complexity: Putting Plerimorphs into Society: Culture and Values

At Str. VII: Here we move to the executive leadership—the
CEOs, the COOs, the presidents—of large corporations.
In its essence the work is concerned with judging what
the requirements of society are, nationally or internationally, and deciding what institutions to provide to satisfy them. A twenty- to twenty-five-year-plus future must
be envisioned, and conceptual pathways and alternatives
must be constructed which provide starting routes toward

that future, by developing new plerimorphs, transforming existing ones, or divesting others.

Culture and values push to the forefront—the culture and values of nations and of societies, and their relation to your own corporate culture and values. Your corporate value as expressed in your corporate balance sheet will reflect the judgment society makes about how successfully you provide what it values and about how much it believes your long-term envisionment coincides with its vision of where it wishes to go.

- *Main characteristics:* Just as sixth-order complexity repeats second-order complexity but in a much more complex global world, so a seventh-order complexity mirrors third-order complexity, but here also in a greatly expanded world. At third-order complexity the executive must construct alternative plans for producing ranges of specific outputs—things, designs, services, analyses. At the level of seventh-order complexity (Str. VII) the executive (now among the most senior of all executives) must also construct alternative plans, but they are now called strategic plans for producing new or modified SBUs—new ventures—and placing them out in W^3E; in short, it is now unified complex systems (plerimorphs) themselves which constitute the output:
  - For example, a Str. VII corporate chairman and CEO is expanding his company, developing two additional Str. VI EVP roles as a base for growing between five and seven new SBUs: some already partially grown within the company but in need of capital infusions to enable them to grow into true Str. V companies; some to be developed to capitalize upon new products in fields at one re-

move from existing business; and some to be added
by acquisition of new small companies with interesting products and outstanding young potential talent—a double gain. He has worked out a
number of alternative strategic paths, has agreed
them with the board, and is currently pursuing
one of them which calls for penetration into related fields both at home and abroad—a program
which is planned to see the corporation well into
the twenty-first century.

In short, at Str. VII you must develop and pursue *alternative strategic plans,* out in the PESTI W³E space, producing unified complex plerimorphs as your output,
involving internationally supported financial resourcing.

PROBLEM SOLVING AT LEVELS OF LESSER
COMPLEXITY

So much, then, for the qualitative changes in the nature
of task complexity at each adult work stratum. There are
two phenomena embedded in the foregoing descriptions
which I shall now extract and examine. The first phenomenon is a hierarchy of four states of task complexity:
touch-and-feel shaping; diagnostic accumulation; alternative logical tree pathway; and parallel processing.
Each state characterizes the work of a particular work
stratum (for example, Str. IV: parallel processing, two-
to five-year T/S). The second phenomenon is that each of
these four different states of task complexity may reap-
pear in a higher stratum in a more complex or higher-
level setting. These two features are illustrated in Table
3.1.
    This scheme can be further extended from data ob-
tained by work on the assessment of mental handicap
carried out by Ian Macdonald and Terry Couchman (see

TABLE 3.1
HIERARCHY OF STATES OF TASK COMPLEXITY

——————— 50Y ———————		
Str. VII	Alternative Pathways to the Development of Whole Systems	
——————— 20Y ———————		
Str. VI	Diagnostic Accumulation of Significant Events in World Environment	
——————— 10Y ———————		
Str. V	Touch-and-Feel Shaping of Whole Systems from Within	
——————— 5Y ———————		
Str. IV	Parallel Processing Concrete Systems	
——————— 2Y ———————		
Str. III	Alternative Logical Tree Pathways	
——————— 1Y ———————		
Str. II	Diagnostic Accumulation of Tangible Events	
——————— 3M ———————		
Str. I	Touch-and-Feel	
——————— 1D ———————		

Macdonald, 1978a). They found that mentally handicapped individuals live in a world of complexity which is strikingly similar to the above four states of task complexity but in relation to a much more limited and concrete world and requiring the continual assistance of an aide. They formulated this material into an assessment form (Macdonald and Couchman, 1980).

Thus, in their scheme the first-order task complexity is one in which the individual will sit and rock and do nothing unless prompted by an aide, whereupon simple tackling of a problem may occur by touch and feel. The prompting requires to be carried out with respect both to setting goals and to deciding how to achieve them. For example, if the individual is hungry he will not be sure

what to do about it. But if an aide should suggest a sandwich and show him how to get it, he will, with help, be
able to feed himself. Given both a goal and a path he will
be able to *shape* an action.

In their description the first level (called Mode A) is
described so as to explain that even when goals are set
"the person still needs to have the plan told or shown to
them, step by step" (p. 273). In "Five Levels of Mental
Handicap" Macdonald (1978a) explains: "in the first, or
most dependent stage a person cannot achieve any
goals. . . . There is no independence, activity is dependent
upon external assistance in the form of staff aids . . ."
(p. 4). He further states, in a Unit Paper (1983), relating
the mental handicap levels to language:

> However, there is no articulate language, instead there
> are sounds, noises, gurgling, etc. The point about such
> utterances it that there is some sense of expression of
> need although it is the full responsibility of the other
> person or the outside world to distinguish the nature,
> the type of need and the extent of response and also the
> extent to which the need has been satisfied. Again the
> concept of self and outside world is tenuous therefore
> the other takes primary responsibility for making de-
> cisions as to the nature and behaviour of the outside
> world [p. 5].

At level 2 the individual will be able to *accumulate
simple* data necessary to follow a path if he is aided to
construct a goal. Thus, if the aide suggests a sandwich,
the individual will himself be able to reach for it without
having to be shown how to do it. Macdonald (1983) explains: "The difference from stage 1 is that the plan is
not an exact repetition of previously taught behaviour
but contains some slight variation sensitive to the external situation" (p. 5).

He goes on to say that this stage "involves nominal identity, reflected in the use of language for example, dog, car, house (nouns only). Therefore things *are* and their names are actually part of them. However, there is a beginning of primitive sets but still totally located in visible objects presented by the outside world" (Macdonald, 1983, p. 5).

At level 3 the individual will be able to choose possible paths to a goal, but once committed to his goal and path he is on a rigid and inflexible *action* from which he cannot readily be shifted, slowed, or diverted. He cannot entertain any alternative unless he has thought of it himself. This level is that of the handicapped who are prone to temper outbursts if attempts are made to dissuade them from doing what they have determined to do.

Macdonald and Couchman (Macdonald, 1978a) describe this level 3 as follows:

> [T]he characteristic . . . is that the goal and plan are fixed, indeed welded together, precluding alteration. It is a perception of the right way to do something in relation to me. A very simple black and white value system is used. There is very little, if any, toleration of frustration. . . . There is no attempt to accommodate . . . to the needs of others. [External refusal] creates repeated requests and demands which are characterized by repetition. . . [p. 274].

The person in stage 3 will be less amenable than in 2 or 1 but at the same time more capable of action and survival, especially in a physical sense. At this stage a sense of identity, a concept of self, has emerged. However, the brittle ego is unable to cope with holding two options at once. Choice is characterized by wholesale total acceptance or rejection of complete goal/plan packages.

In the paper relating to language, Macdonald continues: "There is a singularity about behaviour which is seen totally in terms of me and my needs without consideration of other people. . . . Language reflects this stage of development with the first use of the words me, and mine" (p. 275).

At level 4 a more flexible pattern of behavior emerges. Others might have their own *alternatives* to the individual's desired or chosen course of action. The individual must understand that other people may have such alternative points of view or desires and *parallel process* his own pathways with theirs.

This parallel processing is described in the Chart of Initiative and Independence (Macdonald, 1983):

> However, this perception of others' needs is limited. . . .
> It is less egocentric (than stage 3) but the toleration of delay and the ability to cope with frustration breaks down if the goal itself is threatened. Thus a person may ask "Can I go to the shops?" If the reply is "Yes, but can you wait until after lunch?" this could be tolerated. If, however, the answer raised doubts about the goal . . . then the anxiety (as in stage 3) would begin to arise.

In the MoC Unit Paper (1983) Macdonald explains this as the: "First stage of initiated action with flexibility represented as me and a changing world. Self and needs are still fixed. However, there is an introduction of verbs and primitive sentences. A sense but not necessarily clear articulation of intentionality. Understanding that you are also me or a me" (p. 6).

At level 5, individuals are able to function at the *touch-and-feel shaping* level as unskilled or semiskilled operators or clerks. They are in fact capable of living on their own. If they have been labeled mentally handicapped it will be because they were put in that stream in early childhood and have been rendered dependent by institutional care. They can be aided to assume an independent role in real life. This level-5 activity is referred to by Macdonald (1978b) as ". . . the final level which corresponds to effective independence. It is of note that where level of opportunity and capacity correspond, staff in practice no longer use the terms 'mentally handicapped patient or resident.' The reticence to use the term does not seem to stem only from a general dislike of 'labels', but, whatever the IQ score, if a person shows this capacity it seems inappropriate to use the term . . ." (p. 262).

From the Chart of Initiative and Independence it can be seen that "there is an understanding of rational argument and the goal and plan . . . are both potentially open to modification and substitution" (p. 6). This understanding is summarized in the MoC Unit Paper (Macdonald, 1983) as the first complete sense of self in terms of I, reflected in language as the comfortable use of the personal pronoun. Others are also recognized as alternative I's. It differs from other levels in that the world is now populated with individuals all using personal pronouns. Consequently, the person can actually leave him- or herself temporarily and consider others' needs. This is clearly not such an egocentric world and recognizes that other people have needs and wants.

Finally Macdonald describes this level 5 as an overlapping level, the last in mental handicap and first in ordinary life:

> It is the first conscious sense of self in terms of: I am and I am me. Boundaries are clear but may be painful. There is now a sense of control and effect on the world. There is now the first use of the personal pronoun "I". "I" is the entity. This is the first point at which there is a clear articulation of intentionality in terms of an active agent in the world in collaboration and compe-

tition with other active agents in the same world [Mac-donald, 1978a, p. 275].

This pattern of problem-solving activities in individuals we categorize as mentally handicapped will be recognized as practically identical with the development of infants and small children. Breast-feeding coincides with level 1, the preverbal overcoming of feeding problems by touch-and-feel shaping at the breast.

At level 2 the child has begun to speak, so that simple verbal suggestions can be given and understood. The act of speaking itself requires the accumulation of simple observations in order to get the sense of words as referring to classes of concretely "pointable-at" things—minimally to the "something" at different times. Words are only partially abstract in the sense that they are not detachable from specific things or events either at hand or recently observed. At level 3 the same pathway construction held on to with the same impatient rigidity is seen in children as in the mentally handicapped. It is accompanied by the same temper tantrums when an ongoing activity is interrupted or stopped.

The beginning of socialization in turn calls for the parallel processing characteristics of level-4 complexity. Maturation to this point gives the child a broader sense of the needs of others in relation to its own needs. It will have matured out of its single-minded concern with its own immediate goals and into a broader self-consciousness which includes other-consciousness and hence the ability to interact with others in true common endeavor.

But neither the child nor the mentally handicapped adult who has matured to this level-4 cognitive power is yet able to cope with the complexity of employment work. The reason is that they are not yet able to deal with the cognitive categories required in work. They can cope with such concrete constructs as pens, pencils, chalk, ball-points, or lights, radios, TV sets, and cookers; as point-able-at things. But they will have difficulty in handling the more general idea that this pen, or this pencil, or this piece of chalk, or this ballpoint, are all writing imple-ments; or that this light, or radio, or TV, or cooker, are all pieces of electric equipment. And this second level of abstraction in which words can replace pointable-at things as entities, is necessary to be able to achieve the touch-and-feel shaping required for the level of task com-plexity of the workshop or the office (although the men-tally handicapped adult might just be able to cope in a protected environment, for example, farm work in a small village setting).

The next move, to level 5, would thus be a move to the touch-and-feel shaping which was also the level 1 described above for the ordinary Str. I organization level. That is to say, level 5 at the top of the child/mentally handicapped sequence overlaps with the bottom of the ordinary adult sequence of work stratification.

A QUINTAVE STRUCTURE OF TASK COMPLEXITY

If we put these findings together we get the following pattern. The fifth level of child/mentally handicapped task complexity overlaps and coincides with the first level of task complexity to be found at Str. I in ordinary work systems. Then when we move up to Str. V we find that it is both the top of the five strata making up the orga-nization levels of whole systems and at the same time at the bottom or the beginning of a yet higher series of touch-and-feel shaping diagnostic accumulation, alter-native pathways, and parallel processing, at the corpo-rate levels of organization.

This pattern is very much like the octave of the west-

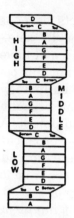

FIGURE 3.2. Scale of C Major.

ern musical scale. An octave contains seven notes and one repeated note; for example, in the scale of C major the first note, C, reappears as the eighth, and the same eighth note C is then the first note of the next higher octave (see Figure 3.2). The note C is always both the first note (1) and the eighth (8) in the scale. That is to say, the first note in the octave is a dual: it is both the bottom of the scale above and the top of the scale below.

Using this analogue we derive a quintave pattern of states of task complexity with the four states recurring in groups of five but operating in increasingly complex worlds. The first order of task complexity—that of touch-and-feel shaping—acts as the dual bottom and top of each quintave, as shown in Table 3.2.

The question then is, what are the differences between the quintaves? Direct observation suggests the answer. The entities which compose the world in which we live come in a hierarchy of domains of entities of increasing complexity. These entity-domains are reflected in the quintaves. The qualitative changes in entities occur in the following pattern.

TABLE 3.2
THE QUINTAVE PATTERN OF TASK COMPLEXITY

		QC-5	(Touch-and-Feel Shaping)
		QC-4	Parallel processing
Quintave C	Str. VII	QC-3	Alternative Pathways
	Str. VI	QC-2	Diagnostic Accumulation
	Str. V	QC-1/QB-5	(Touch-and-Feel Shaping)
	Str. IV	QB-4	Parallel Processing
Quintave B	Str. III	QB-3	Alternative Pathways
	Str. II	QB-2	Diagnostic Accumulation
	Str. I	QA-5/QB-1	(Touch-and-Feel Shaping)
		QA-4	Parallel Processing
Quintave A		QA-3	Alternative Pathways
		QA-2	Diagostic Accumulation
		QA-1	(Touch-and-Feel Shaping)

Quintave A

Those tasks which fall into Quintave A task complexity
deal only with the very simplest kinds of concrete entity.
Those entities may be described as things and events
which are immediately present in the sense that they can
be pointed to, or which have been recently observed. As
long as the person (child or mentally handicapped adult)

is in the presence of the thing–event, he or she can cope for the time being without outside assistance. But outside aides are required when it comes to changing from one event to a next one. The entities of Quintave A really are this immediate thing–event and not the next one. Examples would be to point to *this* piece of chalk for *this* line or drawing; or *this* pan for heating *this* water for *this* cup of coffee.

Quintave B

The entities of Quintave B are what might be thought of as composing the world of ordinary things and events. It will be noted, however, that "ordinary" in this sense is qualitatively and substantially more complex than those levels of the world of things and information among which the Quintave A population are functioning. Things and events are no longer necessarily immediately pointable. Absent things and events can be actively considered, discussed, and worked over verbally, even though the particular things being considered have never been observed but are known only through their category name.

This stepping away from the immediate touchable world of work is possible because that world can be chunked into secondary categories of the kind described above: the categories of writing implements, electrical equipment, wearing apparel, furniture, and so on, which make it possible to get away from the immediacy of categories such as hats, cats, or bats which are made up of this hat and that hat, and so on. Moreover, because things and events can now be dealt with by fully abstract words and therefore need not be immediately present to be worked with, information and problems are set free to be dealt with imaginatively. They can not only be worked with in the perceivable present, but also reworked in memory, and hence used as iterative learning experience; and they can be worked over in anticipation, as hunches or hypotheses about what might be, and about what might be done about what might be—as in "what-if" planning and scientific work.

Quintave C

It is notable that at Str. V, which is not only the top of Quintave B but also the beginning of Quintave C, the full-scale whole-system plerimorph emerges. The "ordinary" things and information of Quintave B are chunkable into subsystems (subsets) such as production technology systems, competitive price structures, sales systems, pay structures; or into scientific findings, or intellectual systems, and so on. These in turn can be categorized into social institutions such as strategic business units, or into systems of hypotheses and theories, or into economic and political programs, or into technological systems. It is these plerimorphs which then become secondary sets of Quintave C.

The fact that nature can be chunked into such categories opens up much wider horizons for human endeavor at that level of capability. The mental economy lies in being able to work with complex networks of ideas as things which can be related and used as mental building blocks. All three regions of work—memory of the past, perception of the present, and anticipation of the future—are unfolded wide open. In effect, the temporal and spatial horizons are opened up in all directions—past, present, and future.

Quintaves Below QA and Above QC

Below Quintave A we would have the world of the prenatal infant in whom the nature of mental functioning is a matter of speculation beyond our present concerns. The ability to function at level 1 Quintave A (QA-1) would be necessary for survival in the neonate.

As far as a possible Quintave D is concerned, it is noteworthy that very senior executives at Str. VIII (QC-4) and Str. IX (QC-5) tend almost uniformly to become interested not only in the vast enterprises they lead, but also in the interrelationship between those enterprises and the societies in which they function in their mutual impact. The clue here would be that the next domain of natural chunking of things and information would be in the form of the large corporate systems or theoretical or political systems which make up societies, and that individuals working at those levels would assume societies to be the things which they were working to change.

This concern about societies gives a possible clue to the nature of Quintave D. If we refer back to QB-4 (alternative systems of production) we will see that it looks upwards toward the Str. V work of QB-5 in that it is concerned with volume of output and its cost, and therefore is involved in notional profitability which becomes actual profitability at Str. V. By the same token, if Str. VIII (QC-4) is looking up to Str. IX (QC-5/QD-1) in its societal orientation, then QD-1 might be concerned with the shaping of societies.

The last conclusion in fact leads to speculation on a possible hypothesis about Quintave D. I think we are encountering at these levels those few rare individuals who actually modify societies, by working out new political systems, or large-scale corporate forms, or theoretical or intellectual systems: the QD-1 individual is capable of shaping these societal subsystems; QD-2 is capable not only of shaping such subsystems, but of reflectively articulating how a society is shaped and what kind of society he is trying to shape; QD-3 is a linear societal subsystem creator, but sees no alternative—he is the creator of dogma—far-reaching in social impact but dogma nevertheless; QD-4 is able to value and to teach toleration, and to value systems and dogma which might be alternatives to his own creation. I leave it to the reader to try to fit individuals into these categories, and to speculate on the nature of a possible Quintave E—connected perhaps with the construction of universals or of societies as a whole?

THE DUALITY AT QA-5/QB-1 AND AT QB-5/QC-1

There is a true duality at the top and bottom of each quintave. The first such duality is where QA-5 and QB-1 overlap—both in domains of task complexity characterized by touch-and-feel shaping in problem solving. The second is where QB-5 and QC-1 overlap—also in domains of task complexity characterized by touch-and-feel shaping, but now in relation to entities which are plerimorphs as compared with the ordinary world of extended things and events at the lower level. I would hypothesize the existence of similar dualities at the level-5/level-1 overlap making up the touch-and-feel shaping category at the top and bottom of each quintave.

Experience suggests the following characteristics of the duality at the QA-5/QB-1 and the QB-5/QC-1 levels. One of the features of the way the world of complexity is handled in Quintave A is by the use of aides—parents, siblings, relatives, friends, professional helpers—who must be at hand to help the individual maintain successful contact with the wider world of things and events which lies beyond the immediately present world of pointable-at things and events. This need for immediately available supervision continues at QA-5 into the workplace at Str. I. The people concerned are the so-called unskilled and lower-level semiskilled, for whom it is necessary to provide supervisory assistants (sometimes called leading hands, or junior foremen, or supervisors) to help the accountable manager by acting for him in a limited way on each shift. These supervisory assistants may specify tasks, teach and train on behalf of the manager, and report to the manager how the subordinates have been getting on.

When, however, you get to the middle and top of Str. I, there are the higher-level semiskilled and the skilled operators and office staff who are also working by touch-and-feel shaping. But they can now work without continual direct supervision of their activity.

At the QB-5/QC-1 transition there is an equally established duality. It exists in the recognized distinction between two levels of leadership and complexity adopted by leaders of plerimorphs. First, there are those leaders of plerimorphs who are oriented almost exclusively downwards and outwards. That is to say, downwards toward their immediate subordinates and to the directing of their activities, and outwards to their markets and suppliers, so that they can maintain control over the whole. They operate as the true QB-5 top level of Quintave B, and do so effectively.

Then there is an equivalent complexity at the upper part of Str. V (the QC-1 complexity) which is not only oriented downwards and outwards but which calls for touch-and-feel shaping tasks oriented upwards toward the strategic development task complexity which is inherent in the tasks of the Str. VI and Str. VII corporate levels of organization.

This distinction within Str. V leadership is described in terms of those strategic business units, CEOs, or diocesan bishops, or army major-generals commanding divisions, who make substantial inputs into the outlook of the corporate entity, as compared with those who do not. The upward orientation is seen as a function of the more capable and experienced leaders who have become able to take up the full complexity of the tasks of the Str. V role, as against those who have not yet done so. In the terms used in the present analysis, it is a matter of the transition within Str. V from still being gripped within the Quintave B world to entering the first stages of the Quintave C world complexity.

QUINTAVE STRUCTURE: SUMMARY

If we put these findings together, we get the following pattern. The fifth level of child/mental handicap task complexity overlaps and coincides with the first level of task complexity to be found at Str. I in ordinary work systems. Then when we move up to Str. V we find it is both the top of the five strata making up the organization levels of whole systems and at the same time at the bottom or the beginning of a yet higher series of touch-and-feel shaping, diagnostic accumulation, alternative pathways, and parallel processing at the corporate levels of organization. Figure 3.3 sets out a summary of the task complexity quintaves. The progression of quintaves is shown, each with its four levels of task complexity. The organizational strata are indicated, with their equivalent categories of task complexity from QA-5/QB-1 to QC-4.

The question, of course, is how human beings are able to deal with this hierarchical pattern of task complexity which occurs in nature. That question will be the subject of the next chapter, in which we shall explore the hypothesis that there is a hierarchy of categories of cognitive complexity which is isomorphic with the categories of task complexity, individuals being able to deal with

78

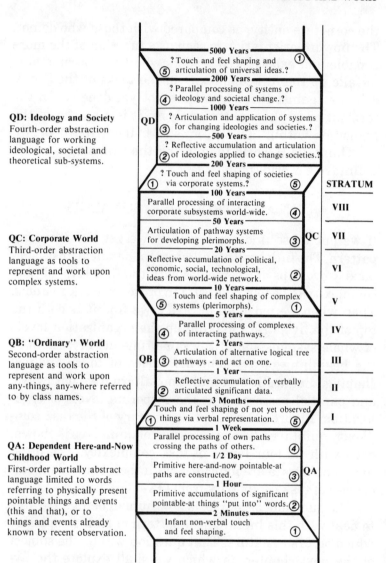

FIGURE 3.3. The Task Complexity Quintaves

external task complexity up to their own level of cognitive complexity.

REFERENCES

Evans, J. S. (1979), *Management of Human Capacity*. Bradford, UK: MCB Books.

Jacobs, T. O., & Jaques, E. (1986), Leadership in complex systems. In: *Human Productivity Enhancement,* ed. J. Zeidner. New York: Praeger.

Jaques, E. (1961), *Equitable Payment*. London: Heinemann Educational Books Ltd.

—— (1964), *Time-Span Handbook*. London: Heinemann Educational Books Ltd.

—— (1965), Speculations concerning level of capacity. In: *Glacier Project Papers,* ed. W. Brown & E. Jaques. London: Heinemann Educational Books Ltd.

—— (1976), *A General Theory of Bureaucracy*. Exeter, NH: Heinemann Educational Books Ltd.

—— (1982a), *Free Enterprise, Fair Employment*. New York: Crane Russak.

—— (1982b), *The Form of Time*. New York: Crane Russak.

—— (1986), Development of intellectual capability: A discussion of stratified systems theory. *J. Appl. Behav. Sci.,* 22/164:361–384.

—— Gibson, R. O., & Isaac, D. J. (1978), *Levels of Abstraction in Logic and Human Action*. London: Heinemann Educational Books Ltd.

Macdonald, I. (1978a), Five levels of mental handicap. In: *Levels of Abstraction in Logic and Human Action,* ed. E. Jaques, R. O. Gibson, & D. J. Isaac. London: Heinemann Educational Books Ltd.

—— (1978b), Assessment of mental handicap: The Leavesden Project. In: *Health Services,* ed. E. Jaques. London: Heinemann Educational Books Ltd.

—— (1983), Quintaves: Five-level system of five levels. *Unit Paper, Measurement of Capacity Unit*. Uxbridge, Middlesex, UK: Brunel University Institute of Organisation and Social Studies.

—— Couchman, T. (1980), *The Chart of Initiative and Independence*. London: NFER/Nelson.

McNeil, H., Jaques, E., & McNicol, W. (1969), *Report of a Review of the Organisation of the Council and Export Programmes of the Board of Trade*. London: Board of Trade.

Richardson, R. (1971), *Fair Pay and Work*. London: Heinemann Educational Books Ltd.

Rowbottom, R. W., & Billis, D. (1978), Stratification of work and organisational design. In: *Levels of Abstraction in Logic and Human Action,* ed. E. Jaques, R. O. Gibson, & D. J. Isaac. London: Heinemann Educational Books Ltd.

Stamp, G. (1981), Levels and types of managerial capability. *J. Mgt. Studies,* 18/3:331–342.

—— (1986), Some observations on the career paths of women. *J. Appl. Behav. Sci.,* 22/4:385–396.

Chapter 4

Cognitive Complexity

What kinds of psychological processes may we assume will be necessary to cope with the complexity of tasks which have been described in the preceding chapter? A starting hypothesis would be that they must be isomorphic with the discontinuous patterns of complexity of the external information sources. Such isomorphism would be essential if human beings were to be able to cope with the world and to survive.[1] If we do assume isomorphism, then we will need to search for a hierarchy of four cognitive processes corresponding to the four states of task complexity. The first of these four processes would have to manifest some form of duality. And all four would have to be able to be moved up or down as a quartet (or quintave with the bottom step repeating at the top), by operating in worlds made up of entities of grossly different orders of complexity.

It was the recent realization (T. O Jacobs, personal communication) that there has to be complete conceptual separation of cognitive complexity from external task complexity that made it possible to address this question of isomorphism directly. And the first question which had

[1] Isomorphism between mental processes and the structure of the environment has always been one of the central tenets of gestalt psychology, and has proven an effective explanatory principle.

81

to be answered was: what could be the central characteristic of this hierarchy of cognitive states. There was
one set of ideas which was immediately to hand, which
helped to resolve the issue. That set of ideas was contained in the concept of a hierarchy of sets of levels of
abstraction—for here we had both a hierarchy of levels
and increasingly abstract categories, with which to work.
Categories in turn are most readily expressed in terms
of sets and that was the key.

The definition which emerged was that *cognitive process complexity* has to do with the complexity of the sets
(or categories) which the individual is *able to construe* in
tackling a problem: not sets with which the individual
has been provided and has learned to use—for we all
know how to do that—but the unique purpose-made sets
put together by the individual specifically for organizing
the field of information for any particular task. It is a
matter of construing, in the sense used by Kelly (1955).
It may be apparent that the concept of set as used here
is that of the consciously articulated, the verbalized, set.
Sets, or categories, in this sense, are the function of language. When we speak of cars, telephones, or running,
or writing, we refer to categories of things or actions
which have already been construed and framed and which
have an established usage or meaning. They can therefore be pulled into play in a nonproblematic way for
everyday use in accord with the dictionary rules of definition.

THE CONSTRUAL OF SETS IN DECISION MAKING

A set is any well-defined list or collection of elements. By
"well-defined" is meant a definition which makes it possible to determine whether or not any element is or is not
a member of the set. There are two ways of specifying a

set. The first is simply by listing the members: as, for example, in listing Mr. and Mrs. Jones, and their two sons, John and William, as the set defining that particular Jones family.

A second way of defining a set, and this way is the one we shall mainly employ in our argument, is to state what it is that characterizes any member of the set. Thus, the Jones family could be defined as anyone who is living and who is either descended from Mr. and Mrs. Jones or related to them by birth or by marriage. Such a set would include Mrs. and Mr. Jones, plus John and William plus any other children they might have, and so on.

Our cognitive mental activity is organized in sets or categories; we cannot think without them. Speaking in sets is like speaking prose. We do it automatically, and from the beginning. Every time we speak of a pen, or of writing, or of a letter, we are speaking of things or activities which are members of sets of things or activities. It is this membership of sets, this categorization, which gives the words their meaning: it makes them understandable.

These examples of sets are examples of one of the two major categories of sets. This first category comprises those sets which have already been construed and are part of the normal universe of discourse. They constitute our language. The characteristics of these sets are defined in dictionaries. That is what dictionary definition of terms is about.

But there is a second great category of sets; namely, those unique new sets we form every day in the process of thinking and of making decisions. Sometimes we make our decisions by touch and feel, without construing explicit sets. Such decision making is called for in the touch-and-feel shaping described in the previous chapter as characteristic of the task complexity at the top end of each quintave—the QA5/QB1, QB5/QC1, QC-5/QD-1 boundaries. But more often we have to bring together data in the form of objects or events or values which we consider to be of significance; bringing them together in some particular way in order to arrive at a conclusion. Let me give some examples.

Decision making by touch and feel occurs every time you choose a particular course of action because it seems the right thing to do, or it appeals to you, or you just want to do it, or you feel you have no other choice, but without building up a case in order to decide—as in choosing a particular dish in a restaurant, or in tightening a bolt "just enough," or in exerting the right amount of force in lifting a heavy weight.

By contrast, a detective attempting to solve a mystery must proceed by building up a case step by step and piece by piece. He will be seeking clues; that is to say, discrete pieces of information which when assembled later on may produce a solution. In order to do so, he must develop hunches or articulate hypotheses, which provide the context within which he collects his significant pieces. As he accumulates more information, he may discard some data which he initially thought might be significant, and recall some which he had discarded but which now seem to fit. Finally, the various clues fall into place, and there is the "Eureka" experience which accompanies the discovery of the solution.

This account—familiar enough in Sherlock Holmes or Agatha Christie stories—illustrates the cognitive process worked in construing a set. The set in this case is the solution to the mystery. The members or elements of the set are data which when fitted together (within the boundary of the set) are significant for the solution—and significance for the case is the bounding principle or definition of the set.

This set can be drawn in simple terms as shown in Figure 4.1. *We may term it a unique, primary, discrete set.* It is *unique* in that it has been construed specially for this particular case. It is *primary* in that its members are data of immediate direct observation, and are not subsets. It is *discrete* in that it is not operated in relation to any other sets.

Let me now define three other types of sets (Figure 4.2). One type comprises *interactive primary sets,* which are primary sets, as defined above, but which are operated in relation to each other rather than discrete, either by adding sets together or breaking them apart, or by over-lapping them (the operations of union and intersection) as illustrated in the familiar Venn diagram.

The next is the *secondary set* (Figure 4.3), a set whose members are subsets; that is to say, it is a set which is

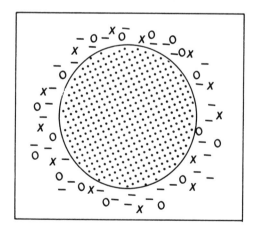

∴ Members of the set (significant data)

− O X Data which were rejected as not of significance.

FIGURE 4.1. Unique, Primary, Discrete Set.

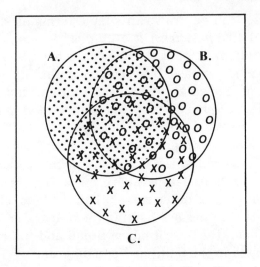

FIGURE 4.2. Interactive Primary Sets (Venn Diagram).

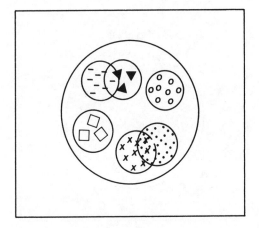

FIGURE 4.3. Secondary Set.

composed of subsets, as illustrated (sometimes called a class of sets in set theory).

The last is the *partial secondary set* (Figure 4.4), which

FIGURE 4.4. Partial Set.

has as its members a combination of subsets and of data of direct observation as illustrated.

With respect to subsets, I shall, for our present purposes, define the following characteristic. It is possible for the observer to observe directly within a set either its elementary data or subsets. But it is not possible to observe the data *within* a subset. A kind of polaroid principle will be assumed; that is to say, the walls of sets and their subsets will be taken as made of glass and polarized at right angles to each other, so that it is possible to look into a set and to see any primary elements plus the outer walls of any subsets, but not possible to see through subset walls to any elements inside them. For example, in variance accounting you get your sets of data in the form of subsets including all the costs which are, say, within ± 2 standard deviations from the mean, plus the exceptional items which are outside those limits. If you want to see the data within the subsets you have to analyze them out.[2]

ISOMORPHISM BETWEEN COGNITIVE SETS AND STATES OF TASK COMPLEXITY

It may have been apparent that in my detective example above, I was describing the nature of cognitive processes which might be employed in solving a task of a level-2 state of complexity. The task complexity is expressed in the second-level diagnostic data accumulation required for its solution. The cognitive equivalent of this state of task complexity is to construe a unique primary discrete set. The elements of this set are the data of direct observation—the clues. The set is the final pulling together to make the diagnosis of who-done-it. This set of significant data is *unique*—it has not been construed before; it is *primary*—its elements are data of observation, and it is *discrete*—it is not joined or otherwise operated in relation to any other sets.

A *second-level complexity proposition,* therefore, is that the *construing of primary, unique, discrete sets* in the cognitive world of the individual is isomorphic with second-level states of task and information complexity in nature.

----

[2] This whole analysis in terms of set theory takes on greater significance and power if it is assumed that human cognitive categories are best formulated in terms of topological sets; that is to say, sets whose elements are all interconnected in a living way by rules of connectedness, which give much deeper meaning to rules of inclusion and to the idea of fittingness—to the idea that things do or do not fit together. General topology also provides the possibilities of a systematic mathematical foundation for analyzing cognitive sets in terms of: identification of boundaries and pathways; connectedness, and simplicity and complexity of connections; set density; sequence and distance; neighborhood; union and intersection; product topologies, and so on; and a range of principles in the form of so-called laws and theories.

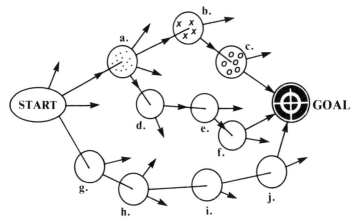

FIGURE 4.5 Construing of Interactive Primary Sets at the Third Level of Task Complexity.

A *third-level complexity proposition* is that the *construing of interactive primary sets* (Figure 4.5) is isomorphic with third-level states of task and information complexity. Recall that third-level task complexity is concerned with the construction of alternative pathways to a goal. Such pathways are ordered as logical trees, in that they consist of a series of choice points each of which must be organized into the range of likely possibilities at each point. Each of these possible choice points must be construed cognitively as a primary, unique, discrete set, so that diagnostic decisions may be taken. But then, in order to consider the various possible pathways, you have to be able to look down through the union of sets (a.b.c.), in relation to each other, or similarly (a.d.e.) or (f.g.h.i.), in order to get the full sense of each one of these construed possible tasks.

This concatenation of *related successive primary sets* is thus isomorphic with third-level states of task complexity. This isomorphism can be seen, for example, in the use of information by managers operating third-level complexity problems at Str. III. They get cost and output data in primary sets; that is to say, in various categories such as labor costs and consumable supply costs, or outputs of various categories of product. But they can examine all the elements of these sets in detail—the overtime cost of this section or that section; or the cost of this or that consumable; or the specific size of this or that order. And they can combine and recombine their cost or output data in different sets, or relate various sets of cost data to output data.

A fourth-level complexity proposition is that the *construing of partial secondary sets* is isomorphic with the fourth level of states of task complexity. The foundation for this proposition is that whereas information at the third level of complexity can be dealt with by categories of direct data, this picking over all the data is no longer possible at fourth-level complexity. Thus at Str. IV, a manager or an individual contributor must be highly selective about all the information which is available —seeking and using what is necessary, and avoiding what is not absolutely essential.

This necessary putting aside of information, leaving only essential elements for consideration, can be seen in the variance accounting practices described in the previous chapter, which leave only the exceptional data for consideration. It is the basis of the so-called principle of management-by-exception, which in fact applies only to Str. IV general management. It is also to be seen in military organization, where at brigade level (Str. IV equivalent) the commander must know how to set terms of reference for his intelligence staff, to ensure that he gets only essential elements of information (EEI) and not all the information; for example, he must know about this and that sector of his terrain, but cannot possibly know the whole of it.

The functioning of partial secondary sets in connection with level-4 parallel processing is illustrated in Fig-

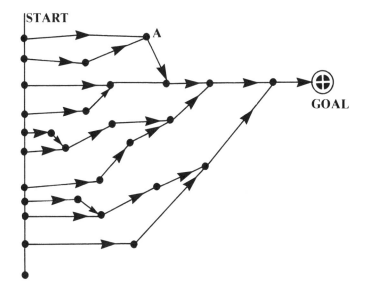

FIGURE 4.6. Construing of Partial Secondary Sets at the Fourth Level of Task Complexity.

ure 4.6. If progress to node A is late, the decision has to be made as to whether to pour more resources into that pathway to catch up, or to slow down all the rest, or to put resources into other paths, or introduce a new path, or to revise the whole pattern of the parallel pathways. In order to make such a decision, the executive must be able to have selective information and not the whole of the information about each pathway. To have all the information detail would be overwhelming.

DUALITY OF FIRST AND FIFTH LEVELS OF COMPLEXITY

Finally, it may be noted that I started this analysis of isomorphism with second-level rather than with first-level complexity. That starting point was not accidental:

that isomorphism is the easiest to describe. I have left the first level and fifth level categories to the last because they require an analysis of duality. I shall now undertake that task.

A *fifth/first-level complexity proposition* is that the *duality of construing secondary sets, plus the use of primary sets as single items,* is isomorphic with the dual fifth/first levels of task complexity making up the duality of the top/bottom of each quintave. The assumption is that the transition from the fourth level of complexity to the dual fifth/first level of complexity is isomorphic with a transition from partial secondary sets to full secondary sets, and that the duality is expressed in the secondary sets being transformed into primary sets, and primary sets into discrete entities. Let me explain.

I have described in the previous chapter how fifth-level task complexity at the top of a quintave is transformed into first-level task complexity which begins the next higher quintave. The information complexity is too great to be gripped in well-ordered articulated form, even with PERT chart procedures. Decisions must be taken by the touch and feel of the situation and of the forces at play and their second- and third-order consequences.

I explained this complexity in terms of how, at QA5, categories such as pens, pencils, and chalk, or lights, radios, and batteries get combined into higher order categories such as writing implements and electrical equipment. Such higher categories are isomorphic with secondary sets as shown in Figure 4.7. But note carefully the structure of these secondary sets and their subsets and primary entities.

In the first place, the primary entities which are used for work in Quintave A are things to be pointed to, and the sets are categories of pointable nonverbal entities encapsulated in a name. That is to say, a child will point

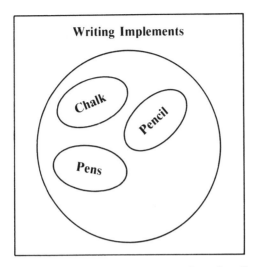

FIGURE 4.7. Higher Order Categories as Secondary Sets.

at something (which we would call a pen) and name it "pen." The entity is the nonverbal thing which is pointed at, and which must therefore be physically at hand, or at the least, recently observed. And the primary Quintave A set is the named category of things of that kind which are pointed out. Language is in this sense only partially abstract.

This statement that entities at Quintave A are things-at-hand which can be pointed to does not mean that children cannot learn to speak about things which are not present, for of course they do so. But it does mean that they cannot *work* with specific things at a distance which they have not seen, cannot construe unique new sets with them in order to solve problems. Words are only partially abstract, and problem solving remains tied to the physical tangible present until Quintave B cognitive complexity is achieved, a transition which occurs within the QA5/QB1 duality, as follows.

The secondary sets of QA5 are made up of subsets which are named categories of pointed-to tangible entities. But the tangible entities have now disappeared within the subsets, so that the individual must now, for the first time, work with "intangibles"; namely, the named sets of tangible entities, which have now become subsets of a higher order category.

This process was foreshadowed at QA4, when tangible entities were grouped in subsets, as elements within partial secondary sets. But these partial secondary sets also contained free primary data—the "exceptions"—and it was these exceptions with which the work was done, the subsets being put to one side for the time being so that the primary data they contained would not create information overload.

In contrast to QA4, the individual working at QA5 must therefore be able to work with what were previously primary sets (e.g., that pen), which have now become complex entities; namely, not "that thing" called a pen, but "a pen" which has not yet been seen, and which may not necessarily be at hand to be pointed at. *A symbol has replaced a tangible entity as an intangible thing with which work can be done.*

This transition from first-order concretely present tangible entity with partially abstract name, to second-order abstract symbol is of course a major shift in human development. But it does not take place completely at QA5. It is partial in two ways. In the first place, as described in the previous chapter, the individual working at QA5 must still have access to a supervisor, or leading hand, or NCO aide, or teacher, or other kind of aide at work, in order to be able to sustain an organized state in the complexity of the QA5 world. And in the second place, the individual can still maintain some contact with the concrete world of tangibles, by keeping a grip on the linkages between, say, electrical equipment, radios, and refrigerators, and "those things" to which you can point.

The full transition occurs with QB1, at which stage of complexity the individual has become comfortable with using symbols as entities, and no longer needs to cling to the regular return to the security of knowing that after all is said and done, entities "really are" those things to which you can point. In this sense it can be said that at QB1, the primary sets of QA have now become entities, and what were secondary sets at QA have now become the primary sets of Quintave B. Thus one full quantum step in level of abstraction and consequent-complexity of entity occurs between Quintave A and Quintave B. In others words, the Quintave B world has a conceptual depth which the Quintave A world does not have.

In the same vein a change in level of abstraction and in the nature of complexity of entity between Quintave B and Quintave C occurs in the QB5/QC1 cognitive band. Here again it is a change in which primary set becomes entity, and secondary set becomes primary set. More specifically, the secondary sets at QB5 were whole systems (plerimorphs) such as a strategic business unit. The subsets (or primary sets) were subsystems of the SBU such as competitor systems, labor force, pricing structures, factories, sales organizations, capital structure, investments, value systems, executive development programs, and so on. It is these subsystems which are now handled as entities by touch and feel. The SBU CEO must be able to sense the likely consequences of changing forces and situations for the myriad subsystems he controls. The variables are limitless in number: he must be able to judge which are the particular subsystems which are most likely to be significantly affected; and he must ensure that possible second- and third-order consequences are assessed and taken care of.

At QB5, the SBU CEO will be dealing with his SBU as secondary set, and the subsystems as subsets. He will be directed outwards to the business environment, and downwards within his SBU. But with growing experience, he will mature to QC1, at which stage his outlook will have been transformed to one in which the plerimorph (his SBU) has become the primary set, and the previous subsystems will now be treated as things or entities. At this stage, while still operating with touch-and-feel approach, he will be able to look upwards to impact upon corporate policies and strategies, as well as outwards and downwards.

This work with plerimorphs as sets, and their subsystems as entities, is then the situation which obtains through the rest of Quintave C. What would be called the "ordinary" data of observation (entities) at Quintave B get left far behind as those exceptions which last appear on the scene at QB4. At the QC levels, these QB entities get taken into account only by breaking into the lower levels by personal inspection and observation, or by digging into lower level data for purposes such as checking on the impact of existing policies or getting ideas for new policies or strategic thrusts by soaking up some detail.

Thus it is that the Quintave C world has the depth of being lived in terms of entities which are primary sets of QB entities, which entities are in turn primary sets of QA entities. The level of abstraction increases by quantum leaps from quintave to quintave. Or to put it in other terms, the symbolic value or intensity of language goes through the same qualitative changes. The world of the individual who is working at, say, QC3, is thus a very different world from the individual working at QB3 or at QA3. The fact that the same apparent words may be used, at each of these levels, obscures the fact that there are great differences in the depth of meaning attaching to these words.

A final speculation may be called for with respect to Quintave D, and the transition from Quintave C to Quintave D at cognitive band QC5/QD1. The process we are following would require that we ask what the secondary sets would be which contained plerimorphs as their subsets. The answer to that question is self-evident enough; the institutions which contain plerimorphs are what might be termed large-scale corporate bodies—both social bodies and bodies of ideas. Examples of such corporate bodies and bodies of ideas are: large industrial and financial corporations which contain a multiplicity of SBUs; churches which contain dioceses; political associations which contain regional associations; large universities which contain schools or faculties; systems of theories; and value systems.

Quintave D, therefore, may be said to be the level at which plerimorphs become entities, and large corporate bodies and bodies of ideas become primary sets. It is these large corporate bodies and bodies of ideas which constitute the subsystems of societies. And it is through these subsystems that societies may be changed. Quintave D work, therefore, may be regarded as oriented toward changing societies by changing the large corporate bodies and the bodies of knowledge and values, out of which societies are built.

THE STRUCTURE OF UNCONSCIOUS MENTAL WORK

In chapter 5 of *The Form of Time* (1982) (see chapter 10, this volume) I suggested that the processes by means of which choices were made and decisions taken must in the final analysis be unconscious and remain unconscious.

Conscious knowledge and conscious and logical mental manipulations have a function in setting: the context for our actions; the limits in terms of rules, regulations, policies, and objectively known facts and constraints within which we are working; and the direction in which we are going. But they do not explain that final putting together of everything we know into the mental cooking pot of assumptions about risk and about probabilities of outcome, the felt utility of given prospects, and just plain hunches about what it might be best to do, which meld together to produce a decision which we learn about as it surfaces into conscious awareness.

We can then consider how these unconscious mental working processes are organized. That they cannot be statically organized, as in the case pro tem of conscious knowledge, must be clear, because if they could be mentally gripped as static entities they could be made conscious. They are undoubtedly dynamically organized processes or flows. My proposition would be that these flows are organized in the form of the processes of set construal which I have described.[3] That is to say, the flows are organized in the form of set patterns, or interactive primary set patterns, or patterns isomorphic with the flow of partial secondary or secondary sets in form. I would emphasize that I am referring to the *patterning of flows* and not simply the conscious outcomes of those flows, much as you might refer to the patterns of movement in a metal plate set vibrating by a violin bow, which produces Chladni figures if sand is sprinkled on its surface.

---

[3] I have been interested in Ignacio Matte-Blanco's work (1975) on the unconscious as infinite sets. Although his approach is not the same and his conclusions are hardly identical, I nevertheless feel that there is a similar sense of the nature of unconscious processes and their pattern or form which informs our work.

REFERENCES

Jaques, E. (1982), *The Form of Time*. New York: Crane Russak.
Kelly, G. A. (1955), *The Psychology of Personal Constructs*. New York: W. W. Norton.
Matte-Blanco, I. (1975), *The Unconscious as Infinite Sets*. London: Duckworth.

Chapter 5

Maturation of Cognitive Power

THE GROWTH OF TIME HORIZON IN
INDIVIDUALS

I now propose to turn to the question of how cognitive power matures and develops in people. In order that there shall be no confusion, let me recall my context. Cognitive power is but one component of the attributes which form a person's ability to work. The other attributes include knowledge, experience, skill, temperament, character and values, and type or quality of articulation. I am concerned in this chapter only with cognitive functioning. It is not that knowledge, experience, value, and skill are not important: but how such equipment is acquired is very different from the regular patterns of maturation of cognitive functioning. And the question of how temperament and values change or develop with time is yet another question—and one which will also be left aside at this time. Let me turn, then, to the question of the development of cognitive functioning in its own right.

It is a self-evident fact that human beings are not born fully matured in cognitive power. How then does the process of maturation occur? The theory of discontinuity of cognitive state and of quintaves suggests that there are a number of different questions here which need to be teased out from one another. One question is whether people who eventually mature, say, to be able to operate in mode QC-2 at Str. VI show signs of not-yet matured QC-2 potential earlier in life. If they do, do signs of QC-2 potential first show some time in childhood, in early adulthood, throughout life, at different times in different individuals, at the same time in all potential QC-2 individuals?

Another question is whether an individual's potential to function at a particular cognitive level or in a particular cognitive mode is inborn—constitutionally given—or whether the potential per se can be modified by education, or by occupational or social opportunity. And if it can be modified, then by how much? Is everyone capable of developing to any cognitive level, or is there a constitutional base which sets the maximum limit of growth and development? These questions are of course among the politically loaded issues of developmental theory, and need to be addressed with great care. In order to proceed systematically, let me develop further the concept of the time-horizon of the individual.

At any particular point in people's careers there is a maximum time-span at which any given person can work. If people are employed at levels of work below that maximum time-span they feel their capabilities are being underutilized, and they experience boredom and frustration. If people are employed at levels of work above that maximum time-span, they become disorganized and anxious and are unable to cope. If people are fortunate enough to be employed at levels of work that coincide with the maximum time-spans which they are capable of achieving, then they feel comfortably employed, and so long as their work is of interest and they have the appropriate knowledge, skill, and temperament, they will derive satisfaction from that work (Jaques, 1968, 1976; Evans, 1979). It is this maximum time-span at which a person is able to work at a given point in time that I referred to above as that person's time-horizon. This time frame gives a measure of a person's cognitive power and ability to handle conceptual complexity at that time (Jaques, 1982a). The temporal-horizon sets the limits of the world of purpose and intention which people can construct and pattern, and within which they live and organize their active lives and aspirations. In connection with the foregoing questions about intellectual development, let me present some evidence of regular and predictable tracks of growth and maturation of time-horizon.

The curves shown in Figure 5.1 set out my hypothesis about the rate of maturation of time-horizon. The hypothesis set out in these curves expresses the rates of maturation and growth of the cognitive power of individuals. This hypothesis was originally derived from a regularity noted in the real earning progressions of individuals (that is to say, their earnings corrected to a common base for movements in the earnings index) in over a dozen different countries. There is an underlying trend in these progressions which is expressed in the array of curves shown here (Jaques, 1961, 1968). My hypothesis was that the regularity in the trend of the earnings progressions reflected a regular trend in the growth of level of cognitive function in the individuals in the samples; or, as I would now express it, the growth in earnings reflected a drive in the individuals toward achieving a growth in level of work, and this drive in turn was the expression of their growth in time-horizon.

That there is in fact a growth in time-horizon that corresponds to these curves has been demonstrated in a number of studies described in the references cited above. One key study has been the tracking of the careers of almost 200 individuals whom I have had the opportunity to follow for periods of between eighteen and twenty-five

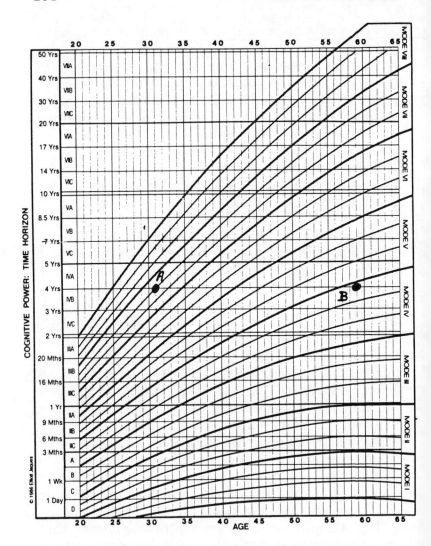

FIGURE 5.1. Time Horizon Maturation Curves.

years. At various times during those periods I was able to obtain: measures of the time-spans at which they were working; their actual pay and their felt-fair pay; their sense of the degree of comfort of fit between their level of capability and their level of work; and, if there was a felt mismatch, then we were able to get measures of the level of work in positions which they felt would be just right for them.

These data have been analyzed by Dr. Tom Kohler of UCLA. He has found a strong regularity in the "comfort curves," as he has called them, of individuals. These comfort curves conform very tightly to the progression curves of my hypothesis—some 95 percent of the actual curves staying within the bands designated Mode I, II, and so on, on my chart. The general trend of these comfort curves is shown in Figure 5.2, and Kohler is now publishing the results of his study.

Let us examine these curves more closely, starting with the significance of the Mode I, Mode II, and so on, bands just mentioned. It may be noted that there are lines running horizontally across the charts at one-day, three-month, one-year, two-year, five-year, ten-year, and twenty-year time-spans. These horizontals set out the boundaries of Str. I, II, III, IV, V, VI, and VII. The bands have been picked out in such a way that each one encompasses all the time-frame maturation curves which reach the relevant stratum at full maturity. Thus the band designated Mode III encompasses all the maturation curves which eventually reach Str. III.

In the case of the higher modes (V, VI, VII, VIII) it will be noted that they do not reach full maturity by the maximum age of fifty-five years allowed for on the chart in Figure 5.4. The data suggest that people of these very high potential levels of capability do not reach full maturity in cognitive level by normal retirement age. And

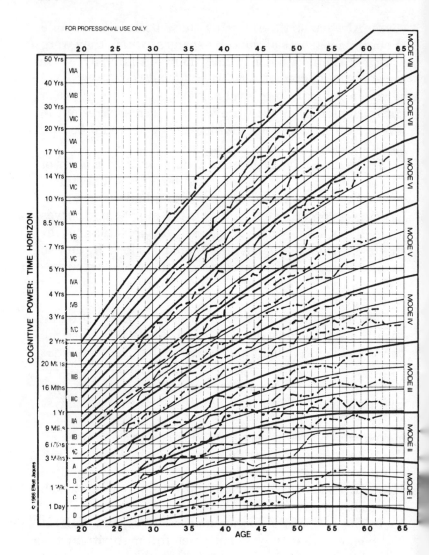

FIGURE 5.2. Regularity of Typical Progression "Comfort" Curves.

indeed, at the very highest levels it would appear that individuals are afflicted by senile deterioration and death before their potential cognitive power can reach full maturity—a hypothesis that is supported by the careers of many of the very greatest composers, artists, judges, politicians, and outstanding leaders in other fields.

These hypotheses are, of course, inconsistent with the findings from IQ ratings which suggest full maturation by the age of eighteen of whatever it is that IQ rates. The fact that IQ matures fully at such an early age emphasizes the gross limitations of IQ rating as far as giving any indication of cognitive development is concerned.[1]

A MULTIPLE-TRACK THEORY OF DEVELOPMENT

It may now be apparent that we have constructed a third group of discontinuities, to add to the discontinuities described in the previous two chapters. The first is a discontinuous hierarchy of levels in task complexity and the structure of organizations. The second comprises discontinuities in the nature of cognitive capability of individuals, reflected in a discontinuous hierarchy of four cognitive states grouped in an encompassing hierarchy of quintaves. And the third is a discontinuous series of developmental bands within which the maturation of in-

---

[1] It has been put to me that the time-horizon maturation curves represent "merely" an increase in experience beyond the age of eighteen. That that assumption cannot be valid is shown by the fact that the time-horizon curves mature in a regular and predictable fashion. This regularity cannot be explained by experience alone, although experience is certainly one necessary condition for the maturation of time horizon. Fortunately, ordinary everyday life confronts the individual with a panoply of social, economic, familial, political, and intellectual problems which provide more than enough opportunity for full maturational development of cognitive power to occur.

dividual cognitive power as measured by time-horizon will occur.

The consequence of this third hypothesis about discontinuities in maturation bands is of some interest. It reveals the fact that most developmental theory has been wedded to the notion that everyone matures along the same track, but some people mature further along that track than do others. I would now substitute a multitrack theory in which individuals are conceived of as maturing along any one of several possible maturation bands. It is as though we were to move from a single-track railway system to a multiple-track railway system: a number of new explanatory principles become available. Let me explore some of them.

There are two very general implications of this construction: they are first, that each person will mature in level of cognitive power as measured by time-horizon, within one particular maturation band; and second, that in so doing each person will cross a number of work strata, each stratum being characterized by a particular cognitive state. The greater the cognitive power of the individual, the greater the number of strata to be crossed. There are complexities here which need to be carefully teased out and examined.

Let me take a specific example. Say, on Figure 5.1, an individual A has matured to a time-horizon of four years at the age of thirty-one. There are two points to note: first, he will be capable of working in Str. IV at that age; and second, he is maturing in the Mode VII cognitive band and will have the potential to reach Str. VII by somewhere between the ages of sixty and sixty-five. It may be noted that Str. IV implies work at cognitive level QB-4, and Str. VII implies work at cognitive level QC-3.

We now encounter a prime question inherent in the

theory of stratified systems which I am following. The question is: how does an individual of high-level potential function at lower levels while he is maturing? For example, what would be the cognitive state of A at age thirty-one: Mode QB-4—parallel processing, or Mode QC-3—alternative pathways? And, how would A compare in cognitive state with, say, B, who is fifty-nine years of age and also at four-years time frame and who, according to our theory, would be both operating at QB-4 and fully matured in QB-4 so that there would be no inconsistency between his current cognitive state and his potential cognitive mode?

The answer to this question is an interesting one, and has been worked out in field studies carried out over the past ten years by Dr. Gillian Stamp and colleagues. Building upon work done by John Isaac, Brian O'Connor, and Roland Gibson (Gibson and Isaac, 1978; Isaac and O'Connor, 1978), she has developed a procedure for the assessment of level of cognitive power both current and potential (Stamp, 1978). This procedure, which she has named Career Path Appreciation (CPA), comprises a card-sorting procedure based upon the Bruner cards (Bruner, Olver, and Greenfield, 1966), a choice of phrase cards describing various preferred ways of working, and a brief interview to ascertain the time-span of work in which the individual currently feels comfortable.

With this procedure Stamp has been able to ascertain both the individual's current time-horizon and the dynamic strategies used in approaching problem solving. She is able to place individuals at low, middle, or high in a particular stratum, and by the same token to place them in a particular cognitive maturation band.

Thus, for A and B above, she would be able to place A in mid-Str. IV and maturation band VII, and B in mid-

Str. IV and maturation band IV. Her studies show that both A and B would be currently operating in cognitive state QB-4, but with a difference. B's performance would consistently show a QB-4 parallel processing approach set firmly in quintave B; and with little if any comprehension of how to go about working at any higher level: his temporal-horizon would end abruptly at about three to four years. A's performance, by contrast, would be expressed in a QB-4 tactical approach, but it would contain signs of QB-5 and higher, on the phrase cards, for example. Moreover, in interview A would manifest clear signs of comprehension of QC modes of working: and most striking of all, would have already taken for granted that people might be engaged in constructing worlds ten, twenty, and twenty-five years ahead even though accurate forecasting could not produce such temporal horizons. In other words, A uses a context of not yet fully matured QC-3 cognitive strategies as the foundation of working at QB-4.

In short, the conclusion that Stamp arrived at is that individuals will express their currently matured time-horizon in their work, but at the same time will show clear evidence of comprehension of their potential cognitive mode and time-horizon. I have had extensive experience of this phenomenon. The temporal-horizons of men and women in the younger age groups, for example, are of particular interest. The high-potential group readily understands the world in long time-horizons, even though they are not yet mature enough to work at that scale of temporal extension. By contrast, the lower-potential individuals simply do not see the more extensive context. It is as though a four-foot tall person, one five-feet tall, and one six-feet tall, standing side by side look out across a field punctuated by three-foot high fences. How much of the distant fields they would see would be markedly different!

DEVELOPMENT OF COGNITIVE COMPLEXITY IN CHILDHOOD

How then does cognitive functioning as here defined develop in childhood? We are just getting studies of this question under way, within the following hypotheses.

I have replotted the time-horizon progression array set out in Figure 5.1 onto a double logarithmic scale so as to make it possible to do a crude extrapolation of these curves back to earliest infancy. On the assumption that the progressions would be in line with the sigmoid curves characteristic of biological development, I drew the extrapolated curves as shown in Figure 5.3. It will be noted that the higher the cognitive mode the later in life does a person's cognitive power continue to mature and increase.

The idea then occurred that the work of Macdonald and Couchman described in the previous chapter might give a lead into the nature of cognitive capability in children. Their findings about cognitive levels in a population of mentally handicapped adults are very suggestive of the cognitive states found in infancy and early childhood in the type of population studied by Piaget. The correspondences that occur are listed in Table 5.1.

The hypothesis is suggested that the bottom quintave of the cognitive states—Quintave A—expresses the stages of development in children. Some children may develop much more rapidly than others through the stages; and the stages extend throughout adulthood in the so-called mentally handicapped; that is to say, among those who never develop beyond the first four cognitive states.

On this further assumption that the Quintave A cognitive states will be traversed by children in the course of their development, I have hypothesized the modes within QA as shown. My rough hypothesis was that the children with the very highest potential would cross from

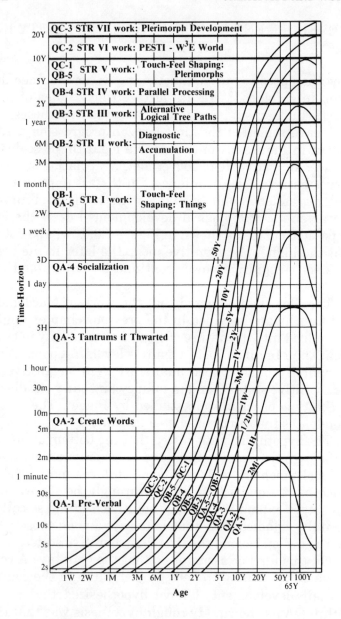

FIGURE 5.3. Progression of Development of Cognitive Maturation.

TABLE 5.1
CORRESPONDENCE OF COGNITIVE LEVELS

	Quintave Theory	Piaget's Theory
Level QA-5	Ability to operate in an adult world at Str. I	Period of formal operations ability to reason by hypothesis
Level QA-4	First stage of concern about alternatives and about the interests of others	Period of concrete operations: combination, dissociation, ordering, and correspondence which acquire the form of reversible systems
Level QA-3	Rigid fixation upon own goals; disregard of needs of others; tantrums if stopped	Period of preoperational thought
Level QA-2	Primitive primary set construal	Sensorimotor period
Level QA-1	Complete dependence upon an aide	

the egocentric temper-tantrum QA-3 stage to the social-
izable QA-4 capability of understanding that others may
have alternatives, at perhaps six months to one year of
age, and that that same stage might be reached in those
with the potential to reach Str. I or II in their adult
working careers at about five years to seven years of age.

By the same token, the age at which a child is able
to understand and to act upon the meaning of yesterday,
today, and tomorrow might turn out to be diagnostically
of great importance. I refer here not just to an under-

standing of the meaning of the words but to a genuine behavioral understanding; that is to say, to the ability to start on some activity on one day with the realization that it will certainly take until the following day to complete it, and to carry the activity through without getting into a fit of rage and abandoning it when bedtime arrives with the project only half finished. My hypothesized developmental curves would predict that Mode-VII children will be able to handle the tomorrow's time-span by the age of three; Mode-IV children by the age of six; and Mode-I persons by the age of twenty-one. These predictions will shortly be tested in our work.

These ideas are mere speculations at present. I put them forward to complete my account. But parents and teachers of young children seem to be familiar with the phenomena described. Our initial studies will include cohorts of five-, ten-, and fifteen-year-old boys and girls from different social and ethnic backgrounds. The hypotheses are at least precise enough to be falsified, reinforced, or modified.

COMPARISON WITH PIAGET AND FREUD

Two additional points must be made with respect to the developmental concepts being described and those of Piaget and of Freud.

First, it should be reemphasized that I am dealing only with the development of unconscious cognitive processes and their complexity. I have not been considering the development of knowledge, or skill, or values and interests, or of emotional or temperamental characteristics or character. These factors are, of course, of importance for the ability of individuals to use their effective cognitive power in any given environment, and in determining for what purposes that cognitive power will be exercised, and how it shall be expressed. But they do not develop in the same way that cognitive complexity and power develop. They cannot be said to follow any natural maturational paths, nor is their growth predictable.

The present work, therefore, is most closely allied to the studies of Piaget on intellectual development. And here, as I have pointed out, I have assumed multiple developmental pathways or cognitive modes, as against his adherence to the usual assumption that there is just one single pathway. This difference is important in the following sense; the moment you assume multiple pathways, you must try to explain why they occur. In trying to do so, I have been driven to the following hypotheses; namely, that the difference in cognitive mode is an expression of the fact that individuals operate with the same underlying mode of cognitive categorization throughout life, but as they mature, they are able to apply that mode to increasingly complex problems. Let me elaborate this point.

Compare two individuals, A and B. Let us say that A is able to operate with partial secondary sets (level QB-4), and B is able to work with diagnostic accumulation and primary set construal (QB-2). The hypothesis: that each will operate with his own type of set formation from early childhood through old age.

But with maturation, A will be able to use the higher level cognitive capability and partial secondary set construal to get to QA-2, and QA-3, earlier than B, and to operate at those levels more quickly and more imaginatively than B. And so it will be throughout life. They are on different maturation tracks, and using different cognitive tools, and will always work differently at every level.

This hypothesis, which I shall not pursue here, suggests a different view of cognitive (intellectual) development than has been current so far. Some consequences of this approach are being sorted out at the present time.

Second, with respect to Freud and psychoanalytical theories of development, as elaborated, for example, by Erikson (1950), and in a related sense, by Dan Levinson (1979), it may be noted that there are similarities in that regularities in maturation are being assumed, but Freud is dealing with the maturation of developmental stages of the whole person, and not simply of cognitive complexity. The conception here is again that of a single track rather than a multiple track system, it being assumed that everyone follows the same sequence of stages—there being an assumed underlying physiological foundation. Whether or not the quality of development of these stages and the time of their appearance would be affected by cognitive maturation is a matter for further reflection; as is the question of whether there is but one developmental track or a multiplicity of them.

A NOTE ON "PREDESTINATION"

Hypotheses of the kind I have outlined about intellectual or cognitive capability and its development seem inevitably to give rise to criticism on political grounds; the hypotheses are held to be politically reactionary on racial grounds or on the grounds of their being neofeudal in the sense of putting each person into his or her own fixed slot in life. These criticisms are of substantial importance and warrant comment.

As far as racial issues are concerned, it is gratifying to be able to report that Dr. Stamp has now obtained evidence that her Career Path Appreciation procedure is effective regardless of cultural, social, racial, or economic background. Studies have been carried out, and followed up over a period of up to twelve years, in cultures as diverse as Namibia and the Solomon Islands, as well as the United Kingdom, United States, Denmark, and Italy, and preliminary analyses show a striking lack of variation due to culture.

It would appear, as I would most certainly hypothesize, that individuals mature in time-horizon and thus in cognitive power under the impact of the problems presented by everyday life, regardless of whether those problems have had to be faced under the exigencies of school learning or under the exigencies of survival in a setting of social and educational deprivation. Who is to say which is likely to provide the greater stimulus?

Let me emphasize that I am talking about maturation of cognitive power only. I am not talking about the social and economic opportunity to exercise that cognitive power in education or employment and so to develop the psychological tools and orientation needed to advance in our society. If these hypotheses about development turn out to be valid, it would mean that whether or not individuals have adequate social, educational, or occupational opportunities for developing particular psychological tools and orientation, their cognitive power will develop nonetheless. If, however, they do not have the opportunity to learn and to develop the appropriate psychological tools and orientation for work which matches their cognitive power and complexity, people will fall behind in their ability to compete in their societies, and they will be frustrated, fed-up, and feel unjustly treated. Moreover, if the discrepancies between cognitive power on the one hand, and appropriate psychological tools and orientation, and work opportunities, on the other are great, people will fall seriously behind in status and in achievement. Some will work zealously to overcome this disadvantage, and a few will become social reformers. But many others will become alienated, and may seek antisocial or delinquent outlets for their ability, or instigate more or less violent social change. It is precisely because maturation in cognitive power occurs despite social and economic opportunity that the social alienation and resentment can occur—led by those with the highest levels of underutilized cognitive power. Any society, to be a decent society, must provide the opportunity for individuals to gain the tools and orientation necessary for them to be able to use their cognitive powers to the full, and must ensure the provision of full employment opportunities for all. (I have argued this case in detail in *Free Enterprise, Fair Employment* [1982b]).

Indeed, it is the viewpoint which states that educational and social opportunity are necessary for the maturation of a person's level of cognitive power which I find difficult to understand. For that view contains the implicit assumption that under generations of subjugation with social, educational, and economic deprivation, subject peoples would have produced populations of intellectual morons. Human nature and the maturation of cognitive power would appear, fortunately, to be more resilient than that.

Finally, I would note that the assessments of cognitive power that I have described are a very far cry from the world of IQ ratings. My whole orientation is toward the performance of individuals in work—in planning and carrying out purposeful goal-directed activities—and in construing their picture of the outside world and constructing their own internal worlds in doing so. This orientation has little relationship to IQ ratings with their failure adequately to separate individual cognitive power from culturally dominated knowledge, skills, and values. Such ratings lean too heavily upon culturally learned answers and language, and upon ability to learn what is taught in schools whether or not you have been to school or even like that kind of learning.

SOME PRACTICAL APPLICATIONS FOR EDUCATION

But now let us examine some potential practical consequences of this approach to intellectual development. I shall consider three such applications: a problem-solving approach to education; assessment and grouping of students; and the transition from school to work.

The use of problem-solving exercises, or projects, has a history of regularly coming into fashion and just as regularly going out of fashion again. It should have a solidly established place. One of the implications, however, of stratified systems theory is that problem-solving projects should be tailored to the time-horizon of the pupils. It is having to complete goals which require substantial periods of time to achieve, which puts individuals on their true mettle.

The time scale would extend from five to ten minutes in younger children and in less capable children, and on up to two to three months for some of the older more highly capable children. The significance of such projects is that they allow pupils to experience their cognitive power to the full. And with such experiences they will find their ability to cope with uncertainty being pulled out to full stretch. The art is to design appropriate projects to the time scales involved (see chapter 7, this volume).

The difficulty with such projects is that they do not readily fit in with standardized and "objective" grading. The substitute for such grading could, however, be that of a teacher's recording of the maximum time-span over which students could be targeted to pursue and to achieve given goals. The time-spans thus identified would provide as useful a piece of information about a student's potential in work career as any amount of so-called objective examination results.

Problem-solving project work might be facilitated by having students of roughly congruent time-horizons in the same class. Before describing such groupings, let me make one thing clear. I am not arguing either in favor of comprehensive schooling or against it. To the extent, however, that some opportunity for grouping on the basis of cognitive complexity is deemed to be desirable, then our work would point to the following principles.

On the assumption that it is possible to assess level of cognitive ability in time-horizon, in children as in adults, then grouping in terms of cognitive mode should follow the pattern shown in Figure 5.4. The following groups have been separated out; namely, those children maturing in Mode I, those in Modes II and III, and those in Modes IV and higher. Roughly 45 percent of schoolchildren would fall into each of the first two groups, and the remaining 10 percent in the third group.

The rationale for such a grouping is that the Mode I group works in the same way, and at any given age, in roughly the same time scale. They are most comfortable in concretely specified situations, with a penchant for physical doing. The Mode II and Mode III groups operate in longer time scales, and require opportunity for expressing their capabilities for reflective formulation of what they are doing, as well as for formulating what might be, as illustrated above.

The third group should be composed of the students in Mode IV and above. The reason for keeping this group together is that they are all operating in a frame of reference in which it is comfortable to handle generalizations. This ease with general categories is in contrast to the Mode II and Mode III groups, who, while they can

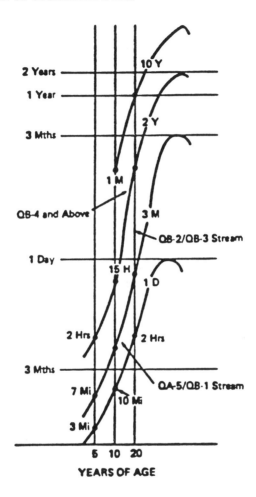

FIGURE 5.4. Cognitive Maturation at School Age: Three Educational Groups.

formulate what they are doing, nevertheless require to
be solidly and concretely in direct physiological–perceptual
contact with the object of their doing.

It might be that by, say, fifteen years of age, those
students who are operating in maturation Modes VI and

VII and who will eventually be capable of operating at strategic levels of work should be given the opportunity to work together. There are, however, so few (less than 1 percent) that special classes might be impracticable. They should, however, be recognized and identified, and given special educational opportunities consistent with their extended time frames and capabilities.

There might, of course, be many reasons why children with the capability to work at these cognitive levels may not exercise their capability to work and study. Effective performance can be hindered or disrupted by emotional disturbance, lack of motivation, social alienation, family economic distress, or lack of support. But there is no sense, where grouping of children is being carried out, in compounding these difficulties by grouping children of high cognitive power (long time-horizons) but low achievement, with students of equivalent achievement but significantly shorter time frames. To be required to work below one's time-horizon is frustrating, demotivating, soul-destroying. It would be much better to keep students together with those of their peers who are their equals in cognitive power, and to remediate whatever shortcomings in psychological tools and orientation are impairing their achievement.

Finally, on the transition from school to work, I would want to gear this transition in accord with the groupings described. The longer the time-horizon of the student, the longer there should be the opportunity to continue with "purely academic" study. Vocationally oriented education might start at fourteen to sixteen years of age for the Mode I students. This age could be extended up to, say, twenty-one or twenty-two for the Mode II and Mode III students. The students at Mode IV and above should have their educations left as open as possible throughout undergraduate studies; they should have their vocational tapering-off after finishing first degree level—in professional schools such as law, medicine, engineering, or perhaps by going straight into work without a vocational educational transition period.

In all the above I believe there is a substantial advantage to be gained by considering students in terms of their cognitive power as measured in time-horizon and ability to handle complexity, rather than to place an almost exclusive focus upon IQ or examination grades. It gives students a chance to show their real work potential regardless of social, racial, or ethnic background, and regardless of gender. And it puts the proper emphasis upon the ability to do work as found not only in answering examination questions but in doing sustained, purposeful activity to produce creative outputs.

But it may be appreciated that the general thrust of my whole argument has been in the direction of the importance of providing opportunity for everyone, from childhood to old age, to have the opportunity to exercise their cognitive power to the full in purposeful activity of satisfying and challenging complexity; and to have the opportunity, further, to acquire the knowledge and skills necessary for doing so in their society.

REFERENCES

Bruner, J. S., Olver, R. R., & Greenfield, P. M. (1966), *Studies of Cognitive Growth*. New York: John Wiley.

Erikson, E. (1950), *Childhood and Society*. New York: W. W. Norton.

Evans, J. S. (1979), *Management of Human Capacity*. Bradford, UK: MCB Books.

Gibson, R. O., & Isaac, D. J. (1978), Truth tables as a formal device in the analysis of human action. In: *Levels of Abstraction in Logic and Human Action,* ed. E. Jaques, R. O. Gibson, & D. J. Isaac. London: Heinemann Educational Books Ltd.

Isaac, D. J., & O'Connor, B. M. (1978), A discontinuity theory of psychological development. In: *Levels of Abstraction in Logic and*

Human Action, ed. E. Jaques, R. O. Gibson, & D. J. Isaac. London: Heinemann Educational Books Ltd.

Jaques, E. (1961), *Equitable Payment.* London: Heinemann Educational Books Ltd.

——— (1968), *Progression Handbook.* London: Heinemann Educational Books Ltd.

——— (1976), *A General Theory of Bureaucracy.* Exeter, NH: Heinemann Educational Books Ltd.

——— (1982a), *The Form of Time.* New York: Crane Russak.

——— (1982b), *Free Enterprise, Fair Employment.* New York: Crane Russak.

Levinson, D. (1979), *The Seasons of a Man's Life.* New York: Knopf.

Stamp, G. (1978), Assessment of individual capacity. In: *Levels of Abstraction and Logic in Human Action,* ed. E. Jaques, R. O. Gibson, & D. J. Isaac. London: Heinemann Educational Books Ltd.

Chapter 6

Notes on the Psychological Meaning of Work

I

The conclusions to be drawn from extensive field work may be summarized in one general statement. When level of work is measured by time-span, a felt-fair differential payment scale can be found: payment that is consistent with this scale will be found satisfying by members fully established in jobs; work will be done in a relatively efficient, competitive, and decisive manner within the limits of the form of organization adopted; and there will be freedom from grievances about differentials between members and between groups or grades of members.

The above statement assumes a definition of work as the totality of discretionary activities that a person does in discharging the responsibilities he has contracted to undertake in order to earn his living. Moreover, concealed within the statement—in the prescription for measuring level of work—is the notion that what is experienced as one's level of work has to do only with the use of discretion and judgment, 'and has nothing whatever to do with the prescribed limits of one's work. These definitions of work and of level of work can no longer simply be taken for granted. Before proceeding further, we must examine them, discover what their implications might be, and see whether any justification can be found for their use.

II

I have limited my use of the idea of discretion and judgment to discretion and judgment that eventuate in definite and observable actions, in decisions that end in someone doing something—issuing an order, setting a policy, writing a report, machining some metal, making a drawing. I have excluded from this definition any idea of decisions that someone makes in thought, but that do not eventually get expressed in action observable by others. It is executive discretion and judgment that are being considered—the use of discretion and judgment in doing something, which may be preceded by thinking about it, but is not confined to thinking about it.

Discretion and judgment are demanded when there are more ways than one to go about doing a particular job. In executive systems, a person's being confronted with alternatives applies only to parts of any job. Every job is limited in some of its aspects, in the sense that complete freedom to use discretion or judgment is definitely not allowed. When we talk about discretion and judgment, therefore, we are talking about those aspects of a job in which the person is *allowed* to choose, and indeed *required* to choose, from among alternative ways of doing something, as opposed to those aspects in which he is *prohibited* from choosing and must follow a prescribed policy or method. In nonmanual work this process of choice is usually experienced and described as deciding, or making and acting upon decisions; in manual work it is experienced as judging, or getting the feel of, or guessing just the right way to do a task—just how much more pressure is needed in drilling something, just what tool angle should be used for cutting, or just when a process has reached the right color and appearance.

The prescribed and the discretionary components of a job interact in the following way. The prescribed elements constitute a boundary around a job. They set limits to what the person in the job may do. They state what he may not do. They also state the things he must do—the regulations, the policies, the methods, the routines, to which he must conform. Within these limits the person must use discretion. He must use his own judgment. He must choose what he thinks is the best course when faced with alternative possibilities. He must seek alternative possibilities. From this point of view, being able to set precise limits to a job is a positive and constructive action of immense importance. It frees a subordinate to concentrate his use of discretion within his own field of operation. It limits uncertainty within manageable bounds.

Realistic regulations, routines, and procedures may thus have a liberating rather than a constricting effect on initiative and the use of discretion. Failure to have clear limits established for him bogs a person down in problems that are not germane to his immediate job, and this causes inefficiency. The advantages of setting firm and stated limits in this way are commonly subscribed to in the notion that it is important for members to know where they stand. If we now turn our attention exclusively to the problem of discretion and judgment, it may be appreciated that this is not to minimize the importance of the prescribed limit of work. It is merely to state that prescribed limits are not relevant to our present considerations of payment and status.

An important feature in discretion and judgment, and a feature that may lead immediately to the heart of our problem, has to do with the nature of choice. When someone is faced with a decision, he is faced not only with the problem of choosing which is the best course of action, and then of following that course. He is also faced with the opposite problem. He must decide against the other courses open to him; he must give up these courses; he must put them aside. Everyone must be familiar with the experience of arriving at a difficult decision and having, because of circumstances, to act upon it, although still not sure whether or not it was the wisest course to take. How desirable some of the rejected courses often become in retrospect, while one is waiting to discover from the results whether the course chosen will turn out to have been a good one! Gnawing doubts and uncertainties of this kind give rise to much of the worry that attends difficult work.

A further complication must now be added. Executive work does not consist of one decision and the job is done. It consists of a continuous series of decisions. No sooner is one choice made, and the consequent path negotiated, than the next corner is reached, and another choice is required. Some paths lead up blind alleys; other paths lead to the final objective, but are more difficult or take longer; and some paths lead through expeditiously. Only when the task is completed is it possible to get it into perspective—sometimes clearly, sometimes only vaguely—and discover which choices, if any, might have made it easier. Furthermore, in jobs at higher time-span levels (commonly in all jobs over several months' time-span) there is more than one task to be done at a time. That is to say, there is more than one series of decisions to be negotiated—some long, some short, and none of them in phase with each other. Decisions with respect to entirely different tasks have to be made in succession.

Reinforcing the doubts that may be stimulated in decision making is the uncertainty, always present, that arises because better alternatives may remain unrecognized and unknown. There are always better alternatives that have not been thought of. Decision making calls for a fine balance to be held between, on the one hand, choosing right away from among the best alternatives available so as to do what needs to be done at the time, and on the other hand seeking, trying out, and bringing into play at the appropriate moment new means for doing the same job in a more effective way. This fine balance is exercised by everybody in every job—manual and non-manual, managerial and nonmanagerial—most often intuitively and without thinking about it. Sometimes, usually at higher levels in organizations, intuitive exercise of the balance is reinforced by setting up special development and research jobs or departments.

When a person is well settled in a job that is "just right for him," he ordinarily does not experience doubt and vacillation and indecisiveness. His job carries a challenge to judgment and discretion. But the challenge is of such a kind that he can at least detect differences between the courses of action from which he must choose only one and commit himself to it. A too easy job is one in which the best course of those available is so self-evident as to require no effort of choice. A too difficult job is one that presents courses of action between which the individual is simply unable to perceive any difference: all the courses appear equally attractive or unattractive, equally sensible or impossible; and choosing and deciding become a matter of gambling, or tossing a coin, with the sense of despair that goes along with such a position if one's job hangs in the balance.

III

Since decision making as we have described it involves the giving up of those courses of action that have been rejected, the capacity to tolerate uncertainty will be seen to play a considerable part in the capacity to do work. Tolerance of uncertainty, and the giving up of alternative choices in order to choose a particular path to a goal, are characteristics of personality that can be seen to grow and develop in the individual. In the very early days of infancy, immediate gratification of needs is required if frustration is to be forestalled. As tolerance grows, a greater capacity develops to put off desirable events or pleasures with the promise, if delay is accepted, of getting something better. The capacity to choose a delayed course of action, rather than immediate gratification, is one that does not ordinarily develop until after the second or third year, and may not appear until much later, even in rudimentary form.[1] For to choose a delayed course means to be able to weigh the chances for or against a greater return if delay is accepted. Couched in these terms, our illustration may be seen to be a description of an early and primitive form of investment behavior—a prototype of later patterns of investment decision. The gratifying prospects of success are weighed against the anxiety or worry attendant upon the possibility of loss in the event of failure, or, more simply, against the frustration and loss of liquidity or immediate gratification arising merely from waiting, even in conditions of relative certainty.

As the individual grows and develops, he becomes capable of tolerating for increasingly long periods of time the uncertainty arising out of committing himself to a

[1] Melanie Klein has frequently pointed out that the duration of gratifying or frustrating experiences in early infancy has a profound effect on later development (Klein, 1955). The infant's reactions to these early experiences, in particular those having to do with the periods in between feeding, and the absences of his mother, establish a rigid foundation upon which there later grows the capacity to tolerate uncertainty for greater or lesser periods of time.

course of decisions. There is no reason to believe that this capacity develops to the same degree in everyone. Individuals vary considerably in what we may term their time-span capacity; that is to say, the length of time for which they are able to tolerate the effects of exercising discretion on their own account in pursuit of a living. It is likely that intellectual ability sets limits to time-span capacity, but is not itself the sole factor of importance. Low intelligence precludes high time-span; but high intelligence does not necessarily mean high time-span capacity, any more than high intelligence automatically leads to vocational success. If our analysis is correct, emotional makeup as well as intelligence must enter in view of the importance of the factor of being able to tolerate uncertainty. To take an extreme example, high intelligence does not in itself compensate in work for emotional instability and impulsiveness. In the short term, good results may be achieved, but impulsiveness and instability will weigh against a person's capacity to discharge responsibility over any extended period of time without review.

IV

The capacity to exercise discretion for longer or shorter periods of time is an outcome of the capacity to anticipate the sequence of events that will follow from any particular action. This anticipation may be conscious, or intuitive, or a mixture of conscious imagination and intuition. Perception will, of course, become more cloudy the farther into the future the chain of events is traced in one's mind. It may be that the length of time into the future that likely consequences can be traced is related to the capacity mentally to organize previous experience.[2] One possibility that suggests itself is that a person's time-span is that period of time over which he can look back and perceive in an organized way a continuous sequence of events leading up to circumstances in his current work situation.

Thus, as we get to the higher and higher time-spans, we may be dealing with greater capacity to utilize longer and longer stretches of past experience. Statesmanship illustrates the point. A statesman must be of historical bent, and requires to have (apart from other historical knowledge) the past fifty or one hundred years of a nation's history available in a living way within himself to be brought to bear upon making decisions of state. By way of contrast, academic historians and archeologists are not necessarily in possession of time-span capacity equivalent to the number of years that the period they are studying occupies in the past. We are concerned with the capacity to organize past experience as connected with the present in a continuous sequence. The work of the historian and the archeologist is in this particular respect usually directed toward the unconnected past. Their time-spans would be measured by the discretion and judgment they use currently in the present, in plan-

---

[2] At deeper levels psychologically, this capacity to organize previous experience is connected with the quality and intensity of unconscious anxiety, in particular of what is termed paranoid anxiety. In her paper, "The Importance of Symbol Formation in the Development of the Ego" (1948), Melanie Klein has shown the relationship between severe inhibitions in learning and the inability to deal with extremes of unconscious infantile sadistic impulses. It is these extremes of sadism in very early infancy that give rise to the deep-seated paranoid anxieties, which have a profoundly inhibiting effect on learning and upon all work in general. Anxieties of this kind militate against the ability to use past experience, and hence will diminish time-span capacity. In severely disturbed individuals, the capacity to do work is reduced practically to zero.

ning, organizing, and carrying out historical or archeo-
logical studies of the past.

V

From the point of view put forward, work may be described as a kind of investment behavior—investment in
one's foresight, one's ability to foresee the consequences
of one's actions. The bigger the job, the bigger the problem
of investment, in the sense that the longer is the series
of decisions to be negotiated and the longer the periods
of foresight required. *So also, the longer is the period of
uncertainty about the wisdom of the investments being
made.* For an employed person, the investment is of a
special kind. He is authorized to invest the resources of
his employer in his own foresight for the time-span governing the job.

Work in the above sense of investment and foresight
may be contrasted with scientific prediction and gambling, in both of which a sequence of happenings is predicted with a known degree of certainty. The probability
of a given result, or the odds on any particular outcome,
can always be stated. Executive work contains some scientific knowledge and prediction, and some elements of
gambling. But it is different from either of them in a very
important respect. Its central feature is the mental working out of the various alternative paths, and the choice
of what seems the best, without the benefit of any knowledge whatever about the probability or degree of certainty of a given result occurring. This mental working-
through is mainly unconscious; it takes place automatically most of the time, and only makes itself felt when
a person finds himself faced by a difficult problem.[3]

[3] This notion of work is made explicit in the Latin use of *labor* and
opus. Labor is the work or toil that precedes and accompanies the

We may thus carry our psychological definition of work one step further. What is experienced as size of job, or level of work, is the experience of the passing of time during which a series of decisions is made and a sequence of actions carried out without the individual's being able to know until some time later how good has been the discretion and judgment applied. The size of a job is the maximum period of time demanded by the conditions of the job with respect to one's being able to tolerate making fresh decisions in the face of continuing uncertainty. Weight of responsibility has been translated into time of responsibility. Being weighed down by too much responsibility means, in these terms, being exposed to continuous uncertainty for such long periods as to induce insecurity, lack of sureness, and anxiety.

VI

An important question now poses itself. Is it to be construed that an individual has a given capacity at any given stage in his development to undertake work of a particular maximum span of time? Findings on this subject, though limited in scope and number, are consistent, and do suggest such a construction; although, just as with other characteristics of personality makeup, a person's time-span capacity at any given time need not be taken as absolutely fixed and incapable of change.[4] If we pursue

---

carrying out of the task or *opus*. *Labor* is often used in the sense of the toil or effort that must go on inside oneself in order to set to the task. It is recognized as an emotionally trying process. *Hoc opus, hic labor est.* The ability to toil underlies true knowledge and wisdom—to both of which are often attributed pain and tribulation, an attribution that is due largely to the content of emotional toil.

[4] Time-span capacity is a compound of intelligence and emotional makeup. As such it would be modifiable under the same conditions as other deep-rooted personal characteristics like stability or temperament. Ordinarily educational or training procedures would be ex-

the implications of such a construction sufficiently far, we may discover that it will help us to explain certain otherwise puzzling matters, although our explanations may not always be in accord with established or traditional views.

Explorations of their work history with individuals employed at Glacier[5] and elsewhere suggest a regular pattern in the development of the time-span capacity of each individual. Examples of what were deemed by the individuals to be the biggest jobs they had done at various stages in their careers were analyzed in terms of the maximum time-span of discretion carried. When these maximum time-spans were plotted on a graph with respect to age, a regular progression could be found, as illustrated in Figure 6.1.

When the findings from a number of individual analyses of the above kind are put together, curves of the general shape in Figure 6.2 are suggested. Time-span capacity gradually increases until middle life, at which time the increase slows or stops. At the lower time-span levels, the process of increase probably stops in the early thirties, and there may be some subsequent recession. The tailing-off process appears to occur toward the mid-forties at higher time-span levels. At the very high levels, time-span capacity may increase throughout life.[6]

---

pected to have little, if any, effect in bringing about consciously planned attempts at individual development. It is likely that more intensive procedures would be required, aimed at deep-rooted personality change, of the kind to be achieved with full-scale individual psychoanalysis.

[5] The Glacier Metal Company, a London engineering company in which much of my original field research was carried out.

[6] The curves appear to be of the type of normal growth and decay processes, the full train of which is not encompassed within the normal span of life. The peak of the process is reached in the early thirties at the lower time-span levels, and very late in life, or not at all, in the very high time-span range. Hence, more of the phase of diminution or decrease in capacity is seen in the lower time-span range.

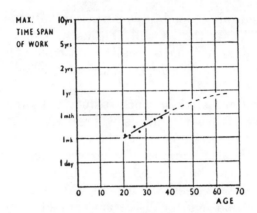

FIGURE 6.1. Individual Time-Span Capacity vs. Age.

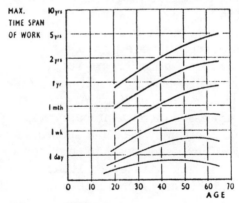

FIGURE 6.2. Overall Development of Time-Span Capacity.

The pattern of the curves suggests the need for two conceptions: that of the *current time-span capacity* of an individual—his time-span capacity at his current age; and the *potential time-span capacity* of an individual—his maximum likely time-span capacity in the future. The above curve is that of a person with a current time-span capacity of about six months, and a potential time-span capacity of something over one year.

It has not escaped our attention that the work from which this family of curves has been derived is based upon a very far-reaching assumption. We have assumed that any given individual has a time-span capacity that will exert a strong force in determining the level of work he will seek and carry successfully at any particular point in his career. Moreover, we have supposed that people seek out careers in terms of their developing time-spans, so that in maturity they may achieve a level of work adapted to their potential time-span capacity. This assumption must be critically scrutinized and assessed. Let us therefore elaborate it further, and examine it in more detail.

VII

Our thesis is this. Individuals who work full-time, and who elect to work in industry, will press toward finding work at a level corresponding to their current time-span capacity. We have carefully limited our thesis to work in industry; and to persons who are dependent for their living on full-time work. How far this thesis might apply outside these limits will not be considered. It is too big a question. It would extend, for instance, to the question of persons whose work is a vocation, and who are held to accept work at lower levels than they are capable of managing, because of the satisfaction of a personal or ethical kind to be derived from the particular content of the responsibility. It would also extend to artists and others engaged in creative work, or to persons in individual professional work. These areas of work must remain outside the present analysis. The data are not available for considering them.

The meaning of the above thesis can be described as follows. A person in a job that is consistent with his cur-

rent time-span capacity and that allows for the taking on
of added responsibility as his current time-span capacity
increases with age will experience a sense of well-being
so far as the work content of his job is concerned. And he
will not be experienced by his manager as either pushing
or slacking. If his work is at a level higher or lower than
his current time-span capacity, he will take steps to gain
work at his own level—either by pressing on through
special effort to get increasing responsibilities, or else by
arranging matters so as to off-load responsibility onto his
manager or onto his colleagues. The farther his job is
from a level of work corresponding to his current time-
span capacity, the greater will be the effort he will put
into gaining work at his own level. A person who has
been actively pushing to change his level of work will
reduce his efforts to do so as he approaches work at his
current time-span capacity. He will go on pushing only
if he is frustrated in his efforts to gain his correct level
of work.

   In the foregoing, due emphasis must be placed upon
the fact that we have formulated our propositions in
terms of an individual *seeking* a level of work consistent
with his current time-span capacity. These propositions
do not mean that every individual finds his correct level
of work all the time; nor do they mean that an individual's
time-span level is fixed and immutable. It is readily apparent, for example, that in times of depression, or of
rapid change in industrial organization, or of shifting of
population, individuals become dislocated to a greater or
lesser degree, and are likely to find themselves depressed
in level of work. Under such conditions, our thesis would
state, each individual will exert strenuous effort to regain
his proper level of work. If there are too strong barriers
counteracting these efforts operating against too many
people at any one time, as in times of economic depres-

sion, the dammed-up pressures toward higher levels of work will contribute significantly to the explosiveness of the situation that may arise.

What we mean when we say a person will press for work at his own current time-span capacity may be illustrated in the following three examples.

1. In Figure 6.3, let AC represent the actual course of the development of a particular individual I in his career in terms of maximum time-span of work achieved. Our thesis would lead us to expect that circumstances at E had frustrated his normal advancement. We would predict that he would begin to exert increasing pressure to get ahead. He would continue to exert this pressure until he regained his appropriate level of work at, say, point D. At this stage, the additional pressure would drop off, and he would proceed along his normal course of advancement toward B. Occasion to study their circumstances with individuals who could be described as being in such a position has shown that they exert these additional pressures by such means as: seeking and getting a change in job within the same firm; seeking a new job elsewhere; applying for a managerial traineeship; decid-

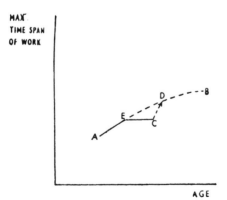

FIGURE 6.3. Time-Span Development in Individual I.

ing to undertake first training and then work in an entirely new field, even where this might mean an initial drop in status and income.

2. If individual II with a time-span curve shown in Figure 6.4 was working in a job whose range of level of work was XY, the following predictions would be made. He would not have been appointed to the job in the first place until he was approaching the age of thirty. He would begin to become dissatisfied with the work available to him—finding it too easy or too dull—if he was still in the job as he approached the age of thirty-five. Our own experience is in accord with these predictions. We have become familiar with persons in such circumstances beginning to think again about their careers and futures, as they approached the upper limits of current jobs, and contemplating a change to another job with more scope, or else seeking promotion.

3. Another type of situation, whose occurrence is not unfamiliar, is that of the person who feels his job grow out from under him. The level of work in his job may be reduced by standardization or by other change in method or work content. Or its level of work may be increased

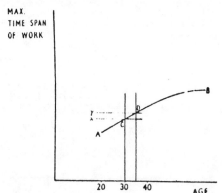

FIGURE 6.4. Time-Span Development in Individual II.

as a result of organizational expansion of new types of work calling for a higher level of discretion and responsibility. Changes of this kind are constantly occurring to a greater or lesser degree in the flux and flow of market conditions and new technology. Such circumstances could be predicted to have the following characteristics.

If level of work drops, the individual will start to exert pressure toward a higher level of work, or else he will resist the changes in method that are reducing the level of work in the job he occupies. When it is resistance to change that takes place, the resistance usually manifests itself in terms of arguments about wages and salaries, rather than about changes in work. In the absence of objective measures of work level, money is more readily talked about than the work that gives rise to it. In our experience, the managers and the members concerned with such situations end up equally frustrated, even though makeshift solutions are found. A much more satisfactory outcome has been observed to be experienced when the justification or lack of justification for the change in work content has been argued out and resolved; and when, in addition, principles have been agreed for changes in jobs for the individuals whose current jobs suffer reduction in level of work.

When an increase in level of work occurs in jobs, the effects will be different from those following a drop in level. If the increase in level is not too much in advance of a person's own rate of increase in current time-span capacity, then he may succeed in adjusting. If, however, the rate of increase in level of work is too rapid, the mental and emotional strain upon the individual may become intolerable—showing up in the form of what is commonly experienced in industry as difficulty in coping, evading responsibility, overburdening of subordinates,

failure to plan ahead, and, as a final outcome, even reaching the stage of personal illness.

VIII

The above thesis and the three illustrations raise a very
important question. Is it considered that no persons fully
employed in industry in order to earn their living ever
permanently accept work of shorter time-span than is
warranted by their current time-span capacity? It is commonly argued that precisely such an abnegation of advancement often enough occurs in our society. The
motives described for such behavior are various. Some
individuals are reputed to set aside advancement in order
not to have to part from their working group. Others are
said to avoid too great responsibility at work, in order to
pursue hobbies, or avocations, or voluntary services of
benefit to the community. The lesser responsibility at
work is supposedly compensated for by the greater emotional satisfaction derived from the activities outside
work. The thesis outlined would suggest that these commonly held notions ought not to be accepted at their face
value. A further critical examination may be warranted.

Reexamination of the following experiences in the
light of the above thesis tended to support the notion that
the commonly held view of these matters may well not
be in close accord with reality. One has had the opportunity on a number of occasions to note persons who had
renounced higher levels of work that they were reputedly
capable of doing, and who had subsequently been per-
suaded, for whatever reason, to accept promotion to the
higher levels. On such occasions, the reactions of the persons concerned have been characteristic and consistent.
One might have expected a more or less grudging acceptance of the new responsibilities, with indications that

the work could be done if the person chose to do it. But such was not the case. The common reaction was breakdown in the face of the new responsibilities. A person who was good at his previous job had been lost for one who was a failure at the higher level. Such evidence, it is recognized, is very far indeed from the sort of evidence that would allow any definite conclusions to be drawn. But it has been found to be very difficult to discover instances that support the commonly held view and that can bear detailed scrutiny.

This question that we have raised will have to be left open. The material presented, however, does allow the issue to be formulated in a manner that can be examined. It is suggested that patterns of individual development in terms of job successfully held will not show evidence of voluntary acceptance of work below the level to be expected in the normal course of development. Thus, curves of the type illustrated in Figure 6.5 are most unlikely to be found in circumstances where the individual concerned expresses satisfaction with his work and position, and is seeking no further advancement. The anticipated outcome, according to the present line of thought, has been presented in the first example above.

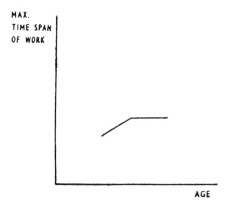

FIGURE 6.5. Time-Span Development of Individuals Avoiding Their (Higher) Level of Work.

The mechanisms that might make for each individual seeking his own proper level of work may, however, be considered. If a person not in training works at a level below his true capacity, he will experience strong group pressures to accept his full level of responsibility. The difficulties or problems—and sometimes even crises—that arise day in and day out in industry jeopardize everyone's economic security. As each difficulty is encountered, everyone connected with a job, managers and colleagues (and subordinates, if any), are all to some extent disturbed at their work. Everyone ordinarily wants to see the difficulty overcome as quickly as possible. The persons with the capacity to help resolve the difficulties are expected to show their mettle. And, if it is thought that some difficulties might be obviated if a given individual would only assume his full measure of responsibility, that individual will become the butt of resentment—either open or disguised.

Added to the personal effects of this resentment is the acute discomfort built up in individuals when they see crises and difficulties on the horizon that they judge they could help to prevent if they themselves had more authority. Where the capacity to do so really exists—that is to say, where it is not merely a fantasy of wishful thinking—then there is great internal pressure to take on the size of responsibility that gives the authority. Moreover, to be underemployed means the constant irritant of reviews of work at shorter periods than are emotionally acceptable. To have sufficient free play for uncertainty is a powerful driving force.

It is posited that individuals who can withstand such group and internal pressures are unlikely to be found. But it is possible that the morale of a factory could be such that a group or individuals just did not care whether or not crises and difficulties arose. In such a case it might well be that individuals could obstinately tolerate being underemployed, and indeed derive some satisfaction from it. But such situations are most unlikely to remain stable. The individuals will not remain content with their underemployment. Nor will the work get done. The usual outcome is an explosion of some kind—in the course of which either a sorting out is achieved, or there is a further buildup to another explosive outcome.

With respect to overemployment, the situation psychologically is more simple. To have too great responsibility means the anxiety-provoking situation of insufficiently frequent review of one's work, and hence the piling up of uncertainty. Even if the work proceeds satisfactorily, there still remains the feeling of being neglected or overlooked. Sufficiently frequent review of work is a necessity for the peace of mind of an individual, as much as it is a safeguard for the economic security of the organization.

IX

The foregoing analysis of the time-span capacity of individuals may suggest some reasons why changes in companies, and in the internal organization of companies, often take place in the way they do. It may be predicted, for example, that a company *that is operating successfully,* with a managing director and a team of immediate subordinates all below the age of forty or forty-five, must expand and develop. If they are below thirty-five, the company will expand rapidly. These predictions derive from the assumption that such individuals are at a stage of increasing time-span capacity, and would be seeking greater scope for their capacity. A successful company with a managing director and immediate subordinates over the age of fifty-five would be predicted to have strong internal forces acting in the direction of the organization remaining stable—neither contracting nor expanding—but threatened by eventual contraction if replacements are not found within five to ten years.

The implication of our assumption is clear. Whether or not changes occur in the size of business of a particular firm will depend directly upon whether the time-span capacity of the individuals in charge is consistent with the level of work being done. If their time-span capacity is growing beyond the level of work in the firm, they will grow the firm. If their time-span capacity is stable, and they are capable of doing the available work, the firm will tend to be stable. If their time-span capacity is below the level of work required, the firm will contract to a level consistent with their time-span. External considerations like market potential, while providing opportunity for growth in various directions, and setting limits in any given direction, will not cause any *particular* undertaking to expand or contract. Such a conclusion is consistent with everyday experience. Of a number of firms catering for the same market, it is frequently the case that some grow more rapidly than others, and, indeed, that some contract while others are expanding. Or, if there are numbers of firms dealing with a contracting market, it does not necessarily mean that all the firms will contract. One or more of them may well expand—either by incorporating some of the others, or by seeking other markets that they can enter with new types of product.

We may now also be able to describe in systematic terms a situation of frequent occurrence in industry, and one that may be among the commonest sources of psychological stress in organization. It is likely to be a rare occurrence that the individual members who are colleagues in a firm will be of an age and a rate of time-span development so geared to each other as to allow for smooth development in which they will always remain colleagues. We may take, for example, a firm that is doing well, with a managing director of thirty-eight, working at the four-year time-span level, and subordinates of age range, say, of thirty-two, thirty-five, forty-five, and fifty-five, doing work of the one-and-a-half-year time-span level. Such a firm will be likely to expand. Within five years, the managing director will be at the six- or seven-year time-span level. His subordinates, instead of being at one level, will have spread out. The youngest will have developed to about the four-year level, the next to the three-year level, the next to perhaps just under the two-year-level, and the oldest will have remained at about the one-and-a-half-year level. The firm will have to have increased in size to hold the advancing members. The members remaining under the two-year time-span level will not be able to carry the newer responsibilities likely to be thrust upon them. The group will be faced with the difficult problem of bringing some new members over the heads of some of its older members in order to provide the economic security of a job in a successful firm for each one of them and for the members subordinate to them.

It is not our present task to consider means for alleviating the stresses engendered in organization by the uneven rate of development of individuals. To the extent, however, that our analysis applies, a ready technique suggests itself whereby executive groups may judge one important aspect of their own internal stability. This judgment can be made by examining the age distribution of their members in relation to the level of work being discharged. By this means, the changes may be assessed in the levels of work that the individuals will require in the approaching years—and the degree of disjunction likely to arise may be appraised. To the extent, therefore,

that foreknowledge is useful, the above notions may be
of some help.

REFERENCES

Klein, M. (1948), The importance of symbol formation in the development of the ego. In: *Collected Writings*. New York: McGraw-
  Hill, 1975.
——— (1955), A study of envy and gratitude. In: *Collected Writings*.
  New York: McGraw-Hill, 1975.

Chapter 7

Learning for Uncertainty

I

In this chapter I want to concentrate upon one important factor in education—a factor whose existence has been much neglected but which exerts a weighty influence upon the dynamics of the classroom group, causing a restriction in the development of one crucial area in education—the area that relates education most closely to work and to creativity.

My argument runs as follows:

1. The communication and acquisition of knowledge, while an important part of education, cannot be its sole major object. There must also be the object of learning about the worry and uncertainty that accompany work and creative activity; that is to say, of learning how to work and how to learn, and of expanding one's capacity to use knowledge creatively in problem solving. I shall refer to this activity by the phrase *creative application.*
2. But, despite all attempts to construct educational methods and examinations which grade creative application as well as knowledge, our educational rewards tend to go to those students who shine at the acquisition of knowledge whether or not they

can put this knowledge to work, and to the teachers who can transmit knowledge.

3. The problem is partly a technical one of further development of our educational and grading methods to incorporate the students' own initiative and creativity into the program. But it is also partly an emotional problem tied up with the dynamics of the classroom group.

4. The teaching and absorbing of knowledge give both teacher and pupil a secure feeling of certainty—the pupil can reproduce what the teacher produces, and everyone can feel that knowledge thus shared is tangible and real.

5. But this sense of reality is ill-founded, since real-life problems are open-ended in the sense of not having correct answers but only answers that may be shown by subsequent experience to have been better or worse.

6. We all recoil—sometimes consciously but often unconsciously—from the more painful reality that open-ended problems are inevitably accompanied by worry and uncertainty, and never end with a reassuring sense of completeness. It is easier, therefore, for teachers and pupils to collude unconsciously to cling to a relationship based upon the security of knowledge and spurious certainty, than to allow the reality of uncertainty to intrude too far into the classroom.

7. Administrators, educators, and parents are no more immune from unconscious anxiety about the uncertainties of reality than are teachers, so that the classroom dynamic is bolstered up from outside.

8. I shall give an indication of how open-ended learning and creative application can be introduced into education (once we learn to understand our anx-

ieties about the uncertainty of reality), not to supplant the acquisition of knowledge but to counterpoint and spice it.

II

If we wish to find the central aim of our educational system, it is wiser to observe what we do than to listen to what we say we are trying to do. For in what we say we are trying to do there is much variety and difference of opinion: to convey information and knowledge; to stimulate the growth of personality; to create responsible citizens; to develop memory or intelligence or ability; to transmit culture; to facilitate socialization. In what we actually do there is less difference, for nearly everywhere it mostly ends up in examinations and in gradings which test the acquisition of knowledge and are produced as the tangible end product of the process.

One of the central aims of our educational process can be observed to be to learn whatever it is that passes examinations and gets high grades. Whatever else goes on in school, whatever else there may be in the relationship between teacher and pupil, the public reward for teacher as well as for pupil is the exam result, and the exam grades are the key to advancement.

Far and away the most outstanding characteristic of examination passing is the acquisition of the required knowledge. Acquisition of knowledge, therefore, becomes de facto, the main activity of our education. High grades imply high acquisition, and the ability to absorb information; low grades show low acquisition, but do not necessarily tell us much about the ability to learn. There is, however, a disjunction between performance as manifested in the acquisition of knowledge as rated by exam grades in school, and performance in adult life—a dis-

junction with which you will all be familiar enough.
School grades do not necessarily predict university performance, nor do university grades correlate tidily with
work performance and creativity, despite the fact that
work and creating also call for learning.

In broad terms, it is not surprising that there is this
disjunction. It is not to say that the acquisition of knowledge is unimportant. It is simply that in work—whether
it is administrative, research, professional, or creative
—knowledge alone will not see you through. You are
confronted not by examinations but by problems which
have no absolutely correct answer. You have to use
knowledge and judgment in interaction. And your performance is judged, and promotion gained, not in terms
of your knowledge alone—that is largely taken for
granted—but in terms of the quality of your judgment
and your capacity to use your knowledge. Let us, therefore, compare the process of acquiring knowledge with
the process of creative work, for if we can get clear enough
about the differences we shall be able to uncover a significant feature in the dynamic of the classroom group.

III

The process of acquiring knowledge can be understood
only if we can define what knowledge is. I do not, however,
propose to enter into an epistemological disquisition. I
think we may avoid that course by seeking a practical
working definition in psychological terms.

A central characteristic of knowledge is that it is verbally formulated and therefore precisely reproducible.
This characteristic is given in its etymology—knowledge,
from *gignoskein,* a reduplicated form.

But what is it that is verbally formulated?

The raw data of experience are nonverbal, or perhaps

more accurately, preverbal. I shall use the term *percepts* to refer to these new perceptions. We perceive—hear, see, feel—on a wide front, and only a small portion of our percepts are brought into that central focus of conscious attention that allows us to verbalize them. Indeed many of our raw percepts remain tantalizingly unidentifiable and unverbalized. Let me cite, for example, the complex of percepts that build up into our judgment of the performance and capacity of students. When we try to express our reasons for such judgments, our verbal justifications fall far short of what is required and we cannot teach what we have done. In effect, words fail us, but we may feel secure in our judgments nevertheless. It is not that these percepts will always remain unidentified. Experience, inquiry, and research may help eventually to recognize and isolate them so that they can be verbalized. They then become part of knowledge and can be taught.

The process of verbalizing percepts requires that they be organized in accord with man-made rules to form concepts. In effect what we do is to agree among us that this percept and that, and any others like them, shall be included within a given concept which we identify and to which we allocate a word. The perceptions may be things, actions, or relationships. Definition consists of specifying the boundary line (drawing a boundary is what definition means) which delimits which data of perception fall within the concept and which fall outside it. Thus, a triangle is not a thing but a concept in the minds of men, and does not exist in nature. What does exist in nature is a perceivable shape which, in accord with man-made rules, we include within the defined boundary of the concept of a triangle. This distinction between the verbal construction—the concept—and the perceptual experience of specific data is often found to be emotionally difficult to get hold of. Far too many university students, for example, graduate still believing that a triangle is a thing rather than a mathematical concept.

The point I wish to emphasize is that knowledge is man-made. That is why we can be so sure of it. We have made the rules, and set the limits. And it is these rules and limits which allow us to reduplicate it with such precision. In effect we know that two is two, and two plus two make four because we have decreed the formulation. What we know with certainty is the formulation. We can convey the rules to others. And we can thus set examinations to determine whether the rules have been learned and can be regurgitated. The constant danger, however, is that the word to some extent becomes the thing, and we dull and inhibit to the same extent our capacity to perceive.

The acquiring of formulated knowledge thus gives a secure feeling. It is identifiable, sure, and complete. When you know it, you know. You know because you can reduplicate it. And if you do not quite know it, you can work a bit more until you can reduplicate it.

Moreover, the acquiring of formulated knowledge is socially cohesive, and brings the security of group solidarity. You join up with others in the operation of shared rules. You increase your powers of communication. You can show your teacher what you know. And your teacher can show the outside world what you have been taught.

As the gestalt psychologists would express it, the acquisition of knowledge brings with it a sense of closure. You know when the task is complete.

It is this sense of sureness, of completeness, of reproducibility, that gives the psychological experience of the concept being the thing itself—a fact of experience as against a psychological fact. As Abercrombie (1960) has emphasized, this sureness can block creative perception and inhibit flexibility in thought.

In examining for the acquisition of knowledge, objective examinations are the most relevant. But since there is always the desire to examine for more than the mere reproduction of knowledge, essay type exams may be used. But even with essay questions, the demands of objectivity and comparability require that they be marked in such a manner as to put a premium upon the factual content of the answers, with a small allowance for the creative content expressed in the way the reply is organized. The judgment of the individual marker must be kept to a minimum.

IV

When we turn to consider work and creativity, we enter a different sphere of mental activity. In work, the essence of the activity is the exercise of discretion. Indeed, as I have had the opportunity to learn in connection with work measurement, the psychological experience of effort in work lies solely in the exercise of discretion. This feature is the same whatever the type of work at issue; that is to say, whether we deal with so-called creative work, or research work, or administrative work, or manual work, or the work of teaching, the crucial factor has to do with the exercise of discretion. We may, therefore, for our present purposes drop the distinction between creativity and work, and speak of work alone. For the difference between them lies not in the exercise of discretion; it lies in the fact that in so-called creative work the person generally sets his own object and task, whereas in other types of work his object or task is set for him.

In saying that discretion and judgment constitute the sole factor in the sense of effort in work, I do not mean to imply that knowledge is unimportant. Knowledge is essential for work. But it is essential in being one of the tools of work—like a saw, or a microscope; it is not the work itself. There may be work in deciding which fact or theory or procedure to muster and employ, but to the extent that you know your way, you do not have to work to find your way.

For example, as a teacher you know the length of time for given classes, you know specific material that has to be covered and by when, you know the type of exam to be set, you know which category of teaching method you are using—you do not have to start afresh in those things each day. But to help a particular child to advance in a particular subject in the face of difficulty—that is a problem that has to be faced afresh each time. You have to judge from day to day what is the best next step, and how best to handle the matter as you go along. If you knew what to do in the sense of there being an automatic formula to apply, it would be easy. But judging what is best done at any given moment is not easy. It takes work. And you can never be sure that you might not have achieved a better result if you had proceeded differently.

What is it then about the exercise of discretion and judgment that gives the sensation of work and of creativity? We are involved here with a sphere of psychological activity which, although extremely familiar, remains conceptually ill-defined. There is no satisfactory, commonly employed and accepted language for it. We speak about judgment, intuition, "nous," skill, experience, know-how, scholarship, common sense, discretion, discrimination, hunch, and more crudely, expressions like "using your loaf" and "guesstimating."

The sensation itself is one of uncertainty, of worry. We cannot put into words what it is that we are taking into account in doing what we are doing, and in that sense we do not know that what we are doing will get us where we want to go, will achieve the result we want to achieve. We judge that it will, we think it will, but we are not sure, and only time will tell.

Moreover, it is also of the essence of work that, having decided how to set about a task, and having completed it, you can never be sure that if you had decided to do it another way that you might not have done it better or more quickly. You just do not know. Once a task is done it is done. You cannot reduplicate the task and the conditions under which you did it. If you can, then it is no longer a task in the psychological sense; you have created knowledge, and you can lay down procedures for dealing with problems of that kind.

The mental processes involved in work are unconscious. They are mental processes at the preconceptual stage—preconceptual thinking as opposed to conceptual thinking. It is thinking which uses unconscious preconceptions (as described by Bion, 1962) rather than conscious conceptions. It is therefore unverbalizable, and because of that, it cannot be taught by direct formulated communication. It is the kind of experience ordinarily communicated by apprenticeship techniques—whether in manual work, or law, or medicine, or teaching—in which we say to the student, "Watch what I do, and try to get the feel of it," or "I wouldn't have done it that way, I would have done it this way."

V

I would hope that this description of the difference between knowing and working, between the conscious use of concepts and the unconscious flow of preconcepts, is sufficient to point up gross differences, which will be familiar to educators, between education designed to transmit knowledge and education designed to encourage or stimulate creativeness and the capacity to work and solve problems. The distinction between the two is currently most widely expressed by educational psychologists in terms of the educational processes concerned with convergent thinking on the one hand, and divergent thinking on the other. Convergent thinking tends toward the usual and expected, toward retaining the known, learning the predetermined, and preserving what is; divergent thinking tends toward the novel and speculative, toward revising the known and explaining the undetermined. One favors certainty, the other favors risk. In modern Western society our education tends to be concerned with convergent thinking, rather than with the encouragement of divergent thinking. It transmits knowledge and examines for it. It provides some opportunity for creative work and thought, but does not examine for it. And there is always the hope that some inspiration will rub off on to the pupil from the teacher.

And yet our aspiration is strong that education should do more—should inspire, should stimulate students to want to learn, should help to get them intellectually under way, to open their minds to be receptive to new knowledge and to new perceptions, should give them the experience of what it is like to work for data and to solve problems. Existing knowledge is constantly being made redundant as new knowledge is gained. Our students must learn how to go about revising this knowledge, adapting to change.

But consider what would be involved. I am not talking, for example, about improving laboratory methods for the teaching of science. For carrying out experiments that have already been done, however advantageous from the point of view of acquiring scientific knowledge, does not necessarily increase scientific imaginativeness or creativity. Nor am I talking about periodic opportunities for free expression, or for creative projects, organized in a manner peripheral to the syllabus in the sense of not counting for marks. What we are concerned with is the experience of learning to learn, learning about problem solving and decision making, or more precisely, learning about the uncertainty, worry, and anxiety involved in problem-solving, in work, in creating.

VI

If learning to work and to be creative is what we want as one aspect of the education process, why is it so widely experienced as difficult to give it the place in the syllabus and in examinations that we protest it warrants? Here we come to the crunch. Is it because the problem is too difficult technically or intellectually? Perhaps it is a difficult technical problem and would take a good bit of creative work to overcome it. But I think that is not the whole story, nor even the starting point. We have to ask just what evidence there is that we can tolerate a situation in the classroom which is worrying and anxiety provoking. It is my thesis that there is in fact a strong unconscious collusion, central to the dynamic of the classroom group, in which teachers and pupils are involved in keeping the educational process which counts, firmly tied to the transmission of knowledge with its certainty and group cohesion, and to hold at arm's length the individual effort and uncertainty of preconceptual learning.

Consider for a moment what would be involved.

In addition to classes as we have them now—with teaching, laboratory work, projects—there would have to be the opportunity for project work of a particular kind, calling for the creative applications of knowledge. It would be concerned with projects—I will call them cre-

ative application projects—of graded complexity, intensity, difficulty, which could be assigned to students in
such a way that they would eventually find their own
level; that is to say, the level that would put them at full
stretch. The problems would have to be open-ended, in
the sense of having no predetermined solution. They
would have to be genuine problems, and not, for example,
merely the collection of information for a project book.
And the assessment of the quality of the performance
would be a matter of the judgment of the teacher.

In finding their own level, the students would progress
from assignments that were just too easy for them, to
assignments that were just too difficult, and in which
they would be allowed to have the opportunity to experience stress in work, that is to say, to go through the
experience of just being able to cope. The experience
would be akin to what we ordinarily speak of as carrying
responsibility and finding one's responsibilities too light
or too easy, just right, or too heavy and overwhelming.

There are two major problems involved; first, the difficulty of designing such problems of creative application;
second, the difficulty of introducing the experience of
stress as part of the educational process. The first is a
technical problem; the second, involving assessment of
performance and experience of failure, is connected with
the group dynamics in the classroom. Let us briefly consider each in turn.

VII

The problems of designing projects in creative application
are manifold. In the first place, there must be room for
the exercise of discretion by the pupil in the way he goes
about tackling his assignment; he should not simply re-
peat someone else's method. Each assignment would have

to some extent to be unique, in the sense that although the same ultimate object might be set, the conditions under which the problem was set would have to be able to vary sufficiently to call for the exercise of discretion afresh each time, so as to be a genuinely creative application. The problems would have to be able to be classed into grades of increasing difficulty. And they would have to be of such a kind as to make use of the knowledge which the pupil has been taught, but without going too far beyond it.

I cannot readily picture the form that such assignments in creative application would take in school. They are easy enough to arrange where professional education is concerned; for example, in clinical work in medical schools. But even in the ordinary university setting, there are difficulties. Thus, for example, in some universities we achieve something of this end by the sandwich method of education in which students have three six-month work-training periods during their four-year course. They are actually in training at work, being paid, under conditions in which, ideally, the employing organization gives them work and opportunities in which they can use their acquired academic knowledge and take on as much responsibility as they are capable of.

VIII

But leaving aside the technical difficulties for the moment, are we justified in supposing that all would be straightforward if we were only able to think up definite assignments in creative application? Not at all. Let us look at the second problem, that of assessment of performance. The essence of a creative problem is that the result cannot be assessed objectively. Someone must judge the performance. It is like assessing the performance of a teacher. You cannot simply add up the marks made by his pupils, and take the total. Someone has to judge what he has done with the pupils he had working under the particular conditions of that moment.

This same problem occurs in assessing the work-training period of university students. The assessment is difficult, and no way has yet been found to get an effectual rating system which can enable work-training performance to be taken into account in deciding the final grade.

The problem is much the same as that of a manager rating the performance of a subordinate at work. This assessment has always been widely experienced as a great difficulty, although I believe that it is in fact fundamentally simple. The main reason that it is experienced as a problem is that everyone is so busy trying to discover objective criteria which will allow the performance to be measured, thus relieving the manager of the burden of using his own judgment.

Great effort and large sums of money are expended in designing accounting procedures and measurements of output which will throw up an index number, or perhaps a complex of index numbers, which will tell just how well each subordinate has done.

When I say that the problem is in fact simple, I do not mean that I know of any ready and easy method of making the judgments. What I mean is that it is simply a fact that the assessment of performance in work, whether in teaching, or in industry, or in a project problem, must remain basically a matter of judgment; a principal's judgment of a teacher, a manager's judgment of a subordinate, a teacher's judgment of a pupil. To seek a measuring yardstick that will give objectivity and strict comparability is only to complicate the matter and to steer attention away from the main issues.

These main issues in assessment I would see as twofold: first, to ensure satisfactory conditions of assessment; and second, to develop objective aids to assessment. Among the necessary conditions I would include that of continued assessment in many situations; and I would include also the building up of composite assessments based upon the judgments not of just one teacher, but of a series of teachers. These multiple judgments ought then to be processed by the departmental head to whom the teachers are responsible, so that a consolidated judgment may be reached.

Even with these safeguards, and with objective aids, the assessment nevertheless remains a matter of human judgment; and that always seems to give rise to anxiety. We tend to have a very ambivalent attitude toward such judgments. On the one hand, everyone wants to be assessed by those above him—by his teachers, or managers, or headmaster. We need such assessment to help us to know where we stand. For the fact is that the assessments are made whether we like it or not. Mutual assessment is a basic element in all human relationships. If the assessment is a good one, of course we all like it, and would wish it to be taken into account in affecting our careers and our progress. It is when the assessment is below our expectations, lower than our own judgment of ourselves, that the difficulties arise. Why should someone else have got a higher rating? Why should my merits have been overlooked? Surely it is a matter of inadequate judgment, or of prejudice, or of personal dislike? Feelings of hurt, of resentment, of unjust treatment, enter the situation, and individuals may feel hard done by, or that others have forged ahead by currying favor. You will know the kind of feelings I mean if you have ever been passed over for some special duty that you wanted, or for promotion, in favor of someone whom you judged to be less competent than yourself for the work in question. When a place at

a university, or the grade with which you graduate, is at
stake, feelings can run high about assessments based on
judgments about performance in project problems akin
to work, where there is no objective or preset outcome to
provide a base for objective comparability of results. That
may be the reason why, in professional training when
judgment of practical performance becomes a major element in the assessment of performance, grades are commonly not given, the student being either qualified or
not.

IX

The third problem is that of introducing the experience
of stress as part of the educational process. I am not speaking here of chronic failure, or of failure overall. I am
speaking of the opportunity for the student to extend
himself in project problems to the point where he begins
to find it difficult to cope. By this means he would be able
to test and to find the upper limits of his capacity. We
are all familiar with individuals who, under the impact
of stress or of changed or unusual circumstances, begin
to manifest qualities which had previously laid dormant.
Wartime, for example, often makes demands which
stretch a man to the full, sometimes for the first time, so
that his full capacities may be revealed.

The difficulty is that so long as a person is succeeding
in his work, however difficult, it is not possible to know
how effective he might be. The only way to know you
have come to the upper limit is somehow to exceed it. To
exceed it means for the student to experience failure—to
experience the sense of the inability to cope.

Suppose then it were possible to design appropriate
project problems to test the limits of capacity of students.
Once again, anxieties would be aroused. Students would

experience concern. So would their parents. And so, too, would their teachers. This concern readily turns to anxiety if the teachers themselves are not able to contain it, and if the school system is not geared to tolerate it.

X

Let us now consider some implications of these considerations. For purposes of exposition, I shall try to single out and magnify, so as to bring more sharply into focus, what I believe to be a factor of central importance in inhibiting the introduction of creative application into the teaching program. I refer to the anxieties that are generated, two of which I have described; namely, the anxieties connected with assessment, and those connected with the stress of testing the limits of a student's creative capacity. These anxieties are ordinarily not apparent. They are not apparent because the educational process tends to be so solidly organized around the safety of the communication of knowledge. So long as we confine ourselves to this setting, we can produce relatively objective assessments. These assessments allow for comparison between one student and another, whether in the same or in different schools. No anxiety need be aroused, other than a concern that something is lacking, that somehow knowledge is not all, and that there remains a disjunction between formal education and the creative application required in work and in life.

The anxieties do become apparent, however, as soon as the question is raised of introducing exercises in creative application into the classroom as part of the assessed performance of the student. Then the neatness and tidiness of the arrangement is threatened. We have substituted for the assessment of the student's absorption of knowledge—his learning about the culturally available tools for work—the assessment of his capacity to do work. That is to say, we have shifted from concern only with certain cognitive capacities, to concern with appraisal of the creative capacity for work of the whole person. The reality of uncertainty is proclaimed, and anxiety is aroused. One expression of this anxiety is to argue that if practical work is introduced, then academic standards will be lowered. Practical work, however creative, is related to use, and the conjunction of academic knowledge and its use is so often felt somehow to tarnish the intellectual value of the academic work. Creative application therefore tends to be belittled as merely *vocational*—a term of opprobrium.

I have seen this anxiety aroused in students in learning about work. If you create conditions in which they can experience the open-ended nature of the work situation and in which they have to rely upon their own judgment, they become uneasy. They demand more reading references. They want lectures or laboratory classes in which they can get back to the security of formulated knowledge. They want to know what they are expected to do, to observe, to record, to reproduce. They are made anxious by the experience of uncertainty.

Most teachers will have experienced this kind of anxiety among students. They are familiar with the way this anxiety can communicate itself to the teacher. It needs great will and perseverance to withstand it, especially in a setting in which it is not the policy of the school to provide the opportunity for creative application. Moreover, if the teacher has the task of assigning and assessing project problems without himself supporting the general idea, his own anxieties in the situation will ensure that his supervision will be unsatisfactory.

XI

One is led, therefore, to the conclusion that there is an unconscious collusive force operating as between teacher and student to keep the academic situation pure, and free from the anxieties of creative application. To put it another way, there is a strong force unconsciously operating to ensure that the educational situation is well structured, deals with formulated knowledge, allows the student to know what to prepare for exams, and enables him to do well and to get good grades so long as he has learned the organized material. The fact that getting good grades in the repetition of this knowledge gives little indication of subsequent performance in real life, affects the dynamic of the classroom group little if at all.

I use the term *unconscious* because the phenomena themselves are not consciously identified. Nothing much shows unless there is the threat of introducing creative application and uncertainty.

It may be noted that this unconscious collusion is not reality based. As I indicated earlier, the reality of problem solving as it exists outside the school situation is very different from problem solving in school. It is something more than using well-tried concepts to answer familiar questions by means of learned techniques. Moreover, it overlooks the fact that however much satisfaction high marks may give to students, their teachers, and their families, these high marks bear no necessary relationship to eventual performance. There is an apparent enigma here—that of collusion toward unreality in the group dynamic of the classroom. Surely we might expect reality-testing to reign supreme in the educational situation?

That the matter may, however, not be so simple, was suggested by Freud many years ago. It is not necessarily to be assumed that the reality principle will inevitably dominate in human affairs. At best there will always be some conflict between the demands of reality-testing and the demands of those more primitive qualities within us which seek for magical solutions in accord with what Freud termed the *pleasure principle.* One particular expression of these magical impulses is in the power attached to words. Not only, as I have already mentioned, does the word become the thing, but to know the word is to possess control over outer concrete reality. To control the word is to control the thing. Thus it is that the educational process is constantly under human pressure to keep verbal knowledge and its transmission at the center of the stage.

Verbal knowledge is, of course, important. But when it becomes elevated to the topmost position in education, then we may suspect that the dynamic of the classroom situation is being influenced by the pleasure principle to a greater extent than would be desirable. That is to say, to the extent that knowledge dominates the educational object and grading, and creative application takes a back seat, I would seek the reasons less in the technical difficulties of developing techniques for bringing opportunities for creative application into the classroom, than in the unconscious dynamic provided by avoidance of the anxiety and pain of reality-testing.

In short, how to bring creative application into the classroom, alongside knowledge, may be a technically difficult problem. But it is a problem worth tackling, for among other benefits are those of helping students to gain familiarity with the anxiety attendant upon work and creativity, and with the emotional difficulties of reality-testing, particularly the reality-testing of our own personal capacities. We shall never properly tackle the problem unless we get ourselves free from the unconscious collusion in the classroom to seek refuge in a word-dominated world—a world in which the word is the final secure and repeatable reality—as against the real world itself.

REFERENCES

Abercrombie, M. L. J. (1960), *The Anatomy of Judgement.* London: Hutchinson.
Bion, W. R. (1962), *Learning from Experience.* London: Heinemann Medical Books Ltd.

Chapter 8

Theses on Work and Creativity

1. The critical difference between employment work, creative work, and running a business lies in whether there is any external reference for the work, and in the character of the external reference; that is, it lies in the manner in which the object of the work is determined.

2. In *employment work,* the object is set in defined terms by means of an instruction from an employer, who inspects the final product and who must be satisfied if the employment is to continue.

3. In *creative work,* the object is not at all externally prescribed. It derives from the internal world and is produced for an internal audience, it reflects an impulse of the artist to express something which he himself is moved for unconscious reasons to express; there is no external task in either concrete or symbolic terms to be completed; the finished product must satisfy the artist, and, if he is successful, will touch depths in the minds of others, evoke a response, and establish new standards. The creative artist requires that his external audience should also work.

4. In *running a business,* one of the main tasks lies in discovering the object of the work by discovering consumer needs which may be satisfied. This work of discovering what needs may be satisfied at a profit (i.e., understanding the market) is the hallmark of successful

business. There is an external reference for the work but it is not given by instruction; to discover it requires a particular kind of sensitivity to the needs of others.

5. Creative work is therefore wholly symbolic; the finished product is symbolic; and the work itself touches upon and derives from the deepest layers of the mind, unaided by any objective and concrete point of reference. In employment work, there is always an external framework to guide and assess the symbolic work; hence symbolic work does not touch so deeply or so completely upon the unconscious processes. Running a business is intermediate; there is an external framework, but it requires symbolic work to discover it; and failure to conform to it results in a gradual loss of business, and not in an external direct criticism as from an employer.

6. The main differences in the psychology and the psychopathology of the three types of work can, I think, be derived from this starting point.

EMPLOYMENT WORK

7. The general theme to be pursued is that of the connection between employment work (and other types of work as well) and the work of mourning; the relation to the object in work is characterized by temporary states of mourning, during which it is feared that the work is resulting in failure, and the object destroyed instead of being created.

8. In the course of the work process, inner reality and external reality are connected by means of testing symbol formation against an object emerging in external reality and judged by someone else in terms of externally established standards.

9. If the work is successfully completed, inner reality and external reality are slightly better understood, inner

reality is slightly less chaotic, the lost primary object is experienced symbolically inside as good, and hope and confidence are increased in the capacity to create an object on which real and demonstrable value is placed, and, symbolically, in the capacity for reparation.

10. The most primitive fantasies of the relation to the primary object are awakened because the labor of creating a work is carried on for the purpose of gaining a livelihood; that is to say, the value of the labor is directly reflected in the standard of living achieved.

RELATION TO THE OBJECT

11. A task is set by a manager in terms of: "do that task." If he is an effective manager the work is well organized, in the sense of reasonable tasks being set, proper value placed upon the work, and a fair assessment made of the capacity of the individual.

12. The quid pro quo is that the employer will pay a livelihood for the work done—that is to say, the doing of the work has material value.

13. The expected result is always prescribed.

14. Certain limits to the ways in which the work can be done are also always prescribed by the employer; that is to say, there are governing rules and regulations, in the form of limits on time and cost, methods, procedures to be followed, and so on, which the person doing the work is expected to *know*.

15. The task is always set in symbolic terms; that is to say, the work to be done may simply be described in words, or by a drawing, or by what the thing to be made must be able to do; at its most concrete, it will be set in terms of a quasi-symbolic equation; for example, "Make another just like this."

16. That is to say, the task is set in the symbolic terms

of a goal or objective, the essence of a job of work being that the finished product does not exist but must be created.

17. The work process starts with an object that has neither been created nor destroyed; but in the course of the work, either may occur. Unconsciously it is an absent or missing object to be created in order to receive material reward; that is to say, a breast or genital to be restored or repaired.

18. Work represents a challenge in relation to the object. The life-giving forces are to be tested, as they are tested in connection with the testing of potency and creativity in making a baby.

19. The relation to the object may be complicated by the extent to which the relation to the employer giving the instruction unconsciously represents the mother or father demanding that the object be created; that is to say, the lost object restored, and a baby created. This instruction may be experienced as a loving demand, as an intrusion, or as a threat, to be responded to by a show of loving and life-giving potency, by rejection, or by placation.

20. If the depressive position has been sufficiently worked through, the work situation presents the opportunity to work through once again in phantasy the reparative relation to the lost and destroyed primary good object, restore it to the good mother, and have it received with proper valuation, while at the same time strengthening the tie to reality by symbolically matching the phantasy process by a concomitant real activity resulting in success and value in the external world.

21. The relation to the internal objects must be sufficiently good to make it possible to accept the external standards and restrictions set by the employer—the standards for the completed work, and the prescribed lim-

its within which the work is to be carried out; that is to say, the superego must be experienced as basically helpful and not attacking, for the standards and limits to be experienced as helpful in the sense of limiting and structuring the task rather than as restrictive and persecuting.

THE FUNCTION OF KNOWLEDGE

22. The employee must be able to visualize more or less completely the finished work he is to create.

23. Within the limits set, and materials and facilities provided, he must find the best way to complete the job.

24. He must *know* the prescribed limits.

25. He must have enough familiarity with work of that type to *know* some possible ways of doing it and to *know* some of the consequences likely to arise from various courses of action.

26. He will, however, never *know* completely in advance the very best way to do any particular job, since every job differs in some respect from every other, and therefore he must exercise *discretion* in doing his work.

27. He must visualize (in symbolic terms) various ways of doing the job in terms of, "if I do this, then that is likely to happen," and bring both *knowledge* and *symbolic work* to bear upon the problem.

28. Bringing knowledge to bear implies judgment in the sense of *jus-dicare* (to speak the law); that is to say, juxtaposing relevant knowledge so as to get limits to the process of symbol formation.

29. Knowledge can be regarded as an ego-bounding or ego-limiting function, and is thus similar to superego function.

30. It may prove useful to consider the superego as

one part of the ego-boundary region (a kind of circumego),
a region which comprises at least the following content:

a. superego function: prescribing general norms of
   conduct;
b. reality-tested knowledge of the social standards
   and physical properties of the external world;
c. non-reality-tested working hypotheses, or beliefs,
   about the properties of the external world;
d. currently perceived external standards and limits,
   which constitute the externally set framework for
   the job in hand.

31. Knowledge is thus limiting—it states what can
and cannot be done; to the extent that it is accurate
knowledge it is confining in a helpful way, because it
limits symbolic and real action within the bounds of what
is possible in reality.

32. As Ezra Pound has expressed it—"The tradition
is a beauty which we preserve, and not a set of fetters to
bind us."

33. The effective functioning of the ego-boundary (and
of knowledge) will depend upon the degree to which: the
superego has been assimilated by the ego; the superego
is integrated; and the superego and other regions of the
ego-boundary are integrated with each other and with
the ego.

34. A harsh, unassimilated, and unintegrated superego will disturb the functioning of knowledge to the extent that the superego relation determines the quality of
the relation between ego function and the ego-boundary;
knowledge, and thus reality, will be experienced as harsh,
unduly restrictive, and frustrating.

SYMBOL FORMATION AND SYMBOLIC WORK

35. The use of discretion in work implies the capacity to work the task through in one's mind, before actually tackling it.

36. Symbolic work implies new symbol formation, however minute, for the purpose of following through in thought the likely consequences of various courses of action, and making discretionary choice of the best way to do the job.

37. This process of symbolic work may be facilitated by trial actions in reality, in which only a small loss is sustained if the symbolic work does not match up to reality.

38. Under conditions of integration and assimilation of the superego and ego (that is to say, with fusion in the ascendant), symbol formation can proceed in conjunction with and supported by knowledge, and without resort to denial of reality.

39. The process of symbol formation will further be facilitated to the extent that the symbolic requirements of the task fit in with the line of symbol formation which would naturally and spontaneously follow.

40. It is this combination of knowledge and free symbol formation (and the interaction of conscious perception and unconscious processes implied in freedom of symbol formation) which I think describes the ancient Greek conception of "nous"—mind comprising both heart and soul, intellect and feeling, thought and impulse. Yeats expresses it as:

God guard me from those thoughts men think
In the mind alone;
He that sings a lasting song
Thinks in a marrow-bone

41. Symbolic work, however, stirs the deepest anxieties of fragmentation and annihilation, because of the necessity to separate the elements in a situation, consider them apart from each other in order to select the relevant ones.

42. This symbolic separating and choosing, if carried too far, has all the elements of splitting and fragmentation, and is fertile ground for the displacement of unconscious aggression.

43. Moreover, the essence of symbolic work is that it is carried out in the complete isolation and loneliness of the internal world; thus, only if the inner world is integrated will symbolic work of this kind not represent a threat of chaos and confusion, and be carried through to the point of decision.

44. The difference between differentiating and splitting depends upon the presence in essence of simultaneous integration (i.e., a "diffintegration").

45. At some point in the process of symbolic work, and trial, the decision must be made to undertake the real external task, armed with the symbolic work that has been done. It is the point at which reality testing begins.

46. Decision is from *de-caedere*—to cut apart; it implies embarking on the chosen path in the sense of cutting away from the other possibilities (or deciding not to look for others), and pursuing the chosen path in external reality.

47. A decision cannot be said to have been taken unless accompanied by real commitment in action.

48. The point of decision is the most likely to arouse anxiety: it symbolizes cutting and giving birth; it is the point of no return; it implies the loss of the other possible courses of action which have to be given up; it is the moment of success or failure.

49. Anxiety is increased by the fact that symbolic work can never be completed, not only because by the very nature of its being symbolic it cannot be completed in outside reality, but because there are always limits of time to be faced, and lack of information about what the real situation will hold once external work has begun.

50. The art of successful work is to keep the process of symbolic work going just long enough, and with just the right amount of detailed sorting out. A nice balance is required between too early closure and obsessional spinning out.

51. The achievement of this balance requires that the concomitant unconscious processes symbolized in the work task (of working through the reparative relation to the primal object and creating a child) are not dominated by hopelessness and fear, accompanied by obsessional or manic defenses, or paranoid–schizoid regression.

EXTERNAL WORKING

52. At the decision stage, the die is cast, and external work begins in which inner symbolic work and use of knowledge interact with the perception of the emerging real object.

53. From this stage, to turn back and try another path would entail the *real loss* of the external work already done.

54. The developing real object is kept in constant conjunction with the symbolic completed object, and compared with it, and constant fine adjustments are made to the plan of action by means of symbolic work, and to the emerging work by means of action carried on in the light of the symbolic work.

55. Reality testing begins at the stage of external work which follows decision.

56. Completion of the external work calls for unconscious acceptance of the loss in reality of the primary
object, and attachment of affect to the external object
which is being created.

57. The external object will rarely, if ever, be perfect,
nor will the path chosen for creating it. If, however, the
work process has been carried out under the dominance
of libidinal impulses (at depth, with fusion predominating) and a good relation with the internal primal object,
then lost opportunities and the concomitant fear of having lost the object can be coped with by temporary states
of mourning which include mourning for the lost primal
object, and the ego strengthened as a result.

58. The increase in ego strength derives from the fact
that the ability to experience uncertainties, lost opportunities, or mistakes, and to live through and to mourn
the sense of loss that accompanies the full realization of
what might have been achieved, is the basis of that constructive self-criticism which leads to learning from one's
own mistakes.

59. The completed work is compared with the standards explicit and implicit in the symbolically stated instruction.

COMPLETION OF THE TASK

60. The completed work is handed to the manager for
his inspection and, if satisfactory, his approval and acceptance.

61. The employer pays for the value of the work as
already established.

62. Reality testing is completed when the work is in-
spected by or on behalf of the employer.

63. If the work is satisfactory, contact with reality is
reinforced by the reward in current livelihood which is

gained when the primal good objects and the parents are established inside and not confused by introjective or projective identification with the external real job.

Summary

64. The process of normal work is one in which the individual must descend within the depths of his own internal conscious and unconscious world, and there, in lonely and isolated state, carry out the double task of unconscious reparation to the primal object and symbolic creation of an external object.

65. Having thus tested the balance of chaos and of integration within himself, he must then expose his state of mind to the test of scrutiny and assessment by himself and others through the medium of the product of his mind and skill as represented in his external work.

66. In the course of the work, temporary states of mourning are experienced in connection with difficulties in advancing the work of creating the object, with lost opportunities, and with mistakes.

PSYCHOPATHOLOGY OF WORK

67. The processes described above may break down at any or all of the stages outlined. We may consider first of all how psychological disturbance may cause breakdown in work even in objectively good working conditions.

68. Given the ordinary conditions in neurosis of a too harsh superego; anxiety about aggression; hopelessness and lack of confidence in the capacity to repair and restore the primal object; fear of depression and persecution; fear of chaos and confusion in the inner world; insufficient differentiation of the conscious from the unconscious

parts of the mind, and of inner from outer reality, and excessive projective and introjective identification (and underneath all, states of defusion of the life and death instinct, and a deeply repressed primal bad and persecuting object split off from the deeply repressed idealized primal good object); then the following pathology occurs.

RELATION TO THE OBJECT

69. The relation to the object in work is disturbed by excess of projective and introjective identification; the object of the work is insufficiently distinguished from the internal objects.

70. The absence of the object to be created stirs depressive anxiety; hopelessness and despair govern work, and the confidence in capacity to do the job is lacking.

71. Unconsciously the anxiety is that, under the predominance of oral, anal, and urethral sadism, the object will be attacked while it is being created, and a bad product, equated with the destroyed internal object, destroyed or uncreated babies, and with bad excreta, will be the result.

72. The rejection of the bad product by the employer representing the persecuting and castrating parents and objects, and the withdrawal of livelihood, is anticipated.

73. The situation is at the same time experienced internally as an attack on the internal good object and on the ego which is attempting to repair and restore that object.

74. The job of work, and the manager who allocates it, are intensified as persecutors, through projection of bad objects and destructive impulses.

75. Fear of persecution increases hatred of the work and of the employer, and reinforces deeper-lying doubts in the ability to mobilize full capacity in doing the job.

76. Pathological envy and jealousy are aroused—envy

of the employer who has work to give, and jealousy of him for giving work to others; nepotism will intensify these feelings. The process of constructing a symbolic representation of the object to be made is interfered with by anxiety and by the displacement into the symbol formation of aggression directed against the internal object; there results an incomplete or distorted picture of the job to be done.

FUNCTION OF KNOWLEDGE

77. The start of the job is further hampered by external standards and knowledge being perceived as hampering and restricting, through identification of the total functioning of the ego-boundary region with the harshness and severity of the superego which forms a part of that region.

78. Knowledge and helpful limiting regulations are therefore rejected, because they are unconsciously experienced as imprisoning, persecuting, and as castrating in the sense of denying freedom for magical thought and omnipotence; hatred is turned against the ego and its knowledge, and ego function accordingly weakened.

79. Contrariwise, the external persecutors may in turn be identified with, in order to gain control over internal persecutors and destructive impulses; there results a weakening of ego function, characterized by a rigid conformance to regulations and consequent unimaginativeness in work.

SYMBOLIC WORK AND SYMBOL FORMATION

80. Symbolic work constitutes a decided psychological threat under conditions of neurosis.

81. The descent into the internal world under conditions of isolation and loneliness stirs the anxieties of de-

scent into the inner chaos, and the fear either of not being able to return (that is to say, of remaining internally preoccupied and transfixed, or utterly confused), or of returning with some monstrous creation; the anxieties are a small-scale replica of the anxieties of pregnancy and labor, including the threat of loss and of mourning.

82. Thus, Aeneas is warned: "Light is the descent to Avernus. Night and day the portals of Gloomy Dis stand wide: but to recall thy step and issue to the upper air—there is the trial and there the task!"

83. These anxieties are increased by the real doubt and uncertainty which must be experienced in genuine work, in the process of symbolically differentiating the various elements and possible courses of action, picking over them, and selecting the preferred path: real doubt is equated with unconscious confusion and reinforces it.

84. Differentiation under the predominance of destructive impulses is symbolically equated with, and unconsciously becomes, splitting and fragmentation: unconscious guilt and persecutory anxiety are increased, and the process of symbolic work is experienced as inner confusion.

THE POINT OF DECISION

85. The moment of decision precipitates anxiety: the experience of failure is anticipated; reality testing must inevitably be faced under the conditions of work for an employer; unconsciously the moment is that of facing the prospect of failure to repair and restore the good object; desperation is at its height; and there is disruption of the capacity to make the cut away from other possible paths of action.

86. The result is an inability to hold the necessary balance between excessive and insufficient symbolic

work; the imbalance is expressed as indecisiveness and dithering, or as omnipotent and premature action.

EXTERNAL WORKING

87. Finally, the carrying out of the external work is undercut by depressive anxiety.

88. Imperfections in the object and/or the method chosen to create it (and these are in fact likely to be excessive) are seen as evidence of the dominance of destructive impulses and inability to repair and restore; guilt is heightened.

89. The basic response to failure or threatened failure becomes, "if only I had done so and so," or, "I could kick myself"—a sense of paranoid stupidity reinforcing anxiety about self-destructiveness.

90. Depressive reiteration of the badness of the self militates against constructive self-criticism, since it is based upon hatred of the self, obsessional inability to give up the lost opportunity, and use of the lost opportunity sadistically to attack the self (and the primal object) by demonstrating its ineptitude.

91. But, as in all mourning, the greatest danger is the turning of hatred outward; against the object and the employer who demanded that the object be made: both are perceived by projective identification as persecuting, and failure is perceived as the natural objective, since by failure the object and the parental substitute can be destroyed.

92. Aggression against the work is increased by the mobilization of envy toward the employer who is to get the object, expressed as envious spoiling of the work and spoiling of the employer by letting him down.

93. The theme becomes, "Why should I do good work for them," and internal mourning and external creative

work are both brought to a standstill—intensified by the withdrawal of livelihood, which serves unconsciously to stimulate further the aggression associated with the lost primal good object.

DEFENSES AGAINST ANXIETY IN WORK

94. The main defenses against depressive anxiety —manic and obsessional defenses, and regression to the paranoid–schizoid position—are brought to bear in a neurotic relation to work, and impress their features upon the character of the work done.

95. In each case the process of free symbol formation is interrupted or inhibited: the pleasure of symbolic work, which is life-giving, is lost; boredom, unconsciously experienced as death, is never far away; and the loss of the symbolic activity in turn demands to be mourned.

MANIC DEFENSE

96. Under the dominance of omnipotence and triumph, an "I'll show them" attitude comes into work.

97. Excessive ambition and drive may be manifested, with denial of affect, single-minded adherence to work to the exclusion of other spheres of living, and general impoverishment of emotional life.

98. Sadistic destructiveness finds an outlet in triumph-seeking competitiveness.

99. Hatred and contempt are directed toward both the employer and the task.

100. Symbolic work may be dominated by magical omnipotence; leading to grandiosity of plans, a carelessness for detail, and, usually, premature closure of the symbolic work process (or there may occur grandiose elaboration).

101. Success is reacted to by depressive anxiety, because it is experienced as triumph.

102. Failure is experienced as persecuting annihilation.

OBSESSIONAL DEFENSE

103. Symbol formation becomes stultified rather than free, because of rigid adherence to existing symbols and their use for ritualistic purposes.

104. Development is restricted and ambition is inhibited.

105. The unconscious goal is to maintain a state of bliss by means of living in an unchanging world, in relation to an ideal good and unchanging object which makes no demands for reparation because it has never changed.

106. There is some denial of reality (but not psychotic, because of the predominating contact with reality and knowledge of change) by means of a ritualistic compromise in which activity is gripped in an obsessionally fixed frame (*vide* the Platonic notion of the unchanging ideal world as against the changing sensible world).

107. The result is impoverishment of thought because of obsessionally ruminative play with symbols partially supplanting symbol formation, by means of which the destructive impulses and persecuting object are controlled.

108. The resulting work is stultified, excessively detailed, and unimaginative, the process of symbolic work is carried too far, and indecisiveness is the keynote.

109. The reaction to the result of the work is omnipotent denial and excessive appreciation of the detailing, and/or obsessional reiteration of the "if only" feeling.

PARANOID–SCHIZOID REGRESSION

110. Regression is characterized by two main elements in work: confusion and stupidity, and cunning and deceit.

111. The relation to the object, which is experienced as annihilated, is one of hatred and persecutory anxiety.

112. The process of symbol formation becomes intensely threatening because of the close tie with inner chaos and confusion, and is replaced by symbolic equation under the impact of destructive impulses and fear of annihilation, with excessive projective and introjective identification with the object.

113. Inhibition of thought occurs, symbols are destroyed, and work and the organization of work become confused and characterized externally by stupidity, and internally by magically omnipotent creativity and daydreaming.

114. In conjunction with manic defense systems, slyness and cunning are used in relation to the object, bad work is concealed or glossed over, regulations are secretly breached, and untrustworthiness and delinquent irresponsibility result.

115. Failure is reacted to as confirming the persecutory situation, hatred and destructiveness against the object are reinforced, self-criticism is precluded by omnipotent triumph, and fears of persecutory retaliation are increased.

CONCLUDING THESES

116. *These anxieties are increased under the impact of bad management*, that is to say, when work, payment, and capacity are not in equilibrium, as for example:

a. underpayment mobilizes paranoid fears of exploitation, and envy and rivalry;

b. underemployment arouses fears of rejection by the good object and of castration, and reinforces anxieties of not being able to use reparative skills at full stretch;

c. overpayment plus overemployment supports manic grandiosity and denial of fear of failure, stimulates the sense of being idealized and overvalued, and gives rise to dependent toadying mixed with secret contempt.

117. The neurotic individual may seek precisely such conditions of external disequilibrium, unconsciously knowing his ambitions (whether grandiose or self-depreciative) to be out of line with his unconscious knowledge of his true capacity, level of work, and equitable payment for that work.

118. The non-neurotic individual commonly uses splitting to deal with externally foisted disequilibrium; he retains as good a relation as possible with the immediate object (his work and his on-the-spot manager), puts his destructive impulses and objects into the larger surrounding and more anonymous situation of the company, the "boss" and politics, and by means of projective identification uses social systems to reinforce his defenses against persecutory and depressive anxiety and to protect his relation to his work.

119. These unconscious mechanisms do not exclude the possibility of actual exploitation by employers; exploitation and the impulse to exploitation do occur, especially as part of the use of slyness and cunning in the mechanism of paranoid–schizoid regression in managers in the attempt to avoid depressive anxiety in their own work.

120. The psychologically constructive job of managers

lies not in the provision of counseling and welfare services, but in arranging for work to be done efficiently in
the sense of ensuring the employment of individuals at
a level of work consistent with their capacity, and administering payment in accord with the equitable
work–payment scale.

121. Such arrangements are not a substitute for psychological treatment; they are preventive in the sense of
eliminating an important external source of envy, destructiveness, and despair.

Chapter 9

The Work–Payment–Capacity Nexus

I

Taking my experience as a whole with the use of the time-span of discretion, the equitable work–payment scale, and the capacity growth curves, a number of assumptions seem to me to be warranted, some of which I have already stated:

1. We each have an accurate unconscious awareness of the level of work we are capable of doing, the level of work in the role we occupy, and the equitable payment level for both the level of work we are carrying and the level which we are capable of carrying (if these are different).
2. We are each aware of any discrepancies which may exist between our capacity and our level of work, and between our actual payment and the payment which would be equitable for our work.
3. We each have an accurate unconscious awareness of our level of capacity for discriminating expenditure and of our level of satisfaction consumption, and we are aware of the extent to which our actual income may deviate, either above or below, from that which would provide abundance.

4. The development of our potential capacity follows a regular course which can be described by one of the capacity growth curves representing the earnings which would be equitable for work consistent with our capacity at any given age.
5. We are each motivated toward a level of work that is consistent with our capacity, and a rate of progress in our work that conforms to our rate of progress in capacity.
6. We are each motivated toward equitable payment for our work.
7. Each of us will be stimulated toward the maximum psychological equilibrium of which we are capable, by a level of work consistent with our capacity, and equitable payment for that work within an economy of abundance.

These assumptions about our unconscious awareness of the degree of consistency between our capacity, work, earnings, and consumption, and of the sense of balance and of peace of mind with respect to them which we tend to experience when we judge all to be in line with each other, may be at variance with everyday notions and with customary ways of talking about these matters. Work and money are so commonly the source of fantasies and daydreams of wealth and creativity, comfort and security, greatness and power—or, in contrast, of masochistic fantasies of failure, impotence, and destructiveness. Our conscious self-evaluation and ambitions may be subject to gross fluctuation from depressed self-contempt to omnipotent aggrandizement, according to our mood as affected by our unconscious fantasies. We may all have had experience of individuals whose thinking was thus dominated by irrational fantasies—consciously and unconsciously—for greater or shorter periods in their careers, and who became failures because of them.

There is an apparent paradox in this outlook. Our unconscious awareness seems on the one hand to be unexpectedly realistic, and on the other hand and at the same time, to be irrational and emotionally unstable. This paradox is resolved once it is recognized that both processes—reality-tested awareness and fantasy-dominated wish fulfillment—may go on simultaneously in different parts of the unconscious mind. In the neurotic parts of our unconscious minds—and indeed in the psychotic pockets which are a part of the mental makeup of even the most normal persons[1]—the picture we may have of ourselves and our economic condition may be totally at variance with that outlined in the foregoing assumptions.

It is likely that anyone who is capable of earning his own living has developed a sufficient degree of inner reality to be able to make the unconscious judgments about himself and his work of which I am speaking. But the existence of an unconscious assessment of our real capacity does not necessarily mean that this assessment is consciously accepted. Quite the contrary. Very few of us are capable of consciously sustaining an accurate and stable self-appraisal of our capacities and limitations. Some of our deepest unconscious defenses against anxiety would be threatened—fantasy gratification, omnipotence, self-effacement. We repress our knowledge of our true capacity, and retain it repressed in our unconscious mind. This repression makes for emotional oscillations

[1] I refer here to the profoundly important work of Melanie Klein (e.g., 1948, 1957, 1959) in exploring the very deepest layers of the human mind. Her work relating to the existence of psychotic pockets in the normal mind has been further elaborated by Bion (1957), Segal (1957), and Jaques (see chapter 14, this volume).

in our conscious self-evaluation, while at the same time we may maintain our unconscious awareness of our adjustment to work reality. It is only in the exceptional mature and integrated person that the unconscious awareness of work and capacity becomes the sole or even the major determinant of conscious self-appraisal.

At the same time, just because our conscious picture of ourselves and our capacities may be heavily influenced by unrealistic unconscious fantasies, this does not necessarily imply that we will behave unrealistically in our work and economic life. The unconscious reality sense is an extremely powerful controller of behavior in the real world, particularly in that area of the real world where behavior is reality-tested by economic satisfaction or dissatisfaction and, in the final analysis, by economic survival. We are always dealing, therefore, with a typically human situation of conflict in each person between the demands of fantasy satisfaction and the demands of the reality sense,[2] as influenced by the character of the social and economic environment within which he lives and to which he must adapt.

I do not propose, however, to consider here, other than in general terms, the dynamics and structure of inner psychic conflicts in the individual in connection with work, capacity, and economic rewards and consumption.[3] My present concern is more with the economic and work environment and with how these conditions affect individual and group behavior, either reinforcing the reality sense or stimulating and encouraging the operation of

[2] This theme is one of the cornerstones of the psychoanalytic theories of Sigmund Freud, and is vividly presented in his book *Beyond the Pleasure Principle*, 1922.

[3] I have sketched in certain aspects of these complex inner psychological processes in chapter 14, "Disturbances in the Capacity to Work."

unrealistic components of thought and judgment. The effects of these outside circumstances on any specific person will be influenced by the conflicting tendencies within him toward both realistic and unrealistic attitudes and behavior. The specific contents and amounts of these conflicting tendencies will of course differ from person to person. But these individual differences need not concern us for the moment. The effects common to everyone can be considered in their own right. By so doing, we shall be able to get closer to the type of behavior which could be encouraged by equitable payment and sound progress.

II

In exploring the work–payment–capacity nexus, I am fully aware that a person's payment and his level of work are not the only factors which make for his satisfaction or dissatisfaction in his job. There are other important factors: the interest which the type of work has for him; the physical and geographical surroundings; the congruence of the social atmosphere and the temperament of managers and colleagues with his own temperament and general psychological makeup; and many other factors besides.

But just because these other factors exist, it does not necessarily mean that it is not useful to treat of work, payment, and capacity apart. There are in fact some weighty reasons for doing so. The provision of work consistent with a person's capacity, and of equitable payment for that work, may be regarded as fundamental responsibilities of an industrial society to itself and to its individual members. These factors are essential to the optimization of the production of wealth for the society, and to the maintenance of individual health and satisfaction. Direct personal interest in the job, or an equable geographical surround, or congenial colleagues, however desirable in themselves, cannot be considered to be the responsibility of society in the same way that equitable payment and opportunity for full use of capacity may be. This is not to say that these factors are unimportant, but to claim for them an importance as secondary factors compared with the prime significance of the work –payment –capacity trio.

All the various possible combinations of level of work, level of payment, and level of capacity can be described in terms of thirteen fundamental patterns (the three variables are indicated by W, P, and C in the schematic illustration for each pattern):

(a) The individual occupies a position whose range of level of work is consistent with his capacity, $\boxed{\text{C-W}}$, and receives:

1. equitable payment for the level of work: $\boxed{\text{C-W}}$-P

2. payment higher than equity: $\overset{P}{\boxed{\text{C-W}}}$

3. payment below equity: $\underset{P}{\boxed{\text{C-W}}}$

(b) The individual occupies a position whose range of level of work is greater than his capacity: $\boxed{\genfrac{}{}{0pt}{}{W}{C}}$, and receives:

4. payment above equity: $\overset{P}{\boxed{\genfrac{}{}{0pt}{}{W}{C}}}$

5. equitable payment: $\boxed{\genfrac{}{}{0pt}{}{W}{C}}$-P

6. payment below equity, but higher than would be equitable for the work consistent with his capacity: $\boxed{\genfrac{}{}{0pt}{}{W}{C}}$-P

7. payment that would be equitable for the work consistent with his capacity: $\boxed{\begin{array}{c}\text{W}\\\text{C}\end{array}}\text{-P}$

8. payment that is below equity for work that would be consistent with his capacity: $\boxed{\begin{array}{c}\text{W}\\\text{C}\end{array}}$ P

(c) the individual occupies a position whose range of level of work is less than he is capable of carrying, $\boxed{\begin{array}{c}\text{C}\\\text{W}\end{array}}$, and receives:

9. payment above equity for the work level consistent with his capacity: P $\boxed{\begin{array}{c}\text{C}\\\text{W}\end{array}}$

10. payment that is equitable for the work level consistent with his capacity: $\boxed{\text{C}}$-P $\boxed{\text{W}}$

11. payment that is below equity for the work level consistent with his capacity, but above equity for his current work level: $\boxed{\begin{array}{c}\text{C}\\\text{W}\end{array}}$-P

12. payment that is equitable for his current work level: $\boxed{\text{C}}$ $\boxed{\text{W}}$-P

13. payment below equity for his current work level: $\boxed{\begin{array}{c}\text{C}\\\text{W}\end{array}}$ P

These thirteen patterns can be schematically summarized in this manner. I shall use this schematic shorthand to identify the particular pattern I am discussing:

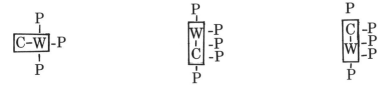

III

There is a general reaction pattern to each one of the thirteen C–W–P situations which is common to us all. Of course there are individual differences within each of these general reaction patterns. But despite these individual differences, there are fundamental similarities in the way we respond to each of these situations, in our feelings about them, in our descriptions of them, irrespective of what we might do about these feelings, of how we might express them in action, or indeed of how we might adjust within ourselves to our reaction. The experience of each of the thirteen C–W–P situations acts as a force stimulating particular feelings and attitudes.

It will be appreciated that each of the C–W–P patterns is dynamic in content. Each of the patterns must be conceived as occurring in time. Individual capacity, level of work in the job, and wage or salary (or the value of money) are each in a state of more or less rapid change. For purposes of description, therefore, I shall assume that all three factors, although undergoing change, are nevertheless changing at the same rate and hence the pattern of the factors is remaining unchanged. I shall assume also that an abundant economy is operating. In an overabundant or an underabundant economy we may expect additional reactions according to the extent of the over- or underabundance.

1. The first pattern, and the most important of all, is the C-W -P pattern. This is the pattern which stimulates in us the maximum psychological equilibrium which we are capable of experiencing with regard to our work and payment. Our work is just matched to our capacity, and there is opportunity for our level of work to increase at a rate nicely attuned to the growth and development of our capacity. Our payment is equitable for the work we are doing, and we can make realistic plans for the future

because we have a good intuitive idea of the rate of increase of our earning power.

Just how much any particular person can achieve a sense of balance in his economic life under such circumstances will depend to a certain extent on how balanced he is in his emotional life in general. The more well-balanced and stable we are and the more able we are to apply our capacities, the greater the peace of mind we will be able to achieve for ourselves. Contrariwise, the more neurotically insecure we may be, the less will we be able to take advantage of our position to help us toward peace of mind. But deep within ourselves we will be aware that our insecurity is a personal matter, and that there is little or nothing that our employer, or society at large, can do by way of underpinning our economic security.

2. Correct work level, and overequity payment: $\boxed{\text{C-W}}$. This pattern gives the possibility of manifest great satisfaction with the employing concern in the early stages. Then some uneasiness and guilt develop, but these feelings remain largely unconscious. There is the fear of envy from less well-placed groups, and of retaliation by them, as well as of the possibility of the favored payment attracting personnel of greater capacity than ourselves. In the long term, personal selfishness and insensitivity—or their opposite, a feeling of surfeit—are aroused. We are likely under these conditions to try various techniques of evasion of the fact that we are receiving relatively better financial treatment than colleagues or other groups.

3. Correct work level, and underequity payment: $\boxed{\text{C-W}}$. This pattern provokes gradually increasing psychic conflict and disaffection. The rightness of the fit of the work to our capacity is a strong attraction. It binds us to the job. But our payment remains unsatisfactory. We feel

unfairly treated as compared with others. Our zest and enthusiasm for our work will be less than it would otherwise be. If our interest in the job was high, it will be lessened; if it was low, we will be stimulated to change jobs. If, however, the circumstances in our occupation, or our personal circumstances, preclude the likelihood of our being able to obtain equitably paid work, we may say and do nothing, but the undermining of our morale will be greater. We fall in, in a veiled fashion, with group protest and criticism of the institution.

4. Too high a level of work, and payment at or above equity: $\begin{array}{|c|c|}\hline W & W \\ \hline C & C \\ \hline\end{array}$-P. These are patterns which are often likely to be associated with the so-called stress disorders of executives. An individual who strives to hang on to a job whose level of work is too high for his capacity is the prey of excessively neurotic ambition and drive—under the dominance of unconscious destructive impulses, of envy, hate, jealousy, and greed. Greed for financial reward above that consistent with our capacity, and for the enhanced status, drive us to hang on; mental conflict and strain result. The impact may be lessened for a time by unconscious collusion with our manager to protect us. But the inevitable break will come in due course—either through personal breakdown (which may give rise to psychosomatic illness), or change in job, or through being taken out of our job (whether by open dismissal or transfer or "promotion").

5. Too high level of work, and payment below equity: $\begin{array}{|c|}\hline W \\ \hline C \\ \hline\end{array}$-P $\begin{array}{|c|}\hline W \\ \hline C \\ \hline\end{array}$-P $\begin{array}{|c|}\hline W \\ \hline C \\ \hline\end{array}$. These patterns are manifestly very unstable. We have the attraction of employment with enhanced status. But we are confronted by the personal strain of work beyond our capacity; and the financial

return is not worth the candle. Very scarce employment or strong neuroticism must be at work if we try to stay in a job in these circumstances. These comments apply the more strongly the more the earnings fall toward or below a level that would be equitable for work consistent with our capacity. The few instances I have come across have been embedded in strong personal disturbance in both the individual and his manager, and have ended (if not worked through) in bad industrial relations and personal breakdown.

6. Too low a level of work, and payment at or above the level consistent with capacity: $\boxed{\begin{smallmatrix}\overset{P}{C}\\W\end{smallmatrix}\begin{smallmatrix}C\\W\end{smallmatrix}}$-P. These patterns may give equilibrium on a temporary basis, where the organization wishes to retain the services of the individual but does not at that moment have a job in which it can utilize his full capacity. With the agreement of the individual, the above-equity payment may represent a kind of retainer fee designed to keep him in the enterprise until a suitable vacancy (or a planned vacancy) occurs.

In the absence of this very special condition, these patterns are calculated to induce disorganization. In effect you have an underemployed and overpaid individual. He tries to take on other people's work, and gets into trouble with them. Conscious or unconscious contempt will inevitably arise for the employer who pays for value not received. Insecurity is equally inevitable: overpayment is never experienced as secure (unless of course one is dealing with a favored family member in a family business). The seeking after windfalls and easy gain is satisfied, with consequent appeal to the weaker areas of character.

7. Too low a level of work, and payment at or below equity: $\boxed{\begin{smallmatrix}C\\W\end{smallmatrix}}$-P $\boxed{\begin{smallmatrix}C\\W\end{smallmatrix}}$-P $\boxed{\begin{smallmatrix}C\\W\end{smallmatrix}}$. These patterns are inclined to
$\underset{P}{}$

induce dissatisfaction, the degree of the dissatisfaction becoming severe at the lower levels of payment. At the extreme, where payment is below equity, our work is doubly unrewarding: not only is our capacity being un-deremployed, but we are not even getting equitable pay-ment for this unsatisfying level of work. Given reasonable employment opportunities, we will probably seek other employment, and labor turnover is practically assured.

It is only under conditions either of severe personal disturbance or of unemployment in a person's occupation that he is likely to continue in such a job. A case that illustrates the former point is the one of a person suffering a nervous breakdown who is glad to be underemployed for a period of some years until he manages to get over the breakdown.

Apart from such catastrophe, it is during periods of unemployment that large numbers of individuals suffer subjection to these unrewarding work conditions. Those who are unemployed are exposed to total dejection. And of those who continue to be employed, a large proportion will be underemployed and payment will be under equity. So that even being lucky enough to be employed in a situation of widespread unemployment may nevertheless involve being degraded and demoralized in work. Added to which is the general effect of the fall in individual standard of living accompanying the decline in the abun-dance of the economy under such conditions.

The main point is that these demoralizing effects which stand out so dramatically in times of economic depression can quite readily occur in times of relative prosperity and full employment in localized regions, in sections of an industry, or in sections of an organization. These are the conditions for boredom and human waste. These patterns obtain for many university graduates in their first experience in industry in management train-ing groups. They are equally the patterns for bright craftsmen who have grown in capacity beyond craft jobs, but cannot get up the ladder. It is of the utmost importance for both efficiency and the well-being of the individual that each person should have the opportunity to work under conditions such that the level of work in his job matches his capacity, and he receives equitable payment for that work.

IV

The judgment we possess about ourselves, our work, and our earnings, implied by these patterns of response to the various W–C–P patterns, is judgment based upon unconscious intuitive awareness, the awareness of experience. The processes by which norms are built up in our minds occur unconsciously. We have feelings about these things—deep inner awareness, or ideas-in-feeling—a sense of things either being in balance or out of balance, and a sense of striving for something more or a sense of ease and peace of mind and satisfaction. We do not have explicit knowledge in the sense that we can put forward valid reasons for our judgments of our level of capacity, level of work, and level of equitable pay. And although equitable pay can be talked about in terms of money, there has been no language at all with which to speak about level of capacity and level of work.

If these assumptions are correct, we are faced by the question of how the intuitive awareness I have described comes about. In what form is it carried in the mind and made available for use? This problem is one aspect of the very general problem of how any sort of social norm is formed, how that norm becomes established in individuals, and how the individual reacts to these norms and uses them.

Intuitive awareness is built up from small increments of experience in which nonverbalized awareness and ideas—ideas-in-feeling—are repeatedly subjected to the testing of reality and modified bit by bit until a moderately realistic set of internal standards is established. At work especially, the requirements of reality have to be subserved—continued employment and survival depend on it. If anyone takes on work at a level above his capacity, he eventually fails in his work. If he accepts a level of work below his capacity, he meets the resistance of his needs to express his creativity and to avoid impotence. He also meets the external resistance of his colleagues, his superiors, and his subordinates (if any) in whom feelings of disequilibrium are stimulated when there is disequilibrium in organization and in payment structure caused by someone occupying a position at a level below the capacity he can exercise. In short, each one is subject to a strong internal and external field of force tending to keep him in a position at a level of work consistent with his capacity. It is our reality sense responding to this field of force which produces our unconscious awareness of the level of work we can successfully carry.

Intuitive or experiential knowledge about capacity and such capacity about level of work interact. The psychic yardstick is the person himself. We sense that this job is too easy, that one too difficult, and this one just right. We sense whether we are working at full tilt and right up to scratch, or whether we possess unused capacity for whatever reason—whether for reasons of disinterest, or of preoccupation with inner psychic conflict, or interference by disturbed home conditions or other worries. This experience through time provides us with the information which allows us to build up our picture of our rate of progress in capacity and in achievement.

Having related ourselves to our work, we are in a position to compare our own job with other jobs, not as we may think by means of job comparisons, but by means of comparisons of our own capacity with that of our friends and associates. I find myself forced to the conclusion that there is great precision in our ability to compare levels of capacity in one another. I think it is done by myriad clues of the way in which the other person talks and thinks, in particular the way in which he organizes his perceptions. In talk and argument and discussions, we learn to sense to what extent the frame of thought within which we operate is broader or narrower, more or less comprehensive, than that of others. It is the sense of talking or arguing on a par with another, or of enfolding the other's capacity or being enfolded by it.

Using ourselves as the yardstick, we are each able to compare our own rate of pay with that of others. My data lead to the conclusion that this judgment is two-dimensional. First, it is a judgment whether a person is earning the same as others of lesser or greater capacity. Second, it is a judgment whether his earnings give the same relative degree of abundance as the earnings of others.

These judgments of current equitable earning levels in relation to work and capacity are, I believe, built up in the first instance from contacts with immediate friends and associates. These contacts very quickly build up into an industry-wide experience of earnings. Friends work within a widely flung network of jobs. They work in other offices, on shops, or factories, in other occupations, and in other industries. They move. New friends move in from other communities. There is consequently a flow of information about other types of work. The same process holds for work associates. They discuss their work. They change. New associates join the firm from other places. Other associates leave, and maintain contact after having gained employment elsewhere. Or they may apply for advertized jobs, and give information about the jobs after interview. Or a person himself may apply for other jobs, or change jobs, or move to another community.

Over the years, by virtue of this flow of information induced by the steady stream of labor turnover, a great deal of knowledge is gleaned about various jobs and the payment associated with them—jobs in different conditions, different industries, and different communities. The level of work in these jobs is judged by the assessment of the level of capacity of the friend or colleague who does the job. A coherent intuitive awareness is gradually accumulated of the extent to which other individuals and ourselves are in receipt of abundant pay, or under- or overabundant pay. Norms of the degree of deviation from abundance that is equitable are thus gradually constructed.

The norms of abundance can be looked for in the experience of the individual himself. Given an underabundant income, we experience unused capacity for discriminating expenditure. Given an overabundant income, difficulties, uncertainties, and the disorganized sense of promiscuity in spending are experienced. For most people, however, experience is limited to underabundance, and fantasies about how much one might spend if one had the money remain unmodified and untempered by the test of reality. Nonetheless, the sense of equity which I have observed in individuals leads me to conclude that, even under conditions of chronic underabundance, there exists in the reality-tested areas of the mind a pretty precise standard of just how much higher a standard of living would be required for the demands of personal satisfaction to be met.

REFERENCES

Bion, W. (1957), The differentiation of the psychotic from the non-psychotic part of the personality. *Internat. J. Psycho-Anal.*, 38:266–275.

Freud, S. (1922), Beyond the pleasure principle. *Standard Edition*, 18:7–66. London: Hogarth Press, 1961.

Klein, M. (1948), Contributions to psycho-analysis. In: *Collected Writings*, Vol. 4. New York: McGraw-Hill, 1977.

—— (1957), Envy and gratitude. In: *Collected Writings*, Vol. 4. New York: McGraw-Hill, 1977.

—— (1959), Infant conflict and adult behaviour. In: *Collected Writings*, Vol. 4. New York: McGraw-Hill, 1977.

Segal, H. (1957), Notes on symbol formation. *Internat. J. Psycho-Anal.*, 38:391–402.

Chapter 10

The Conscious, Preconscious, and Unconscious Experience Called Time

The case for the reality of time may be considered not as a thing-in-itself, a *zeit-an-sich*, but as a concept abstracted and constructed from the experience of succession, of process, of events, of continuity, in our total world; that is to say, from the experience of the occurrence of events in both the external material world and the internal psychological world. The concept of time so constructed is analogous to the concept of space. It is a univocal concept, applying to all types of experience, ponderable and imponderable, objective and subjective, and to experience in thought, imagination, and dreams.

One difficulty, however, is that we tend to reify time, confusing the concept, which is a static idea (as are all concepts in and of themselves) with the experiences gathered together (*con-ceptus*) within the concept. It is thus that we incorrectly speak of the flow of time, as though *time* were the term for something like a river—as for a concrete particular, rather than for a positional noun or a universal category. This reification of time by particularizing it in concrete terms contrasts with our attitude toward space. We do not treat of space as though it were a physical thing, a box, which stays still while we stand in it (not since Leibniz, that is), and when we now refer to the curvature of space we are aware that that is a mathematical construction and not somehow an infinite plasticine ball that has been pressed out of shape.

I shall consider this reification of time, and will show that in raw experience it is our sense of a space–time manifold, or plenum, which suffuses our awareness, and not our sense either of space or of time by itself. In considering this matter I shall suggest that we must recognize three different levels of component which together make up the totality of experience, and which are enfolded within our idea of time—conscious experience, preconscious experience, and unconscious (protomental) experience. I think that the theory of knowledge in general is hamstrung by its failure to separate out these three different components of mental functioning. This shortcoming is especially pronounced, however, in the case of the conceptualization of time phenomena.

I shall argue that it is the failure to recognize the existence of these interlacing components of experience which gives rise to such questions, puzzles, and paradoxes as: does time flow; does it have direction; is there a past as well as a future; is there merely earlier and later; do we live in an atomic unchanging world or in a world of flux and durée? For each of the three elements in experience—conscious, preconscious, unconscious—creates its own characteristic picture of the world, and the answer to each of these questions depends upon which element of experience is assumed: the more conscious, the more discontinuous and static; the more unconscious, the more continuous and the more in directional flux.

Finally, I shall have to establish that reason, logic, and rationality[1] are not solely the prerogative of the con-

---

[1] I make the distinction between: logical, as degree of adherence to formal rules of thought; reasonable, as judgment that action is

scious mind, of conscious mental activity. They are always the outcome of the interplay between conscious,
preconscious, and unconscious mental activity in this
sense: conscious mental activity sets the explicit articulated framework of behavior, including the context of
knowledge within which we act; preconscious mental activity provides the background store of knowledge and
awareness upon which we can consciously draw; and unconscious protomental activity provides the continuously
shifting direction of intentionality, the sense of where we
want to go, wish to go, will to go. This distinction contrasts sharply with more common usage which takes it
that it is in the conscious processes that we find the reasonable, the logical, and the rational, as compared with
unconscious mental activities which (if they are granted
existence at all) are regarded as the seat of the illogical,
of unreason, and of the irrational, or at best as the source
of foolhardy rationalizations.

My reason for bringing into my analysis these questions of the logical and the rational in relation to the
conscious and the unconscious is to pursue the following
argument. Unconscious desires and goals are elements
in rationality. Goals are intentions; therefore intentions
can derive from unconscious protomental sources and at
the same time contribute to rational action. Our experience of goals and intentions underlies the meaning of
the future, just as our experience of memories underlies
the meaning of the past. Our predictions or ideas of the
future, and therefore of the so-called directionality of time
and of flux, can be understood as the expression of the

---

broadly in accord with intent; and rational, as extent to which activity
is reality-based. It is useful to note that etymologically all three terms
reveal their roots in both conscious knowledge and in unconscious
sensing: logic from Gr. *legein*, to collect, gather, and select, as well as
to tell and to speak; and reason, and rational, both from L. *reor*, which
is not only to think, but also to judge, and to deem.

conscious mode of formulation of unconscious states of mind in the present with their ongoing desires, goals, and intentions.

THE REIFICATION OF TIME

Much of the debate about the nature of time is a fruitless debate, arising from the reification of time. We often treat it as a concrete thing. If we did not, we should not get into arguments about the passage of time, or the flow of time, or about the future flowing into the present into the past, or about whether the arrow of time is unidirectional or bidirectional or directional at all, or whether there is a time arrow, or about the possible effects of entropy upon time. These formulations confuse the concept of time as a positional noun and as a universal category, with the experience of the concretely particular events or processes involving concrete particular things, which are the phenomena from which we construct the concept of time.

It can be stated quite simply that time is neither like a river nor like an arrow. *Tempus fugit* is literally not true. Time does not either flow or fly—regardless of such commonplace expressions, when people are engrossed in what they are doing, as "how time flies," or "how time has flown," or "how quickly time has passed." What they mean is that this particular event has taken a greater number of minutes or hours than they had anticipated or realized. Nor does time go in any particular direction, because time per se does not go anywhere or point anywhere.[2]

[2] The concept of time is in this respect no different from any other universal. Universals do not *have* qualities or properties; they *are* qualities or properties. No valid propositions can be made about a universal other than a statement of its existence. For example: the

This reification of time is similar to the reification of space which characterized thinking at the time of Newton. Newton himself employed a static concept of space, not as an ordering of the material world but as a substantial entity which was a container of objects and which thus was assumed to have existence independently of the existence of any material objects. It was this view which was argued against by Leibniz, who saw space as a matter of the relative positioning of objects, and shortly after by Kant for whom space was an a priori category.

The view of Leibniz has been the dominant view of space in modern science, especially in relativity theory. The concept of space has been abstracted and generalized into a mathematical construct. This construct can be subject to any type of mathematical manipulation depending upon the hypothesis used. It can be stretched and curved into any shape—any mathematical shape, that is—and straightened out again, but without our having to picture some kind of physical entity actually changing shape.

With time, however, we behave otherwise. McTaggart's argument (1927) that the future cannot coexist with past and present, and that therefore time cannot exist, is an argument that is based on the presupposition that a time–thing either exists or does not exist, rather than a discussion of the possible usefulness of a positional time-category. And even Popper (1976), in his protests against the idea of the reversibility of the direction of time (because it would mean, for example, that the fact that Hiroshima had been perpetrated by man would be

---

proposition "Man is a category comprising all men" is valid; but "Man is alive" or "Man breathes" are invalid—they require to be formulated as "That man is alive" or "All living men breathe." Or, to take another example, "Red is a color category" is valid; but "Red is shocking" is invalid, and requires to be reformulated as "All red colors are shocking" or perhaps "Some red colors are shocking."

reversed and would disappear from human awareness),
is at the same time arguing that there is a particular
thing called time and that this thing does move, albeit
in one direction only. Similarly, the arguments of Lucas
(1973) and Dummett (1954, 1964), to take but two examples, seem to take for granted that there is a moving
thing called time—the argument being an argument
about its properties.

But what if it should be desired to avoid the reification
of time?[3] What is the alternative? The alternative is to
treat it as a positional noun or as a universal, rather than
as a pointing term referring to a particular identifiable
thing or phenomenon. In doing so, we are forced to ask
ourselves what kinds of data, what kinds of experience,
what kinds of phenomena, are to be subsumed under the
concept. And it is at this point that the questions become
interesting. For we are forced to ask ourselves in what
way do we experience the past; or the present; or the
future? Just what seems to have speeded up? Or what do
we mean when we say that time's arrow or the passage
of time seems to be in one direction?

In order to try to deal with these questions I propose
to consider the idea of time from the point of view of our
conscious experience, our preconscious experience, and
our unconscious experience. I believe it is essential to
carry out this threefold analysis, since the phenomena
associated with time differ for each of the modes of experience. Conscious experience gives us the focused verbalizable perception of things moving or changing, of
events; but this focused perception is organized into a

[3] It would perhaps be better to have spoken of spatiality and temporality, rather than of space and time—but this awkward usage is
unnecessary so long as we keep in mind what we mean when we say,
"What time is it?" (a particular reading on a clock), as against "Time,
what is it?" (temporality as a universal).

static, discontinuous, atomic world in which time phenomena are dominated by the spatialized notion of discontinuous ticks on a clock.

Preconscious experience gives the background or surround to our flitting consciously focused and verbalized
percepts. It is the peripheral awareness in which we sense
the ongoingness of the things we perceive as in motion,
and by means of which we can formulate our sense of the
extension of events in terms of continuous flux and durée.

By contrast, unconscious protomental experience is
unverbalized. It comprises the psychological world of the
continual flow of desires, of passion, of goals and intentions and will. It is the world of primally fused memory,
perception, desire, and intention (the unified field which
exists before we consciously differentiate the separate
parts), combined into what might be termed the moving
present, a present which is felt as moving from out of the
past and into the future. It is these unconscious phenomena which give us the notion of time as having a direction
which expresses the goal-directedness of intentional behavior.

I now propose to consider this threefold categorization
of experience—for which, of course, Freud was responsible—more fully in connection with its significance for
the clarification of the full complexity of the human idea
of time. It will take us into a formulation of a world which
is neither atomic nor in flux, but both; neither continuous
nor discontinuous, but both; made up neither of forces
acting between points at a distance nor of fields of force,
but of both; neither static nor flowing, but both; with
neither past–present–future nor earlier and later, but
both; neither predictable nor retrodictable, but both; neither universal nor particular, but both; neither objective
nor subjective, but both; neither material nor ideal, but
both; neither concrete nor abstract, but both.

This formulation is that of a phenomenal world. But it is not the limited phenomenal world of Husserl, built upon the unnecessarily narrow idea of mental life as exclusively conscious. It is a world of kaleidoscopic interaction of conscious, preconscious, and unconscious phenomena—with a continual restless oscillation between the dominance of one mode then another. It is a world still at one moment, alive and in motion at the next; vague and cloudy, then clear, external and atomic; full of hazily felt intuitive introspect, then acutely organized with known external real objects; an inner world, then an outer world; a world of just-out-of-focus periphery and a world of sharply focused things; a world of passion, feeling, and desire, then of intellectually grasped impassive idea; a world of love and anger, and then of mathematics and cerebral logic; and most of all, a world underpinned by unconscious processes which are simply inaccessible to conscious introspection, processes which can be sensed but not observed, and which disappear under the impact of verbal formulations since their essence is orientation and action and not words.

These varied facts of conscious, preconscious, and unconscious processes are the means by which we construct and experience our world. They are the means by which we act upon our world and react to it, and by which we build up our conception of it—including not just the conception we call time, but also space and space–time, number, quality, form, extension, whole and part, and chair and man and all the other categories we construct from our constitutional endowment playing upon our experience and the way we organize it. Any theory of knowledge must take all these three levels of mental process into account. I shall do so in the following description of the phenomenal roots of the concept of time.

In order to formulate my propositions I shall employ

these terms: *conscious knowledge; preconscious aware-ness*; and *unconscious sensing.*

CONSCIOUS KNOWLEDGE AND TIME: FOCUSED VERBALIZATION

If we consider the flow of our experience carefully and in detail, it may be observed that it is neither a wholly continuous nor a wholly discontinuous one. Our conscious attention flits rapidly from thing to thing, and from idea to idea, and what is in focus at one moment falls into the background the next.[4] But underneath this restless activity there is a continuous flow of unconscious sensing, intuition, hunch, judgment—a sensing which regularly becomes a diffused field of attention replacing the sharp conscious focus, a diffused field which is extremely difficult to get one's hands on and verbalize.

The recognition and identification of these continual shiftings of ideas between conscious focus and diffuse background is a central feature of psychoanalytic theory, and led Freud to his division of mental systems into conscious, preconscious, and unconscious.[5] Consideration of

[4] This discontinuous process may be observed in the following way. If you stare hard at a blank wall, or a printed page, you will observe a rapid oscillation—occurring in fractions of a second—in which the wall or the page is in focus, then disappears for an instant while awareness seems to turn inside, then reappears, then disappears again, and so on. I believe that this inward-turning of attention occurs, for example, in the extremely rapid movement phases of eye movements in reading. It is as though we are constantly maintaining our adjustment between our external and internal worlds by this continual perceptual oscillation between outside and inside.

[5] Sigmund Freud (1923), "The Ego and the Id." Sensitive to the criticisms of philosophers about the idea of *unconscious* mental functioning, he wrote (p. 13): "To most people who have been educated in philosophy the idea of anything psychical which is not also conscious is so inconceivable that it seems to them absurd and refutable simply by logic. . . . Their psychology of consciousness is incapable of solving the problems of dreams and hypnosis." To which I would add, "and certainly incapable of solving the problem of time."

the nature of the experience of time within each of these mental categories will help to resolve the apparent conflicts between the atomistic view of time, time as flux, and time as future intent.

Let me illustrate by the following situation. I am holding a pen with which I am writing these words. If I attend to its movement across the page I may be vaguely aware of its permanent qualities but cannot focus upon them. If I focus upon its being an object—its "thingness"—then its motion clicks out of focus and it seems for that moment to be still. If I note its black color, then I may be vaguely aware of its motion but I cannot at that moment focus upon it. If I note its tapering shape, color and motion disappear into the background. If I listen to its quiet gliding sound as it writes, motion, color, shape, and all other qualities are held perceptually somewhere else, temporarily inhibited and held out of the center of attention.[6] Moreover, as Schachtel (1963) has shown, the process of paying attention by conscious focusing is as much a matter of discriminating by inhibiting those parts of the field you do not wish to perceive so as to leave only that region in the field upon which you wish to focus, as it is of positively focusing upon something. In order to focus upon A we inhibit, block out, push to the background everything which is not-A, so that only the region A is left.

Why should it be, however, that there are certain

----

[6] In "The Ego and the Id" (1923), for example, Freud writes: " 'Being conscious' is in the first place a purely descriptive term, resting on perception of the most immediate and certain character. Experience goes on to show that a psychical element (for instance, an idea) is not as a rule conscious for a protracted length of time. On the contrary, a state of consciousness is characteristically very transitory; an idea that is conscious now is no longer so a moment later, although it can become so under certain conditions that are easily brought about" (pp. 13, 14).

modalities which stand out by themselves as self-contained, formed, segregated wholes, on a take-it-or-leave-it basis? The discreteness of certain perceptual modalities might seem natural in this regard—that is to say, it does not seem unreasonable that one should be able to focus separately upon the color, or the sound, or the smell of pouring coffee, but not all at the same time, since these belong to identifiably different sensory processes. But what about the categories of shape, number, size, movement, constancy—the categories of state or position—which are not connected with any one particular sensory modality? Why should we see the world in terms of ideas of this kind rather than of some other kinds of ideas—kinds which it would be difficult if not impossible to imagine?

It is these categories of state or position which have been explored by Gestalt psychology. They arrive on the scene whole and in their own right, even though they may require a particular culture in order to emerge. Their potential to emerge as Gestalten is, a priori, constitutional, innately given, and not built up out of experience by the association of simpler elements.[7] They constitute natural contents and natural lines of cleavage of experience. They include the experiences with which we have been most concerned: constancy, continuity, distance, motion, and succession, and our sense of space and time. They also cannot be in focus at one and the same time.

If we now turn to time, and focus upon the motion of an object, our conscious awareness of its substantial permanence disappears, and vice versa. If I focus upon how long my pen takes to move across the page, I cannot

[7] It is not necessary to review the voluminous literature in which the existence of a priori Gestalten has been experimentally demonstrated not only for perception but for more complex psychological processes as well. See, for example, Wolfgang Köhler (1929); Kurt Koffka (1928, 1935); Kurt Lewin (1935).

simultaneously focus upon how long my pen is in length (in spatial length, that is). I cannot thus focus at the same time upon the direct percepts conceptualized as space and upon those conceptualized as time. If I focus upon the immediate spatial distance between two different points, then the length of time of processes falls into the background, along with shape, form, sound, color, and a host of other modalities. And if I focus upon the temporal distance between two points in a process, then the focused perception of immediate spatial distances disappears into the background.

These oscillatory processes are familiar enough in the figure-ground perception experiments, as in, for example, the well-known vase and face figure (Figure 10.1). When we see the faces as figure, the vase has become ground, and vice versa; they cannot be seen together in focus. Our experience of the permanence and succession associated with space and time is the same: we cannot experience them in conscious focus together. How then can we expect to experience the space–time manifold? The fact is that we cannot do so. Not in conscious focus at least. Consciously we can experience not a oneness but only a summation of simultaneous points at a distance (giving space)

FIGURE 10.1. Reversing Face–Vase Figure.

and successive points in a process (giving time) by rapid oscillation of attention between formulated conscious knowledge of the two. In this same way, we could consciously experience our drawing as a face–vase manifold only as a retrospective conceptual construction, an intellectual addition of the two aspects.

But what then do these consciously focused mental processes have to do with our conception of time? I would draw attention to the following features. These focused processes are experienced as discrete percepts such as "that pen I see," or "that sound I hear," or more simply perhaps "that thing or object I see"; or else as delineated ideas, such as "that movement I see," or "that melody I am listening to," or "that distance between pen and paper."

The fact of the discreteness, and the putting into words, both contribute to the atomistic view of the world which derives from conscious focused experience. The conscious world is a world of objects, of things. It is a static world. It is a mechanical world, a world in which forces act between objects at a distance from one another. It is dominantly a spatialized world, a world characterized by discontinuity, a world which is describable in terms of geometry and arithmetic and mechanics. The nearest this world gets to continuous flow is in infinite series, with an infinite number of beads strung along a thread at an infinitely small distance from one another.

These discontinuous and spatialized qualities of conscious knowledge lead to the atomistic conception of time. This conception arises from our conscious perception of events as a discontinuous change in position of objects. Thus, for example, the movement of a car is perceived in the conscious perceptual mode in terms of a retrospective construction: "the car has moved from A to B in three seconds" means that three seconds ago I saw this car for a motionless moment at point A, and now I see it for an equally motionless moment at point B three seconds later.

It can thus be seen that our conscious knowledge of time is the time of earlier and later. It is the clock time of the physicist, the time of a succession of later and later temporal points. There is no flux, no durée, in this world. Taken by itself, the conscious knowledge of time conforms to the Parmenidean and Platonic view that all is constant; there is no change. It leads also to the famous paradoxes of Zeno: so long as all is conscious, then all we can have is a series of points of time which, even though infinite in number, nevertheless can never move. The arrow is forever still—at least so long as we believe that all of experience is conscious, that there is nothing more to mental life than conscious mental life.

PRECONSCIOUS AWARENESS AND TIME: THE FOCUSABLE CONTEXT

But the fact is that there is more—indeed very much more—to mental life than mere focused conscious perception and knowledge. The conscious components of experience, the knowledge, are certainly important elements of experience, but they are just as certainly no more important than either the preconscious or the unconscious elements. I shall now consider the general characteristics of the preconscious background phenomena as compared with the focused foreground, and then consider the unconscious in its own right—both, of course, with particular reference to the experience contained within time.

The notion of preconscious mental functioning was formulated by Freud. As he put it (1923), an idea may be in conscious focus one moment, then not in conscious focus, and then it might be brought back into focus again, but "in the interval the idea was—we do not know what.

We can say that it was *latent*, and by this we mean that it was capable of *becoming conscious* at any moment." Then he adds, "The latent, which is unconscious only descriptively, not in the dynamic sense, we call *preconscious*" (p. 15).

The experience of preconscious background is a difficult human experience to come to grips with and to formulate. It is difficult to formulate precisely because it is background and therefore not structured and focused as is the foreground. To formulate is to give organized form to something, and at that point it is ready to be put into words. But if the nonformed is formulated, made into segregated wholes, it loses its nonformed structure and the preconscious becomes conscious—that is what always happens with words.

The fact that the preconscious nonfocused, nonformed, nonsegregated, nondiscrete wholes type of experience is difficult to put into words is no new idea—to put into scientifically rigorous words, that is. It is better expressed in poetic language, where the sense and color and tone and sequence and emotional resonance of the language can perhaps mirror and portray the quality of the experience.

Let me illustrate what I mean by the following example. Hunters know that moving objects are most readily detected by peripheral vision. To use this ability requires that one's vision be focused ahead, but also that somehow one keeps a sensitive awareness of what is going on round about to the side, on the periphery. If something is seen to move on the periphery, the eyes can then be directed toward the spot. But how can one describe what one "sees" peripherally, preconsciously? It is not possible to do so. There is what Köhler (1929, p. 219) refers to as the comparative "emptiness" and "looseness" to the ground, whereas the figure has "the substantiality of a thing . . . a character of solidity and coherence."

But nevertheless we have an awareness of the periphery as well as of the focus of experience, of ground as well as of figure, of preconscious as well as focused conscious, a sense of things going on to the side of perception, around its circumference somehow. It is part of our reality, but it has the quality of a continuous field of regions which are not sharply delineated from one another. The whole area is flat and colorless and boundless in extent, and the field "swims" like a sky of flat moving clouds. In this field space, time, form, and all the other modalities are there together in a state of fused Being and Becoming. The words are impossible to find, for the moment we speak or write of space, time, form, and so on, even if we say they are fused in a field, the mind nevertheless follows the separate words to separate entities, regardless of our statement that they are fused. Consciousness reaches into the preconscious at every opportunity, fixes upon particular areas, brings them out into conscious focus, and atomizes them—objectifies them—verbalizes them. And then, for the moment, they are no longer preconscious but conscious. Freud has observed, "The question 'How does a thing become conscious?' would thus be more advantageously stated: 'How does a thing become preconscious?' And the answer would be: 'Through becoming connected with the word-presentations corresponding to it' " (1923, p. 20).

The preconscious awareness of ground, or context, then, is unfocused, it does not contain things, it is a continuously extended field, never-ending, and it is constantly in flux, shifting and changing in pattern and configuration. In contrast to consciously focused perception which gives momentarily stilled snapshots, preconscious awareness gives a direct experience of movement, of motion—it is like a motion picture but without the focused picture. It is this direct awareness of motion or flux which underlies the meaning of time as flux or durée rather than simply as spatialized points. It is the meaning of time formulated by Heraclitus and by Bergson.

It is in preconscious experience also that we get our direct experience of the space–time manifold; not space and time, but an awareness of a world of spatially extended process, of space and movement in space all intertwined. The space–time manifold per se as a context or ground phenomenon is a description of an aspect of the experience of the background of things, but not in itself perceivable as a thing in focus as figure. The fact that terms like *space–time manifold*, or *space–time field*, or *space–time plenum* are used to refer to it is not accidental. These terms are very general terms which refer to a sense of unformed fullness.[8]

The analysis thus far, therefore, leads us to two of the different modes of describing time—as of everything else. One is the conscious atomistic concept, related to changing things in the focused foreground or figure. The other is the preconscious field concept, related to the awareness of continuous flux in the contextual field or background of experience, in which time is embedded in the space–time manifold. Neither is the more true concept of time. Both are necessary—just as atomic theory and field theory are both necessary in physics and, if our analysis is correct, always will be necessary, not as an unsatisfactory and

[8] *Manifold* refers to the numerous in a general sense; it was used by Kant to describe the sum of everything sensed *before* being organized by the understanding. A *plenum* is the opposite of a *vacuum*: it refers to a totally filled space. Neither of these terms describes focused perception. It is striking also that the general meaning of a field is ground or extended surface, a field as a limited and segregated piece of land being a special usage.

temporary intermediate situation as Einstein thought but as a fact of the structuring of all human mental activity into figure and ground.

Unlike Minkowski, therefore, I would not want to fuse space and time together forevermore and never treat them apart. I shall argue for the retention of both modes of description—the retention of both Bergsonian durée and Heraclitean flux, on the one hand, and the physical time and atomism of Democritus, on the other hand. Meanwhile, we may note in passing that it is theories of durée and flux which are most difficult to put into words, which are most likely to seem unscientific and even mystical, and which constitute the particular meaning of time which Hegel described as killed by words. This difficulty will always exist: discontinuous words cannot accurately map continuous process.

THE SENSE OF TEMPORAL DIRECTIONALITY

Conscious figure and preconscious ground constitute a dynamic whole with a continual restless movement in which ideas or objects pop into focus and then sink back again into the blur of the unfocused ground. With respect to time, this conscious–preconscious interplay has yielded us the immediate experiences which lie at the roots of the atomistic clock time of dating and of earlier and later, and of the time of fluxion and durée. But neither consciously experienced clock time nor preconsciously experienced flux has yielded the direct experience underlying our sense of temporal directionality: spatial directionality, yes; but temporal directionality, no. This point is a subtle one, but extremely important. Let me try to clarify it.

In order to look at directionality, let us consider the immediate experience of spatial direction first. A sense of direction of processes or events in space can come about by two means. First, it can be experienced immediately by the focused perception of an arrow, or of any other pointing sign or symbol, or by the background of aware-

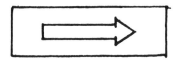

FIGURE 10.2. One Type of Focus for Perception of Spatial Direction.

ness of the movement of an object in a particular direction. Second, it can be experienced as an immediate idea by the reconstruction of a movement; for example, in the idea that an arrow which is embedded in a target can be preconsciously experienced as having moved from the bow from which it was shot, in the direction of the target to which it flew.

When we turn, however, to directionality in time, the flight of an arrow and spatial directionality do not help us. For directionality in time runs from future to present to past, and its direct experience calls for an immediate sense of the coexistence of past, present, and future. But it is no use to say that we can somehow have an immediate experience of an arrow flying out of the future into the past. Such a description would be suitable as a poetic metaphor giving life to an arrow by attributing purpose to it. But recourse to magical anthropomorphism of this kind will most decidedly hold up our argument rather than carry it forward.

Our direct temporal sense of the flight of an arrow, or of any other external movement, is a sense only of earlier and later. To say that the arrow is moving from the bow toward the target is a statement of its direction or sense in space; it is not a statement of its direction in time. We can directly perceive the spatial direction of a movement as something going from "there to there"—all in the present. But we cannot get the same direct sense of past to future in the perception of the movement, precisely because it is all in the present. The arrow can be said to have left the bow at a time t_1, five seconds earlier than it reached the target at a time t_2—so long as we recorded both points in time on a stopwatch. But these earlier and later recordings of time are static: they do not in any way give a direct and immediate sense of future–present–past movement, of future–present–past direction. The bow, the arrow, the target, all exist as spatial points, having moved between two different locations at the two different time recordings, and can so be experienced. But they do not move in any particular direction temporally.

Where then does our sense of temporal direction come from? That is to say, where does our sense of flux from future, to present, to past, come from? To say that A occurred earlier or later than B is a matter of objective record (or at least of objectifiable record): it can be recorded in the external world. When we shift to past, present, and future, however, we would appear to move into the inner psychic world—the world in which past, present, and future all coexist, as Augustine noted, as the present past, the present present, and the present future. They coexist, that is, as the interacting field of present memory, present perception, and present desire or expectation and intention.

I would now draw attention to a very significant circumstance. We have a sense of the coexistence and interaction of past, present, and future because memory, perception, and desire exist as a unified field of force. It is from this unified field of force that we get our sense of temporal direction just as surely as a pointing arrow gives a sense of spatial direction. But the arrow of temporality cannot be physically observed; it is not like a physical arrow somehow pointing from a later time than the present to an earlier time than the present. It is a peculiarly psychological directionality—a peculiarly psychological arrow. It is a mentally felt pointing, an orientation of the mind, sloping or slanting, from what might be thought of as a future time in the field which constitutes the present to a past time in the same present field.

Thus, for example, I note that I am thirsty and get a glass of orange juice from the refrigerator. Such an action comes about through the fused interaction between: a sensed need, a lack, the thirst; a seeking for an idea of something which might satisfy the need; a memory of water in the tap, but then of orange juice in the refrigerator; a playing together of the sensed need, the idea of the remembered orange juice, the sense of what would need to be done to get and drink the orange juice, and the potential satisfaction in doing so; the construction of the intention to get the orange juice; and the carrying along of the memory, need, and intention in the willful action of getting to the refrigerator, pouring the drink, and quenching the thirst. In this example, temporal directionality can be experienced directly in the simultaneous experiencing of the thirst and the intention to quench it in just a few moments.

What then are we to make of this psychological field of force in which past, present, and future rub shoulders with one another, jostle one another, walk together hand-in-hand, work together, cooperate with one another, and pull against one another? A moment's reflection suggests that we are here dealing with living experience, with the present moment in full regalia in all its richness. Let me examine the present past, the present present, and the present future, each in turn.

The interacting past is a highly selected past. It is the past of immediately relevant memory. Particular memories are somehow chosen and drawn from the great storehouse of memory—or somehow extrude themselves—to lend the current meaningfulness of the precipitates of earlier experiences to the handling of the present situation. These memories are alive in the present. How their meaning relates to their meaning at the earlier time of their occurrence can never accurately be known. But they inform the present with their accumulation of wisdom and knowledge (and of errors as well), and indeed sometimes press for particular outcomes as much to satisfy continuing frustrations, leftovers from earlier experience, as to satisfy current need.

If we next move to the organizing present we find an amalgam of current percepts—responses to selected outside circumstances—and current lacks or needs or interests, the things which are astir in the person, and which cause attention to be directed in a manner calculated to search out the most useful information of resources, both from memory and from the outside world. The existence of the orange juice in the refrigerator is winkled out of memory, or presses out of memory, through the interaction of memory and of perceived need.

And then, finally, there is the future, the seemingly nonexisting will-o'-the-wisp. It is the product of our experience of the things we intend to do, to achieve, to create, to bring about. These things are the goals or objectives which we have in mind, which when achieved, or so we believe, will provide us with what we need to satisfy our felt lack, our desires, our expectations. The future is that which we plan to do to express our current interests, to satisfy a current lack, or to bring about what we have decided we want. The future is a statement not of some actual event which has still to get here, but of our will or intention—whether to get a drink, as in our example, or to paint a picture or a house, or to take a holiday, or to create an export sales network, or to preach a sermon, or to land a man on the moon.

Present needs or interests express themselves in selective attention or perception, and arouse memories which in turn influence perception, and lead to the imagining of things-which-might-be. Remembered things and ideas merge with perceived things and ideas, and lead to desired things and ideas, and all fuse in one active field of force generating willed action toward an intended goal. That is what life is about.

Temporal direction, then—the directionality from past to present to future—is nothing more nor less than the fusion of experience, of anticipation, of need and perception, and of memory, into a single force field in action toward an intended, desired, or willed goal. It is the sensing of the goal-directedness of our personal endeavors and behavior.

If this view is correct, that the essence of temporal directionality lies in a person's intrapsychic sense of fused memory, perception, desire, and intention, where then in mental life might such a fused experience—a psychological field of force—occur? Certainly not in the conscious region of mental activity. For there can be no spontaneous conscious knowledge of a memory –perception–desire, or a past–present–future, all together as one focused phenomenon, as a field of force, any more than there can be a focused conscious knowledge of a space–time plenum or field.

We have seen how consciousness is the great abstractor, the great divider, the great still photographer. It creates our knowledge in terms of experience of discrete points at a distance and not of fibrillating fields of force. That characteristic is equally true whether it is conscious perception of the external world as objects, or the internal world as ideas. The ideas too—whether consciously repeated, or drawn from the preconscious, or sliding or erupting from the region of the unconscious—are produced in knowable and verbally formulatable bits. I may construct a conceptual model of a field of force, and consciously know that model as a thing. But that is to know the field of force only at one remove, at secondhand. First-hand knowledge of a field of force by direct experience is not available to conscious mental processes.

Nor can fused past–present–future be found in preconscious awareness. Preconscious mental processes tend to be passive background containing a store of focusable and verbalizable elements. These processes do not generate intentionality, they do not generate goals. Hence they cannot generate the temporal directionality which derives from the sense we have of pressing toward a goal in time.

UNCONSCIOUS SENSING AND TIME: PROTOMENTAL SOURCE OF TEMPORAL DIRECTION

If not in consciousness, and if not in preconsciousness, then where is the dynamic field, the field of force, comprising the coexisting past–present–future or actively interpenetrating memory, perception, and desire, to be found? I emphasize again that I would speak not of each separate element by itself, nor of the intellectual verbal formulation of the field, but of the direct experience, the ongoing active sense of the field, the gut feel of the process. This powerful flow of intentionality is the outstanding characteristic of unconscious mental activity.

For the world of figure and ground, of the conscious
–preconscious system, does not operate on its own. It is
only the surface part of mental activity. Beneath this
surface lie the vastnesses of the unconscious mind—the
protomental region—in which the bulk of mental activity
proceeds.[9] It is in the reaches of the unconscious protomental activity that are to be found the dynamics of human action, the reasons for our doing things, the source
of our desires, goals, and objectives, and our decisions. It
may be clear that I am here using Freud's full concept
of the unconscious system—the unconscious as a part of
normal mental functioning as well as the system into
which previously conscious or preconscious ideas can be
repressed and split off with resulting abnormality in function and symptom formation. I shall be concerned with
normal unconscious functioning and its connection with
time, and not with questions of psychopathology and ab-
normal temporal phenomena.[10]

In considering protomental unconscious life we encounter a problem which if not identified and got out of
the way will gravely obscure the path I propose to follow.
It is the fact that in writing about the unconscious, putting it into words, the essence of the normal unconscious

[9] Tolman (1967, p. 208) described the matter as follows, in connection with animal learning: "The rat must have in some measure
learned unconsciously, before consciousness can begin to appear. He
cannot be conscious until he has already achieved to some degree,
that which being conscious will merely further emphasize. The func-
tional value of being conscious must be said, therefore, to be merely
that of emphasizing and reinforcing field-features, to some extent
already becoming immanent in preceding behaviors. *Consciousness
can achieve nothing really de novo.*" [Italics mine.]

[10] I am here using the concept of normal unconscious functioning
in contrast to the "boiling cauldron" or "horse and rider" theory which
regards unconscious processes mainly in terms of a raging source of
irrational impulse, conflict, and psychopathology, which can be har-
nessed and made reasonable only by the ego and its defense systems.

(as against repressed and split-off unconscious processes), its fluid totally nonverbal character is lost. And so we risk losing the idea altogether.

We encountered similar difficulties in describing pre-conscious processes because they are a continuous field and are therefore ill-dealt with by words which are by their very nature atomistic. But these difficulties are much greater with respect to the unconscious field. Pre-conscious processes are at least available in latent ver-balized form: it does not, therefore, totally macerate the preconscious processes to describe them verbally. Uncon-scious processes are different. Except for the repressed and split-off unconscious elements which must previously have been conscious or preconscious and verbalized, un-conscious protomental experience cannot in any way be adequately verbalized. To describe it in words is the same as describing in words the way in which a two-week-old baby is experiencing his world—or an animal experienc-ing its world. It is not impossible: but it must be con-stantly kept in mind that the *verbal description is a description of a nonverbal process* and not a recording of words used in the unconscious. Unconscious processes are nonarticulatable fields of force. To speak about them is like speaking about an electromagnetic field. The uncon-scious is creatively inarticulate, and is better left so. Fail-ure to recognize this fact has created unnecessary difficulties in analyses of that important area of the ex-perience of temporality, and of spatiality, namely their unconscious experiential substratum.

Protomental unconscious processes, then, are con-cerned with as yet unverbalized human feeling and de-sire, with wishes, will, and intent, with libido, with loving and hating impulses, with primal feelings of envy and gratitude, of potency and omnipotence, of generosity and selfishness—with, in effect, everything that makes the world go round. They lack only the abilities connected with consciousness, to formulate things explicitly, albeit retrospectively, and to employ self-conscious reflexive logical and analytical skills. In effect, in the human being we have the spontaneous protomental unconscious process flowing about and constrained in a conscious logicocritical context.

Perhaps the most important thing about these protomental processes is that they are actively oriented toward something, toward doing something, changing something, achieving something, overcoming something, reducing tension, getting satisfaction, influencing others to feel something or to do something. They are, in short, always goal-directed, intentional.

It is this goal-directedness, this intentionality, of the unconscious protomental world which gives us our direct and immediate sense of temporal directionality. For we may now notice that one of the very significant features of a goal is that it not only states the will or intention to do something or to achieve some state or some condition, but it also includes the intention to do so by a certain time. Goals and intentions are organized in terms of time. They must be. Without a time by which an intention is to be carried out, a goal achieved, there is simply no goal or intention. To intend to do something some time or other, to achieve a goal but by no particular time, is the opposite of intention and will. It is to be will-less, intention-less, goal-less, floating, lackadaisical, spineless. The target time of completion, the willed time of achievement, the by-when it is intended to get somewhere, is as much a property of intention, of goal, of will, as is the redness of a red apple.

Because goals or intentions must de facto have target completion times in order to exist, we are led to the conclusion that unconscious protomental processes are impregnated with a powerful sense of time, saturated with it, dripping with it. Without quite being consciously aware of how it happened, we find ourselves urgently pressed toward reading the newspaper immediately, or with the intention of completing an essay by the end of the week, or with the plan to have a flat redecorated within the succeeding two months. We might change our targets as we proceed, but without a target completion time, even if it is continually changing, it is impossible to organize to get anything done at all.

We may, of course, not carry out the bidding of our unconsciously derived impulses and intentions. And we may modify those impulses and intentions as they become conscious and we are able to adopt a critical attitude toward them. But it is from the protomental reservoir that intentionality springs and in which our sense of the directionality of time thus has its source.

I would put this unconscious sense of temporal direction into words, that is, paraphrase it, in the following way: "I am here, now, at 7 P.M. on October 26. I feel slightly uncomfortable, and have the vague sense that I should be somewhere else. I remember that a week ago I received notice of a meeting which I intended to go to. I picture myself at the meeting and desire to go to it. It starts at 8 P.M., in an hour. I decide that if I get my car and drive to the meeting at once, it will be possible to be there on time. I will myself to go. I am ensconced in present desire, present memory, and present intention."

The effect of this unconscious experience is that at the time of decision, now, there is a past–present–future time axis which points right through my present experience at the moment. Its sensed direction is from my memory of the notice of a week ago of the meeting, through my desire to go, to my intention to be there in one hour. That is to say, this "arrow" of time flies from a week "in the past" to the present, to an hour "in the future." But its flight is nothing more than a mental fiction. It is an important fiction, however, representing as it does my active desiring, remembering, intending, willing, state of mind. Unconscious intention can be oriented from past toward the present into the future because both the past and the future are carried in the arms of the present. It could be represented by Figure 10.3.

This unconscious sense of the dynamic from-the-past-to-the-future orientation of the field of force of will and intention in the case of specifically goal-directed behavior is reinforced by a more general sense of time connected with eternal beliefs and values. Such beliefs and values are felt as operating in a general way over long periods, or for life, or in the hereafter if that is a person's belief. They give a vaguer, weaker sense of temporal direction, however, than the powerfully sensed direction in time of goal-directed intentionality.

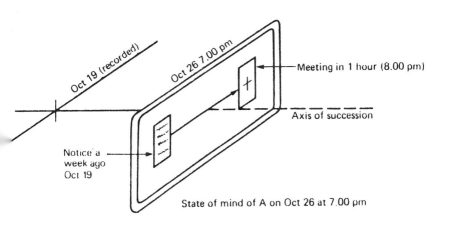

FIGURE 10.3. Direction of an Intent.

THE RATIONALITY OF PROTOMENTAL
UNCONSCIOUS PROCESSES IN DECISION
MAKING

It may seem that my analysis suggests that as far as doing things is concerned, the protomental unconscious processes are the really substantial processes and the conscious processes are ancillary in the sense of being context-setting. That impression would be correct. It is important to recognize that it is the unconscious proto-mental processes which are fundamental, the conscious critical processes being an undoubtedly valuable adjunct. Verbal language, written language, explicit knowledge including science, conscious logic, computer competence, the cortical area of the brain, are all exceedingly useful to human beings, but they are not the central areas of life—or of time. The central areas are in felt rationality, felt goals, memories-in-feeling,[11] felt needs, lacks, or absences which fill out and transform into wishes and desires and then overflow into action.

These felt or lived processes are not localizable in the brain or central nervous system. Nor are they to be localized in something called "the mind" (which then has to be awkwardly placed somehow in "the body" which is supposed to contain it). They are a function of the whole living organism with its sensorimotor system, its thinking and acting, and its touch-and-feel peripheral nervous

---

[11] This is a concept vividly used by Melanie Klein in her psychoanalytic work with children. It describes the manner in which two- and three-year-olds respond to interpretations about past experiences in preverbal infancy, when they clearly get the sense of what is being said, in memory-feeling rather than in verbalized or pictorial memory. Adults also live continuously with such feelings, but they tend to be hidden from conscious awareness by the overlay of verbalized ideas which cover up so much of the richness of experience. See, for example, Melanie Klein (1961).

system as well as its central one. For the protomental unconscious sensing processes in reasoning and decision making are a matter of touch-and-feel, of green fingers, of skill, of nous, of good sense, of judgment, of discretion and discrimination, of shouldering uncertainty[12]—all good solid processes well insulated from too much tampering and interference from the conscious (although sometimes the insulation weakens and impoverishment of personality and of human contact is the consequence).

This view of protomental unconscious sensing processes as a central feature of reasoning and rationality is, of course, not a very common one.[13] I believe, however, that this is because of the widespread tendency to overvalue conscious mental processes, visual perception, and language. Thus, even Freud repeatedly said that the unconscious has no knowledge of time. For example, he stated: "The processes of the system Ucs. are timeless; i.e., they are not ordered temporally, are not altered by the passage of time, in fact bear no relation to time at all. The time-relation also is bound up with the work of the system Cs" (1900). This view is one which has been elaborated by Marie Bonaparte in her article "Time and the Unconscious" (1940). She adds, however, that "The statement that the unconscious is timeless may mean

[12] See my analysis of uncertainty in Chapter 7 of *Measurement of Responsibility* (1956). (See also chapter 6 of this volume.)
[13] Polanyi developed the concept of tacit knowledge to deal with this problem. Thus, for example, he attempts to resolve, by this concept, Plato's paradox set out in the *Meno*, namely: "to search for the solution to a problem is an absurdity; for either you know what you are looking for, and then there is no problem; or you do not know what you are looking for, and then you cannot expect to find anything. . . . The kind of tacit knowledge that solves the paradox of the *Meno* consists in the intimation of something hidden, which we may yet discover" (Polanyi, 1966, pp. 22, 23). I believe that Polanyi would have found himself on stronger ground with the conception of unconscious mental functioning.

that the unconscious has no *knowledge* of time, that time as an intellectual concept does not exist for it. But to say this is to state a truism. The unconscious, the primitive reservoir of our instincts and our will to live, knows nothing of any concept; these are later acquisitions of the intellect. Consequently, it can no more have knowledge of the concept of time than of any other concept" (p. 439).

It may be seen, however, that both Freud and Bonaparte are reifying time. In the consciously formulated sense in which they are using the concept of time, it can of course be known only consciously. But then, clearly, it is equally true that in this consciously formulated sense the unconscious has no knowledge of space either; or of triangles, or of circles, or of redness, or of any other verbally articulated concepts. The unconscious has only a nonformulated, nonconceptualized sense of past –present–future, of memory–perception–desire, and I see no reason to think that this organization is not present at least from birth.

DECISIONS AS TIME-TARGETED PROTOMENTAL UNCONSCIOUS PROCESSES

The rationality and field-of-force organization of the unconscious memory–perception–intention temporally directed field shows clearly in decision making. Decisions are always goal-directed, since a choice can be made only in relation to an intended outcome. Moreover, deciding or choosing are always in the final analysis founded upon unconscious processes. The role of protomental unconscious factors in decision making can be succinctly summed up in the fact that if you consciously know all the considerations that led to a particular choice then you did not make a decision: you were a computer. Let me explain this statement.

The making of choices and decisions is connected with *uncertainty*. If, for some reason, you can be *certain* that a particular goal is called for, or that a particular path to a goal is the optimum, then there is no decision to be made: unless, of course, you wish to decide—for some reason or other about which you would assuredly not be certain—not to seek the required goal or not to take the optimum path toward it.

The factors and possibilities entering into human choice situations are always infinite. The reasons are infinite, regardless of whether the options are finitely limited, as in, for example, gambling on the toss of a coin, or infinitely open, as in most choice situations with respect to action in real life in solving a problem or in satisfying a need. There are always the choices that have been made previously in similar (but never identical) situations; there are all the reasons which have never been thought up before; then there is the possibility of postponement; or of giving up and trying something else; and finally there are all the conflicting desires, aspirations, expectations, hopes, fears, prejudices, influences from others—some conscious and some unconscious. It is out of this amalgam of the formulated, the unformulated, and the unconscious that we somehow decide what to do, sometimes quickly and sometimes with hesitation, sometimes with a confident feeling of a high probability of a satisfactory outcome and sometimes with a pessimistic feeling of low probability. It is because of this inevitable uncertainty and play of unconscious factors that some modern decision theory operates on the basis of establishing probability judgments and of helping decision makers to formulate their view of the degree of uncertainty of their judgment in terms of their sensed probability of a particular outcome (see, for example, Phillips [1974, 1980], Humphreys and Wishuda [1979]).

A judgment of probability is a rational and not a random process; it is an unconscious process made within a conscious context. The context and the outcome of the unconscious judging process usually become conscious, but not the process itself. Conscious knowledge can help to limit the field of choice within which we apply our unconscious rationality. It provides context. It also provides a logicocritical context for the evaluation of progress toward solutions as well as of final solutions, helping to eliminate errors. But it cannot make decisions.

To bring certainty into decision making is a contradiction in terms. It would be necessary to bring all the conditions under control, to confine the situation rigidly and narrowly to a specified number of specified alternatives at each choice point, and to program in explicit terms what is to be done for each choice. Such a procedure has the inevitable effect of removing all the elements of decision. It is this type of control which characterizes the computer.[14] What cannot, however, be built into a computer is what constitutes the decision process; namely, the nonformulated, nonexplicit, nonexplicable, unknown, nonverbalized play of unconscious forces; that is, a property of living organisms only.

In short, then, we have the unconscious sensing of the temporally directed past–present–future field in the unconscious interplay of memory–perception–desire –inten-

[14] The programming of random elements into a computer in no way changes this argument. Human behavior, human choices, human decision making are never random even in so-called trial-and-error learning. Whatever is going on, there is always all-pervasive purpose suffusing the psychological field, as gravity suffuses the physical worlds. When computers can love, get bored, feel bereaved, become overeager and impatient, have their decisions influenced by their own personal sense of responsibility and conscience, suffer disappointment, and experience success and triumph, then they too will make decisions. But they will have become human beings in the process.

tion. We have the awareness of motion, of process, in preconscious background mental activity. And we have the atomistic points of objective time and earlier and later occurrences in the focus of conscious and verbally formulated mental activity. In the interplay of the three processes—conscious, preconscious, and unconscious—we get the human being living his life in space and in time, oscillating between states of contemplation and action, with his knowledge of what came first and what came later, his more limited knowledge of his motives and goals, his reliance upon his vaguer awareness of what is going on round about him, and his dependence upon his unconscious protomental sense of striving and intentions.

REFERENCES

Bonaparte, M. (1940), Time and the unconscious. *Internat. J. Psycho-Anal.*, 21:439–452.

Dummett, M. (1954), Can effect precede its cause? *Proc. Aristotelean Soc.*, Suppl. 28:174–175.

—— (1964), Bringing about the past. *Philosoph. Rev.*, 73:61–63.

Freud, S. (1900), The Interpretation of Dreams. *Standard Edition*, 4. London: Hogarth Press, 1961.

—— (1923), The ego and the id. *Standard Edition*, 19:13–63. London: Hogarth Press, 1961.

Humphreys, P. C., & Wishuda, A. (1979), Multi-attribute utility decomposition. In: *Technical Report 79-2*. Uxbridge, Middlesex, UK: Brunel University Decision Analysis Unit.

Jaques, E. (1956), *Measurement of Responsibility*. London: Heinemann Educational Books Ltd.

Koffka, K. (1928), *The Growth of the Mind*. New York: Harcourt.

—— (1935), *Principles of Gestalt Psychology*. New York: Harcourt.

Köhler, W. (1929), *Gestalt Psychology*. New York: Liveright.

Klein, M. (1957), Envy and gratitude. In: *Collected Writings*, Vol. 2. New York: McGraw-Hill, 1975.

—— (1961), Narrative of a child analysis. In: *Collected Writings*, Vol. 2. New York: McGraw-Hill, 1975.

Lewin, K. (1935), *A Dynamic Theory of Personality*. New York: McGraw-Hill.

Lucas, J. R. (1973), *A Treatise on Time and Space*. London: Methuen.

McTaggart, J. M. E. (1927), *The Nature of Existence*. Cambridge, UK: Cambridge University Press.

Phillips, L. D. (1974), *Bayesian Statistics for Social Scientists*. New York: Cromwell.

—— (1980), *Generation Theory*. Working Paper 80-1. Uxbridge, Middlesex, UK: Brunel University Decision Analysis Unit.

Polanyi, M. (1966), *The Tacit Dimension*. Garden City, NY: Doubleday.

Popper, K. (1976), *Unended Quest*. London: Fontana-Collins.

Schachtel, E. (1963), *Metamorphosis*. London: Routledge & Kegan Paul.

Tolman, E. C. (1967), *Purposive Behavior in Animals and Men*. New York: Appleton-Century.

Chapter 11

Time and the Measurement of Human Attributes

In the course of attempts to measure the level of work assigned into roles, certain fundamental aspects of measurement, not only of work but of social and psychological processes in general, claim our attention. The first is the peculiar and special importance of the dimension of time in such measurement; the second has to do with the more general problem of relating data about human activities to quantitative scales, a problem which applied just as much to physical measurements in its early days. Furthermore, despite the common assumption to the contrary, there is nothing inherently less precise in social measurement than there is in physical measurement, as long as we proceed from simple observation of the processes in which we are interested.

MEASUREMENT IN THE PHYSICAL WORLD

To illustrate some of the main points, I shall consider first of all some basic features of the measurement of temperature. To get at the essentials, it will be useful to have a fresh look at the problem as it appeared to scientists in the fifteenth century, before thermometers had been discovered. In those days the concept of temperature

245

as a potentially measurable quality hardly existed. The prevalent theory was that of heat as a fluid *calor* which could be transmitted from one substance to another; but whether all heat was the same, or whether heat of combustion, solar heat, and animal heat were different, was uncertain.

Imagine then the available data. First and foremost there is the sensation of heat; the sensation of one thing feeling warmer than another, or of things getting hotter and hotter. These sensations are the basic data. It is these sensations which allow us to know about the existence of something we call hot, or cold, or warm, or burning, or freezing. Along with these sensations go our observations of hotter and colder things: flames are hot; so is the sun; ice is cold; fresh water is cool; put a flame under it and it gets hot and eventually it boils; some animals, including humans, are warm to the touch; others, like snakes, are cold. We know that things get hotter and colder, because our senses tell us so.

Let us interject at this moment an observation on the similarities between that situation and our present-day experience of phenomena such as level of responsibility—we can sense when it is higher and when lower; or individual capacity—we can sense our own capacity to be increasing as we mature; or aggression, or love, or envy, or any of a hundred other social and human attributes which we "know" to be greater and lesser, and to be changing in amount, but which we do not, as yet, know how to measure. So with the problem of heat and temperature up until the fifteenth century.

Returning again to the past, there is one other observation that is of outstanding importance; namely, that as *calor* is transmitted to air, the air not only gets warmer, but it also increases in volume. We can observe this phenomenon by warming the air trapped in a test tube held upside down in a dish of water (Figure 11.1). If we hold the tube in our hand, or otherwise warm it, the level of water in the tube can be observed to go down; if we cool the base, say, by holding a piece of ice against it, the water level can be seen to rise in the tube. Clearly, we may conclude, the air is expanding and contracting as it gets warmer and colder.

This observation, and its possible significance for measurement, are not, of course, available simply for the taking. We have to be in a proper frame of mind to pay particular attention to it. For it is merely one datum in the midst of a host of other data and pseudodata and questions which are in many ways emotionally more attractive; for example: What is the nature of *calor*? How is it transmitted from the sun through space? What are flames? Are there flames inside the human body? What happens when water turns into steam, or into ice? These are the fascinating questions. And surely they are more practical and realistic than bothering with the problem of trying to measure what after all is an insubstantial psychological sensation, namely, hotter and colder.

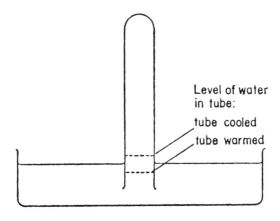

Level of water
in tube:
tube cooled
tube warmed

FIGURE 11.1. Effect of Heating the Air.

But happily it is a characteristic of human scientific endeavor that it does eventually cut through the distraction and obscurity of popular thought to the things that matter. The significance of the column of air in the test tube gains force until someone (the general opinion is that it was Galileo) thinks to graduate it. He puts a mark in the tube at the level of the water when the tube is held in the hand, and another at its level when the tube is immersed in ice. And so the thermoscope is born. Not much can be done with it, but it is a kind of scientific curiosity that we can use to show what happens to a column of air when it is warmed and cooled.

The thermoscope remained a scientific curiosity for some hundred years. What would the view of a modern man be? Would he dare claim to perceive the thermometer nascent in that test tube? To do so it would have to occur to him that the column of water was going up and down and that it was getting colder and warmer, both *at the same rate*. Who could make such an assumption? And if he did, how could he prove it?

What data are available? On the one hand, we have the column of water going up and down. We can all see that. It is directly observable. On the other hand, we have our sensations, our feelings. We can perhaps agree that the test tube is getting colder and warmer, but who knows by how much and how quickly? And how can we possibly agree?

Here we have the prime dilemma and the prime characteristic of all measurement. *Measurement is the process of ordering the psychological experience of magnitude to an external and readily observable scale.* It is a relationship between inner sensations that are not directly shareable and an outer yardstick which we can all observe in common.

Yet someone does break through these emotional and

intellectual barriers, does find his way through the clutter of knowledge, half-knowledge, undigested facts, and fantasies and falsehoods. *He decides to calibrate the thermoscope*: to divide the space between the body temperature mark at one end of the scale and the freezing point mark at the other end into one hundred points. With that one decisive act we have moved from thermoscope to thermometer.

It is not certain who took this step, but it was very likely Newton, for the instrument first appeared in England in Newton's circle at the height of his best work. The instrument was no longer in the form of an open-ended tube, but of a tube sealed off at both ends. And the liquid was no longer limited to water. Colored alcohol and other nonfreezing liquids were also used.

With the use of these first crude thermometers, the study of temperature was transformed. The movement of columns of various kinds of liquid (including soon after the liquid metal, mercury) could be systematically observed, recorded, and compared as they were moved between different baths of sensibly different temperature.

From this point the problem of the development of the thermometer became a technical problem, first of discovering which liquids expanded and contracted with greatest constancy as they were heated and cooled (water, for example, was ruled out, for it was known that after contracting as it grew colder, it began to expand again just before it began to freeze), and second of stating a theoretical basis for the instrument. A major step forward was taken in the middle of the nineteenth century with the formulation of the laws of thermodynamics, and with the development of inert gas thermometers. Then another major step was achieved with the discovery of the behavior of electric currents at different temperatures and the construction of the thermoelectric couple.

Thus it became possible to measure changes in temperature by means of changes in liquids, in gases, and in the flow of electricity. It can be fairly well established that equally calibrated distances represent equal changes in temperature. But it has taken some 300 years to get to this point.

Our brief sketch of the development of the thermometer allows us to illustrate several important points in measurement. One we have already mentioned; namely, that measurement involves the ordering of sensory impressions to an external scale. In effect, it is incorrect to say that we measure temperature; we do not. We measure the length, say, of a column of mercury, and we assume that this measurement corresponds to a particular sensation of warmth or coldness, as a result of the construction and calibration of an instrument called a thermometer. Our construction has been good enough so that we have not yet had the experience of the column of mercury getting observably shorter as the air gets sensibly warmer. Should such a happening occur but once, we should probably have to throw our thermometers away and start again!

Thus it is that it cannot correctly be said that we measure temperature, but, as Bridgman has pointed out, it is our thermometers, our measuring instruments that give us our best mode of defining temperature. All qualities of things, like temperature, length, velocity, redness, are most accurately definable in terms of the operations we go through to measure them.

The next general point has to do with the scale. In the case of temperature it can be noted that we have related our data to a length scale. A length scale is one of three ways we have of representing an equal-interval quantitative continuum in physical terms. That is to say, if we mark our equal intervals and name them 0, 1, 2, 3, 4, 5, etc., then the distance from 0 to 2 is twice that from 0 to 1; from 2 to 6 (4 intervals) it is one half that from 8 to 16 (9 intervals), from 0 to 10 it is twice that from 0 to 5, and so on for addition, subtraction, multiplication, and division.

The second physical scale with these properties is that of mass. If we start with any given weight, and find other weights that exactly balance it, we have a number of units from which we can build up a system of weights equivalent to half, or twice, or three times, and so on, the standard, and establish a scale with the same quantitative characteristics as the scale of length.

The third physical scale is that of time. The recording of time is achieved by establishing an instrument which moves at regular and equal intervals, such as a pendulum or the molecular oscillations in a crystal. From these equal intervals we can build up an equal interval quantitative scale like that of length or of mass.

The problem of measurement, then, can be stated in terms of finding a means of ordering changes in our sensations about the properties of things or of people or of social relationships to changes along the equal-interval scales of length or of mass or of time. Against this background, let us now consider some problems of the measurement of qualities of social life, and the particular relevance of a time scale for such measurement.

MEASUREMENT IN THE SOCIAL WORLD

Our starting point is the measurement of level of work in terms of time-span of discretion. We need not go into detail about the method of measurement; it has been fully described elsewhere (Jaques, 1961, 1964). But its essential elements are as follows:

1. Managers assigning tasks to subordinates always, explicitly or implicitly, assign the maximum period of time allowed for the completion of the task; this maximum *target* completion time is an inherent part of the task.
2. The maximum target completion time sets the framework within which the subordinate can exercise discretion in driving the task through to completion; it sets the time-span of discretion within which he works.
3. The longest of the maximum target completion times assigned in a role, gives the time-span of discretion of the role.

The reason for our taking an interest in the time-span of discretion of a role was that its length was observed to accord with the sensation of level or weight of responsibility. The longer the time-span of the role the greater the feeling of weight; the shorter the time-span the lighter the feeling of weight; increase the time-span and the feeling of weight increases; decrease the time-span and the feeling of weight decreases.

These observable relationships were supported by the unexpected finding that people at the same time-span feel entitled to by and large the same pay; the longer the time-span the higher the payment to which they feel entitled. However, there is the familiar phenomenon that if a manager finds that the responsibility he has assigned to a subordinate is too heavy, he can reduce it by dividing the larger tasks into two or three parts, giving him the first part, then the second part when he finishes the first, and so on. In effect, the manager is involved in progressing the work for his subordinate on a shorter time-scale. Or contrariwise, it will be found that as a manager gains confidence in a new subordinate, he allows him greater freedom by allowing him longer tasks.

We have here the same conditions that we found in the case of the measurement of temperature. There is first of all the sensation, the psychological experience of weight and level of responsibility. And second, there is the objectively measurable datum that seems to vary in correspondence with variations in the sensation. Let us consider each in turn.

The psychological sensation of weight of responsibility is just as "real" a sensation as the sensation of warmth. We have all experienced it. We know when we feel the weight is too heavy, and we feel worried, oppressed, and overburdened. Equally, we know when the weight is becoming lighter, and when it has become too light; oppression and worry turn into relief, which turns into boredom and lack of interest if the weight of responsibility is too light.

That is to say, we are here dealing with an individual experience, sensed in terms of magnitude, of greater and lesser; we can equally sense variations in magnitude, in terms of feelings of weight of responsibility getting lighter and heavier.

The problem of measurement (or definition) of this sensed property of tasks—namely, weight or level of responsibility—just as was the case in measuring the sensed heat of liquids or other bodies, is to find some objectively measurable datum that appears to vary, as did the length of a column of liquid, in concert with variations in our sensation. That datum was found in the assigned time-span of discretion.

Time-span of discretion is just as objective a datum as is mercury in a glass tube. In order to be able to observe it, we must get an explicit and definitive statement from the manager of the maximum target completion time for the tasks he has assigned to his subordinate. These target times, and his subordinate can be informed of them, are objective facts. They are the facts that then govern the behavior of the subordinate in planning and carrying through his work.

Moreover, they are measurable data; they can be ordered to a time-scale. We are thus in a position to examine variations in the subjective sense of weight or level of responsibility, and concomitant variations in the objectively measurable time-span of discretion of the assigned responsibilities whose weight is experienced. The situation is the same as that of being able to examine variations in the sense of warmth, say, of liquids, and the thermometric readings of those liquids. Systematic observation can begin.

TIME AND HUMAN ACTIVITY

It remains, of course, to establish rigorously—as in the case of thermometers—that equal intervals in time-span of discretion represent equal intervals in weight of responsibility. Moreover, a general theory to explain the relationship is needed, and work on the subject is currently under way. This research has led to the occurrence of certain ideas of a general kind.

In the first place, it now seems obvious common sense that level of work should be measurable in terms of time. For work is an activity that occurs in and through time. It is thus no more surprising that we should measure its level in terms of time, than that we should measure velocity or acceleration in terms of space and time.

This statement of the seemingly obvious leads on to other questions. Are there perhaps many human attributes that may turn out to be readily measurable in accord with a time-scale? One at least occurs immediately;

namely, individual capacity or creativity. Capacity and creativity are problem-solving activities that occur through time. Might we not measure a person's capacity if we could find means for measuring his capacity to organize activities through time?

I believe that this line of endeavor is in fact likely to lead to the solution of the problem of measuring the magnitude of an individual's capacity to work. The larger the time-span he can manage, the greater his capacity. Conversely, the size of his capacity can be defined in terms of the maximum time-span over which he is capable of organizing and progressing his work.

Time-span of capacity is readily observable, for example, in very small children. If we observe, for instance, the age at which a child becomes capable of foregoing immediate gratification in favor of promised enhanced gratification the next day, I think we might have a good indication of its potential capacity. The younger the age at which a child becomes able to achieve a one-day time-span, the higher his capacity is likely to be.

In full adulthood, we find individuals capable of undertaking tasks calling for a sequence of activities over periods of months and years, the higher positions in life calling for the longer time-spans. At the extreme, we have individuals whose whole lifetime is one great progressive development without satisfactory closure at any points along the way. In such cases we are dealing with genius; and we have available an operational definition of this quality; namely, a person whose capacity operates in a time-span longer than his own span of life, so that he dies with his talent inevitably incompletely fulfilled.

What other human qualities, individual or social, might also be defined and measured in terms of time-scale I cannot readily suggest. But possibilities that come to mind are properties such as ego strength, ambition, tenacity, and social cohesion. Whatever is the case, it may be useful to keep in mind that individual and social processes are processes, they are dynamic; they occur through time. Time-scale, therefore, may often hold the key to the problem of measurement, and measurement in the natural sciences sense.

REFERENCES

Jaques, E. (1961), *Equitable Payment*. London: Heinemann Educational Books Ltd.
——— (1964), *Time-Span Handbook*. London: Heinemann Educational Books Ltd.

Chapter 12

Quantification in the Human Sciences

Psychology and the social sciences have not as yet come close to achieving the remarkable directness and simplicity which attend measurement in the physical sciences. It will be argued in this chapter that a central reason for the difference between the two fields with respect to measurement is an epistemological one: it is concerned with the clarity of identification of entities and the objective properties of entities in physics, and the absence of such clear designations in the human sciences. How a shift to a 5-D framework might overcome some of these difficulties will be considered.

There are a number of characteristics of natural science measurement which contribute to its elegance and simplicity. The first of these is its ready use of extensive measurement, starting with the fundamental measurement of single properties of length, mass, and time; and its direct and easy construction of ratio scales from this extensive measurement. Then there is the fact that all the measures are reducible to a few primary dimensions, such as, for example, charge, temperature, mass, length, time, and angle, giving a coherent system of units. And finally, the combinations of primary dimensions always have the form of simple monomials, the various measures being relatable by physical laws. These various conditions are comprehensively developed in Krantz, Luce, Suppes, and Tversky (1971).

By contrast, in the human sciences extensive measurement is notoriously difficult and practically nonexistent. Most measurement is characterized by ordinal scaling or interval scaling; and when ratio scaling is established, it is mainly by means of complicated constructions either from polynomial conjoint measures or from differences of interval scales, rather than from simple extensive measurement (Krantz et al., 1971; Roberts, 1979).

The simplicity of direct extensive measurement in physics derives from the primary abstraction and identification of physical entities as material objects extended in space; they are therefore locatable at any given point in time as objects with 3-spatial dimensions in a 3-dimensional Cartesian world, possessing the substantiality of mass. Entity and its fundamental measure dimensions exist in relation to each other and define each other. That simple picture has been modified in contemporary physics with the introduction of field theory from electricity and magnetism but, nevertheless, the fundamental referent of observation and of description remains the identifiable object or recorded datum.

By contrast, in psychology and the social sciences we have not yet made up our minds about the nature of our entities. We are by and large bogged down in 4-dimensional conceptions of atomistic psychic and social states or conditions, such as traits, or intelligence, or responses to stimuli, or social classes, or ill-defined bureaucracies.

Moreover, whereas the natural scientist is concerned to study only entities and constructed objective properties of those entities—objects and their length, density, elasticity, volume, charge, resistance, and some hundred other measurable properties—the human scientist is involved not only with psychological and social entities and their constructed objective properties but also with a third category of data; namely, the human preference for or valuation of all entities, and judgment of their utility. The separation of objectively constructed properties of psychic and social entities from individual preferences for entities, which differ from person to person, has not effectively been established.

A serious consequence of the situation in the human sciences is that it is not always clear whether price, or value, or judgment, or decision, or social class, or political attitude, or social benefit, or utility, or work are psychological or social entities to be counted, or objectively definable properties of entities to be measured, or preferential attitudes about entities to be rated. In the absence of clarity on this construction of knowledge, the problem of measurement becomes exceedingly complex, and unnecessarily so, as I shall endeavor to establish.

The main theme that I shall pursue is that many aspects of these problems of measurement can be resolved by shifting to a 5-dimensional framework for the human sciences. This shift will require the initial abstraction and identification of mental and social entities in terms of episodes with temporal duration. As shown in earlier chapters, the beginning and the planned ending of such episodes can be established and abstracted in terms of the objectifiable (socially contracted) intentions of the persons involved, and the achieved end in terms of the termination of the episode by those persons. The significance of the primary identification of mental and social entities in terms of episodes with duration is that they are full of human purpose and feeling and not trivial. And they are readily subject to simple and direct extensive measurement of the physical science type, in terms of the objective properties of time of targeted duration and time of actual duration of the episode.

It will be argued that the fundamental extensive measurement of time of duration of socially established goal-directed episodes may give the same kind of starting point for measurement of objective properties in the human sciences as the fundamental extensive measurement of length and mass give to the natural sciences.

The construction of such extensive measurement procedures then makes possible a clear distinction between the objective properties of human entities and individual preferences for those entities. The basis for this distinction lies in the fact that the objective measurement of properties demands the absolute zero of the positive real numbers of the ratio scale, whereas in the rating of preferences the zero is at most a point of indifference and negative real numbers are admissible.

In order to achieve the necessary precision of analysis, the term *quantify* will be used to refer to the general process of attaching numbers to entities, to properties, and to preferences and utilities. The specific terms *counting* entities, *measuring* properties, and *rating* preferences (including attitudes, utilities, and values) will then be used to refer to each separate mode of quantification.

WHAT IS "MEASUREMENT"?

There have been continual attempts since the time of Durkheim and Fechner in the late nineteenth century to put psychology and the social sciences on the same footing as the natural sciences with respect to measurement: the comparison is usually with the fundamental physical process of measuring length or mass. There have been those like Campbell, the physicist and measurement theorist, who believed that it was not possible to achieve

QUANTIFICATION IN THE HUMAN SCIENCES 261

this aim because the prime condition of measurement could not be fulfilled, namely, that "a physical process of addition should be found [for the property in question]. . . . The differences between properties that are and those that are not capable of satisfactory addition is roughly that between quantities and qualities" (Campbell, 1920, p. 267).

Others, like Hays, simply note that little or no natural concatenation of psychological data has yet been achieved; he states:

As yet, the social and behavior sciences lack clear agreement about those properties of man and his behavior that might be identified as fundamental *psychological* properties. Thus, for psychological measurement there exists no clear-cut parallel between such mathematical operations as addition and experimental psychological procedures. What exactly should one mean by psychological or behavioral addition? This problem may be solved some day; but at the present time only very primitive attempts have been made. It is safe to say that until the day comes and until psychologists and other behavioral scientists isolate and agree upon the fundamental measurement operations from which other measurement procedures will be derived and justified, the theory of measurement of psychological entities will be more incomplete and disorganized than measurement theory in the physical sciences [Hays, 1967, pp. 17–18].

Hays's argument is based on the fact that it is the "implicit psychological characteristics, abilities, wants, emotions, habits, attitudes, and perceptions, which are not directly observable but which must clearly lie behind their behaviors. In order to measure these psychological characteristics, one must infer their presence and their degree from behavior" (Hays, 1967, p. 19). He likens the psychologist's problem to that of the chemist trying to establish an, also implicit, atomic weight for an element. As I shall try to show, I do not think the problem lies here.

Coombs and his colleagues also seem to agree that: "No natural empirical addition arises in psychology" (Coombs, Dawes, and Tversky, 1970, p. 21). Later in the same work they suggest that "the absence of a natural concatenation (or even bisection) operation in many areas of psychology, has led to the development of measurement models of a different kind" (Coombs et al., 1970, p. 25).

Krantz and his coauthors have given the most comprehensive statement of these difficulties. They have noted that "in the behavioral sciences, extensive measures are virtually non-existent, whereas interval scales do arise from various procedures, including conjoint measurement" (Krantz et al., 1971, p. 517). In their view:

> [T]he attempt to apply extensive measures to the social sciences is beset with serious difficulties. In some instances, no operation is available; in others, the available operation either leads to trivial results or to a violation of the axioms. These difficulties have led to the development of other axiom systems as a basis for fundamental measurement in the social sciences, such as difference measurement and expected utility measurement. . . . Two psychological attributes, subjective probability and risk, are exceptional in that they appear to be extensively measurable" [Krantz et al., 1971, p. 124].

It is to this question of the seeming unavailability of simple and direct extensive measurement in the human sciences, except perhaps under very exceptional circumstances, that this chapter addresses itself. The mixture of views described is characteristic of the general outlook today. There is an inclination to agree with S. S. Stevens that physics-type extensive ratio-scale measurement is achievable in psychophysics but not in the broad area of psychological behavior as a whole.

The difficulties and uncertainties have three main sources: first, a failure to define what is being measured, so that no clear comparisons are possible; second, a failure to note that whereas physics deals with entities and the objectively definable properties of entities, psychology and the social sciences deal not only with these but with individual judgments about entities as well (including values, attitudes, and preferences), getting tangled up between these objectively definable properties and individual judgments; and third, a bogging-down in the world model of physics which excludes purpose and intention, whereas a world model which includes purpose and intention is called for where human activity is concerned, and when used, makes possible the objective measurement of properties. I shall deal with each point in turn.

The unclarity over definition, and the profound practical significance of that unclarity, can be shown in the various definitions of measurement which are used, for example, by the authors I have mentioned above. They are typical of the general outlook. S. S. Stevens, for example, defines measurement as the "assignment of numbers to objects according to rules" (Stevens, 1951). This sounds all right, until one notes that Coombs and his colleagues refer measurement not to objects but to properties. As they put it, "the process by which the scientist represents properties by numbers is called *measurement*" (Coombs et al., 1970, p. 7). But later on they bring in objects and scaling as well as properties and measurement: "The actual process of assigning numbers to objects, or properties, is called scaling" (p. 31).

This confusion between measurement as concerned

with objects or properties or both has serious consequences, as I hope to show in a moment. It is illustrated
in Hays, who defines measurement at first in such terms
as "certain properties of the things studied by the scientist are measured, or given numerical values" (Hays,
1967, p. 1). But then he uses the term *measurement* to
refer simply to classification, as, for example, to such processes as "seeing whether a certain solution is an acid or
a base" (p. 5) by inserting a piece of litmus paper into it
in order to classify it. Thus he writes that "the assignment
of objects of observation to categories according to some
classifying scheme and following some specified rules of
procedure is measurement at its simplest and most primitive level" (p. 7). By the same token, he argues that a
psychiatrist diagnostician determining whether or not to
classify a patient as psychotic is measuring the patient.
Then he applies the term *measurement* to the placing of
runners in a race in the order, 1, 2, and 3 (Hays, 1967,
p. 9), meaning, I suppose, that we measured the first, the
second, and the third runner by means of ranking order.

This indiscriminate use of the term *measurement* to
refer to such disparate procedures as assigning numbers
to objects, or to objective properties, or to individual preferences, and to assign objects or people to categories, is
characteristic of much writing in psychology. Yet in
everyday practice the term *measurement* is not used in
this way. Certainly the physicist does not use it so. He
distinguishes between two quantitative processes: one is
the process of enumeration, of counting how many entities there are, counting their frequency of occurrence perhaps, or counting how many stars of a certain type there
are; and a second is the process of measuring the properties of his entities, their objectively definable properties—their length, weight, temperature, wavelength of
emitted light, hardness, elasticity, horsepower, electrical

resistance, and so on. He does not refer to them both as "measurement." In physics, measurement theory is concerned solely with the assignment of numbers to the properties of entities (objects or events), and not to the entities themselves, or to classification, or to utility, or value or other attributes.

Krantz et al. have substantially clarified the definition of measurement. They define it as the existence of a well-defined homomorphism between an empirical and a numerical relational structure. The properties of the empirical structure must be shown to justify a numerical representation, and that proof constitutes a representational theorem.

Extensive measurement yielding ratio scales is based on the homomorphism of the empirical structure of a set of elements with an ordering relation of some kind and additive concatenation, and the numerical structure of the positive real numbers, the relation of greater than, and numerical addition; that is to say, the homomorphism of $\langle A, >, 0 \rangle$ into $\langle Re^+, >, + \rangle$ (Krantz et al., 1971, pp. 9–12, 71ff.).

Some ratio scales can also be derived by means other than extensive measurement; for example, by polynomial conjoint measurement and by taking differences of equal interval scales (Krantz et al., 1971, p. 518). But these methods of measurement depend on taking more than one attribute at a time, thus excluding the great simplicity of the extensive measurement of single properties in physics.

But even Krantz refers to all homomorphisms of the above type as measurement, including those whose data are based upon individual ratings of preferences as against data based upon the objective construction of properties. Despite the parsimony and clarity of their definition of measurement to cover all attributes, both properties and preferences, I shall argue that the distinction between these two types of attribute should be sustained, and shall show why.

QUANTIFICATION: COUNTING OF ENTITIES, MEASUREMENT OF PROPERTIES, RATING OF PREFERENCES—SOME DEFINITIONS

I propose that we should use the following terminology so that we can discriminate between significantly different processes of quantification, each being of importance in its own right. It is consistent with everyday usage.

The usage to which I am referring is the everyday sense of the difference between counting, measurement, rating or evaluation, and probabilistic judgment. When we ask someone to assign numbers to a pile of carpets in the sense of how many there are, we do not ask him to measure the number of carpets but to count them. If, however, we want to know whether the carpets will fit into a room, we do ask the person to measure the carpets, it usually being tacitly understood from the context that we mean him to measure not "the carpets" but the length and width of the carpets, by means of an objective yardstick. If, however, we want to know whether that person thinks the carpets are worth their asking price, we do not ask him to measure their value, we ask him to value them or to rate their value or evaluate their relative worth by giving us his individual or personal judgment of how he would rate them in relation to other similar carpets at different prices. If, finally, we want to know whether the carpets will wear well in the conditions under which they will be used, we do not ask to have their lasting qualities measured, we ask for a judgment of the probability of length of life (a judgment which might conceivably be aided by measuring certain objectively definable properties, such as the toughness of the jute backing, and taking such measures into account in making the probabilistic judgment).

Even in this simple example, the distinction between counted entity and objective measurement of property would in fact have to be made explicit if the carpet were to be ordered. The distinction in such a case would ordinarily be made in terms of *quantity* and *size*; that is to say, for example, counting out an order for one hundred carpets (counted entities, commonly called "quantity") measuring 15 feet by 10 feet (measured properties, commonly called "size" in such cases).

Now, the question which confronts us is whether or not to use the term *measurement* for all four procedures, as current measurement theory says ought to be done. It would mean a usage in which we would be forced to say, if we were to be consistent, "measure the number of carpets, measure their length and width, measure their value in relation to price, and measure the probability of their lasting." I cannot find that such a usage is employed by anyone, even by measurement theorists.

I propose, therefore, to use the following terms. I am using the term *entity* to comprehend objects, fields, events, episodes, including statements, which are objective in the sense of socially shareable.

I shall shorten the phrase "objectively definable property" to *property* to refer to objectively specifiable features of an entity. These features, such as length or hardness of things, or level of work, or length (temporal) of a contract, are objective in the sense that the way they can be observed, and eventually measured in magnitude, can be stated using a socially established instrument which permits of social agreement regarding the data in the sense that everyone using the instrument will arrive at the same measured quantity. Such properties give the ap-

pearance of being independent of people and consequently
inherent in the entity; but in fact they arise from people's
interaction with the entity, observation of objectifiable
data, and organization of the data in terms of constructs
called properties.

The phrase "individual judgments and preferences
about entities" (including utilities, attitudes, and values)
will be shortened to *preferences* to refer to the different
opinions which different individuals might have about
an entity such as beauty, or benefit, or usefulness, or
other valuation as compared with other entities, in terms
indicating which is preferred. Preferences are thus individual and personal feelings about an entity. They can
never be the subject of objectifiable social norms shared
by everyone, but only of norms which are individual.
Their outstanding characteristic is that they vary from
person to person, and in the same person from time to
time, in accord with personal feeling. I shall continue to
keep the concept of *probability* separate from preferences,
including utility, although I shall not deal with probability at any length.[1]

I shall use *quantification* to refer to the general process
of assigning numbers to entities, to properties, to preferences, and to probabilities. I shall then adopt the usage:
counting of the number of entities, *measurement* of the

[1] The problems of the nature of probability judgments and their
quantification are sensibly discussed by Phillips. He draws attention
to the inadequacies of both the psychophysical models and the infor-
mation-processing models for explaining probability judgments. He
puts forward an alternative model based upon the conception of judgment processes carried on within a hierarchy of mental structures.
This view is congruent with the discontinuity theory of levels of abstraction that I have outlined elsewhere (1976). It may be noted that
probability statements may be applied to the likely truth of retro-
dictive, dictive, and predictive statements about entities, properties,
or rating (Phillips, 1980).

objectively definable properties of entities, *rating* by individuals of the preferences (or utility) they attribute to entities,[2] and *quantified judgment* of the probability of outcome of the as yet unknown.

This terminological specification is critical for the human sciences, and for the demonstration of the importance of the 2-D analysis of time in establishing the nature of entities, properties, judgments, and probabilities in these sciences. In everyday usage, and in the natural sciences, the context will ordinarily let us know what is meant so that language can wander all over from measure, to count, to state the quantity or the number required, or the size, or the weight, or the price, or the size of the bargain. In the psychological and social sciences, however, the context is far from well enough established to allow of such linguistic looseness.

SOME CONSEQUENCES OF CONFUSING PROPERTIES WITH PREFERENCES

Physical scientists do not know it, nor do they have to know it, but when they qualify their entities they do so in terms of measuring their properties but do not get involved in rating preferences. The story in the natural sciences has of course not always been so straightforward. The natural scientist also, at one stage, was beset by confusion between objective properties of entities and anthropomorphic and magical attributions to entities. Indeed, one of the problems of objective definition of prop-

---

[2] This usage of rating allows the term *evaluation* to cover the total process of assessing the outcome and usefulness of given programs. That is to say, a full evaluation might include: a counting of certain effects; measurement of certain properties of the program and its effects; ratings of the social value of the program; and probabilistic judgments of the effects of permanent implementation of a pilot-tested program.

erties is precisely that of how to avoid such anthropomorphic attributions to physical things and to be able to know objectively that one is doing so. This process lies at the heart of the separation of science from magic. For the magical lies in the individual attribution of values to physical things as though these human values were properties of the things themselves. Part of the art of the magician is to make us believe that physical objects have taken on life. This primitive mixing of objective properties and attributed values, of the "real" and the "unreal," of science and magic, persists widely in the everyday world of belief in ghosts, in miasmatic theories of illness, in magical cures, in miracles, in misperceiving things seen in the sky as UFOs, in fears of the uncanny.

In natural science itself it has not always been easy to find the way through to the identification of objective properties. It took Galileo, for instance, to refute the Aristotelean conception that motion could occur only by the continued application of external forces and could not be inherent in things, and so to formulate his law of inertia.[3] Contrariwise, one of the major steps forward in chemistry was the recognition that heat is a property of molecular activity and not a calorific substance, namely, phlogiston, passing in its own right from one object to another. The overcoming of the problem of constructing properties lay in the great explosion of discoveries of scientific instruments which could be used for the objective measurement of such properties—the calorimeters, spectroscopes, thermometers, ohmeters, barometers, telescopes, microscopes, wattmeters, during the eighteenth and nineteenth centuries, and the enormously sophisticated instruments

---

[3] The law of continuous motion of objects unless decelerated or accelerated by external forces.

connected with research into the atomic world in the twentieth century.

In contrast to the modern natural scientist, human scientists have by and large tended to focus their activities upon the study of attitudes and judgments, and the processes of attributing individual values, preferences, and utilities to things. By comparison there is some but not much preoccupation with objectively constructed properties of psychological and social entities, which might constitute empirical relational structures which can be represented by the numerical relational structure $\langle RE^+, >, + \rangle$. Many serious consequences flow from this situation. There is the inhibition of the discovery of objectively definable properties through neglect of the necessary searching, or through searching in the wrong way and in the wrong place. Then there are many unrealistic arguments about values, arguments which are unrealistic and unresolvable in that they are really about objectively measurable properties and could be settled readily and effectively if such measurement were used. And then there is the turning away from purposefully directed mental activity itself, characteristic of behaviorism and other limited positivistic approaches to scientific method.

There are many studies and propositions, for example, in which preferences and properties are confused in the sense of each being mistaken for the other. The consequences can be socially and politically disruptive. There has been the failure to recognize that the level of responsibility in employment roles can be construed as an objective property of the work in the role, extensively measurable on a ratio scale by time-span of discretion, and is not merely a value to be attributed by job evaluation rating procedures[4] or by judgments obtained by so-

---

[4] So-called job or work measurement or job evaluation sometimes means a counting of outputs; sometimes a counting of the various

ciological surveys of the relative status ascribed to various occupational titles.[5]

Then there is the equally common misconception that an employee's performance—which can only in fact be an attribute rated by a manager—is a property of the employee's output to be measured objectively in terms of counting that output. Such thinking has been an effective obstacle in the way of the development of sound systems of differential reward in democratic industrial societies.

Then there are the so-called objective cost–benefit analyses which have become so widespread. In the first place the notion that cost is an objective property of things is a misplaced idea. Cost is in fact a subtle and complex and elusive mixture of material purchases, labor input, and investment—in the final analysis, the totality of labor value and investment value—all of which are attributed values based upon preference ratings. The mythology of costing and pricing is discussed in Brown and Jaques (1964). And in the second place there is the equally unrealistic—I think it would not be too strong in this case to call it absurd—idea that social benefit can be objectively measured, "scientifically evaluated" is the phrase, that it is an objectifiable property of the outcome of a program rather than an attributed value to be judged by policy-makers and those in receipt of the benefit of the

---

movements of the employee and a timing of those movements; sometimes a rating of performance value; sometimes a rating of responsibility; sometimes a rating of the social status of the job title. And the relative advantages of these various processes are argued about as though they were alternative methods of doing the same thing; that is, "measuring the job," for the same purpose, namely, paying for it. But, unfortunately, it rarely means measurement of the level of work in the role.

[5] The results of such surveys are one of the major attributed values built into our ill-conceived sociological conceptions of social class.

program.[6] Social scientists can be of assistance in gathering such attributed value judgments and, as many decision analysts do, in helping the policy-makers to arrive at their own best judgments. But objectively measured benefits as though they could be constructed as objectively definable properties and extensively measured, never!

It is not difficult to list other examples of such confusion between individually attributed values and objectively shareable properties—assessments of the outcome of psychological treatment, productivity bargaining, studies of quality of life, modes of changing attitudes, leadership training, historical materialism, the characteristics of groups—the list is readily enough lengthened. The question is what to do about it. My reply to that question is to turn to a model for the human world which includes purpose and intention. In order to demonstrate how and why such a step can transform the problems of measurement and rating in the human sciences, by pointing to a wide range of readily accessible empirical relational structures, amenable to extensive measurement, let me turn to the fundamental question of the measurement of properties of entities of any kind.

---

[6] For what would it mean to measure the benefit (a common enough phrase, in truth)? It could mean to count the particular outputs from a pilot social program: for example, in an alcohol detoxification program, a counting and statistical analysis of so many alcoholics treated on so many occasions, with an average frequency of so many treatments per person. Or it could mean to measure (or to try to measure) objectively certain inherent properties of the program or its outcomes, such as the low intensity of withdrawal symptoms in individuals. Or it could mean to rate the social value of the program to the alcoholics, and their families, and the community. Or it could mean to judge in quantified terms the probability that implementation of the program permanently on a wider scale might help to deal with the problem of alcoholism in the community. Or it could mean all four. It is important to know which.

ABSOLUTE ZERO-BASED CONCATENATION IN MEASUREMENT

It has long been noted that there are a very few—perhaps three—so-called fundamental methods of measurement in physics. These fundamental measures are length, weight, and time. The sense in which they are most commonly seen as fundamental, rather than derived, is that each is measured in terms of itself.[7] Length is measured by a concatenation of entities of equal length (say, sticks); weight is measured by a concatenation of entities of equal weights; time is measured by a concatenation of equal time intervals, such as swings of a pendulum.

In addition to the concept of fundamental measurement, it may prove useful to recognize that there is an important sense in which length measurement is primary. For both weight and time scales can be reduced to readings upon a length scale (and this is commonly done in our measuring instruments) by any of several means in each case; for example, by measuring time in terms of the rotation of a clock hand about a fixed center point, or measuring weight by equilibrium in rotation about a fixed fulcrum point, both of which can be reduced to readings in length measurement.

The significance of being able to reduce all measures to readings on a length scale is that the length scale gives a direct physical representation of the scale of positive real numbers—including both the continuity of the stick and the discontinuity of the numbered marks on the stick. I shall use this fact in demonstrating that equally fundamental measurement, using 2-D time, is not only pos-

[7] N. R. Campbell (1920) uses such a definition (p. 378), although he uses this categorization as a convenience rather than as the expression of some principle; and Krantz et al. (1971) follow this usage (p. 456).

sible in the human sciences, but that such measures abound naturally—they are all around us, staring us in the face, if we learn to see them. Let us, therefore, scrutinize this process of additive concatenation more closely, using fundamental length measurement for the purpose.

The process of extensive measurement by additive concatenation, as it is commonly described, is to take any unit length and then lay out a series of such lengths, as illustrated in Figure 12.1. This physical procedure establishes an empirical relational structure of the form $\langle A, >, 0 \rangle$ which is a homomorphism into the numerical relational structure $\langle RE^+, >, + \rangle$. The empirical elements can be mapped onto the scale of positive real numbers. In so doing, the same operations of addition can be carried out by arithmetic on the numerical scale, as by the more cumbersome laying out and counting of more and more sticks along the ground (i.e., 4 sticks added to 3 sticks will count up to 7 sticks, the same result as the arithmetical operation $3 + 4 = 7$).

There is a feature of this process which must be noted (Figure 12.2). It will be apparent that the zero in the numerical relational structure means real zero. But the equivalent zero on the sticks has to be explicated as well. It is at the left-hand end of the left-hand stick. It means that the sticks are asymmetrical in position, reading from left to right. And the significance of the zero point at the left end of the left stick is that there is absolutely no more property of length to the left of that point, and absolutely

FIGURE 12.1. Measurement by Additive Concatenation.

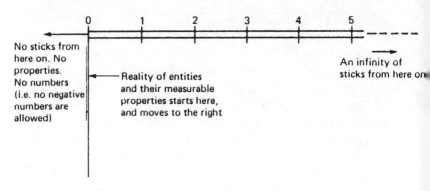

FIGURE 12.2. Significance of the Absolute Zero Point.

no more stick. It is a real zero: it means no more sticks; zero sticks; nil sticks; nothing; no more length, and certainly no negative length. It is an absolute zero: everything stops there.

It is, of course, the existence of this absolute zero, both in the empirical physical concatenation process and in the numerical positive real number model, which squeezes out of this process an equal-ratio scale, one in which 12 = 4 × 3 as well as 9 + 3; that is to say, a scale on which you can multiply and divide as well as add and subtract.

Finally, it is to be noted that the length scale—the physical scale, that is—has a most interesting feature, one which is possessed by no other measuring instrument. This feature is that the physical concatenation process can be represented on one stick, a length rule. It is an actual physical expression, a physical model, of the numerical positive real number scale,[8] illustrated in Figure

---

[8] I have always felt that the first person to mark off an absolute-zero-based equal-ratio scale and use it for measuring ought to have a place in the Hall of Fame between those other two well-known stalwarts of the development of civilization, the person who first used fire and the inventor of the wheel.

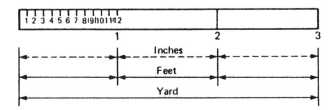

FIGURE 12.3. The Yardstick: An Absolute-Zero-Based Measuring Implement.

12.3 by a drawing of a yardstick divided into feet and inches. It could be further divided into ⅒″, or ⅟₁₀₀″, or even smaller segments. But no matter how finely it is divided, it retains two immediately and directly perceivable features: it is both finitely continuous and infinitely discontinuous. It is a physical manifestation of both the continuous thread and the discontinuous beads along the thread, used to descibe the number scale. In short, this type of rule is a complete empirical relational structure which gives an objective physical expression of the numerical structure of positive real numbers.

It is this feature of containing both continuity and discontinuity which allows the yardstick to be used to measure a 1′3″-long stick as a continuous 1′3″ enclosed within the discontinuous end-points at 0 at one end and at 1′3″ at the other—and to perceive this total state of affairs all at one and the same time. Extensive yardstick measurement of this kind is absolute-zero-based length measurement.

Let us now turn to measurement and rating in the human sciences. I propose to show how we can use extensive measurement to produce ratio scales of the properties of human entities. I shall also show that as far as rating of preferences is concerned, it is possible to generate ordinal and equal-interval scales but not equal-ratio scales. I shall advance a possible explanation for this

fundamental limitation with respect to the rating of preferences.

MEASUREMENT OF PROPERTIES OF ENTITIES IN THE HUMAN WORLD

If against this analysis of measurement in the natural
sciences we move to measurement in the human sciences,
a whole world of natural extensive measurement opens
up—measurement that is as straightforward and precise
as the fundamental measurement of length and mass of
physical objects, and most often with no problem of observer error.[9] To see that world, however, we shall have
to use a world model which retains purpose and intent.
Having done so, we can then measure directly in terms
of time the intended or planned or agreed times to be
allowed for gaining particular objectives as shown in the
descriptions of objectively established goal-directed episodes to be found elsewhere; and we can equally measure
the time taken for the achievement of those objectives.
I refer to such obvious entities and properties as: the
negotiated length of a contract; the time by which someone publicly commits himself to doing something; the
predicted and actual duration of an economic boom or
recession, or the time-scale of economic cycles; the potential five-year life of a parliament; the planned duration
of an engagement; the duration of a football game; the
periods chosen for planning cycles.

These lengths—lengths of time, that is—are true

[9] I shall not go into the question of errors of measurement—either
observer error or errors due to shortcomings in instruments such as,
for example, wear on the knife edge of a balance. But it may be of
interest to note that extensive measurement of a socially contracted
agreement to complete an assignment in, say, two days does not allow
of any observer or instrumental error. A publicly agreed two days is
two days.

measures of significant properties. Take, for example, the length of a contract; if a builder commits himself to finishing a particular job in three months rather than six months, that is a significant and objectively measurable difference. Equally, whether a football player, or a consultant, or a research unit, obtains a one-year, or a three-year, or a four-year, or a ten-year contract is a matter of great substance. And note, to obtain a four-year contract is to have a contract that is twice the length of a two-year contract. Or to add two years to a three-year contract gives a five-year contract. We are dealing here with simple and direct extensive measurement and ratio scaling. A contract of zero time duration is a zero contract: it does not exist.

The same features hold true of all other measurement of the property of the episodes which are the manifestations of psychological and social entities. It is no accident that time, duration, should enter in this way. The temporal length of an episode states its primary existential quality in the same sense that spatial length does for a physical object. The intended and the actual duration of an episode—whether a stated intention or a retrospectively constructed succession—yield two of its basic properties. Unlimited numbers of such natural measurements are available simply for the observing.[10]

[10] N. R. Campbell demonstrates the difficulty of dealing fully with time solely from the physicist's $4(3 + 1) - D$ perspective. He continued to bracket length, weight, and time as the three fundamental measures, even though he remained unsure of time. His intuition told him one thing, but his limited $4 - D$ conception made him doubt his judgment.

In his discussion of the conception of time, he writes: "All temporal conceptions depend on the immediate judgments of 'before,' 'after,' and 'simultaneous with,' " thus committing himself exclusively to the temporal axis of succession, as a physicist should and must do.

But then he adds: "all physical judgments can be ordered in respect of time. But the establishment of this order does not lead immediately

It may at first sight seem trivial and inconsequential to tie the fundamental measurement of properties of human entities simply to their intended and achieved durations. I do not believe that it is trivial. Such measurement is of no less consequence than is the fact that spatial length is the measurement of the basic property of physical entities. There is no special significance in the 3-D spatial length of something: it is what follows from such measurement that counts.

The same holds true for temporal length measurement of human entities. It gives a foundation measure which is not only akin to natural science measurement but is, I believe, the direct homology. As such it is scientifically impeccable. But, because it is a goal-directed temporal measure, this rigorously scientific measure cuts right into the heart of human life: into promises to do something by a certain time, and the keeping or not of those

---

to a system of measuring 'time,' because no satisfactory method of addition can be found. There is no rule whereby I can combine an event that occurs at 3 A.M. with one that occurs at 6 A.M. to make an event which occurs at 9 A.M. (. . . it is impossible to give any definition of the term beginning an 'event is . . .')" (Campbell, 1920, p. 550).

Campbell's difficulty arises from the fact that there is no such thing as an event which occurs *at* 6 A.M. or *at* 9 A.M. Events can occur only *between* 5 A.M. and 6 A.M. or *between* 8:59 A.M. and 9 A.M. That is to say, any event which exists in the sense that its properties are extensively measurable must have duration. And durations can be concatenated. An event which takes one hour can be added end to end to another event which takes two hours, to give a total of three hours of events; just as in physics you can place two sticks end to end and total their measured length.

I believe that Campbell failed to see this simple point because he had intuitively mixed up his physical event time of succession with time of intention and human purpose. From this latter point of view, his example could read, "Starting now at 3 A.M., instead of trying to finish at 6 A.M. take another three hours and try to finish by 9 A.M.," and that statement certainly does contain the temporal addition necessitated by the increase in time-span of intention for achieving the goal. But the addition is now on the temporal axis of intention.

promises; into wishes or longings that something might happen by a certain time, and the realization or not of those wishes or longings; into the anxieties that accompany the commitment to produce something for someone, and the awareness that time is running out and the commitment may not be fulfilled; into the sense of order which derives from things running as planned, in accord with schedule; into the disappointment, or anger or rage, when someone else fails to deliver on time; into the judgments about people's being reliable or unreliable. It is things like these that are at stake in the marriage of intention and achievement in human life: and it is precisely this interplay of intention and achievement which is objectively measurable in terms of time.

DERIVED MEASUREMENT OF PROPERTIES

When we come to derived measurements of properties, however, the situation, as in the natural sciences, becomes more complex. It calls for the development and construction of special instruments, one by one, just as the natural scientist had to do—and the formulating of the theories and laws which underlie their use. It is for this reason that I consider the time-span measurement of level of work (described elsewhere) and the possible time-frame measurement of level of individual capability (described elsewhere) of some interest as possible prototypes. They demonstrate that such derived measurement is at least possible. They suggest that the same search for extensive measuring instruments that proved so important for the development of the modern natural sciences could be equally important for the human sciences. The search for such instruments is not all that easy. They are not there, like ripe fruit, ready for the picking. But, on the other hand, unless they are specifically sought, as a matter of consciously informed effort, they will never be found at all.

It might, however, still be argued, I suppose, that objective derived measurement of truly human activity is impossible, is a contradiction in terms, for the subjective is not objectively measurable. Thus, for example, it has been asked about the measurement of level of work in time-span of discretion, "Where is the separate objective yardstick? Is not time-span of discretion based simply upon the subjective judgment of the manager about how long it should take his subordinate to complete certain tasks? Surely it is just a matter of subjective judgment, like rating any attributed or preference value. Another manager would have judged differently. It is all individually subjective. There is no objective socially shareable yardstick."

This argument might seem to be justified. There does not at first sight seem to be any materially objective yardstick like a foot rule or a spectrometer. But there is an objective independent instrument nonetheless. This instrument lies in the objectively definable procedure or operation of getting a manager to make an objectively shareable committed decision about the maximum target completion time he will allow for a given assignment—not his judgment against someone else's judgment, but a *binding decision* in the sense of being objectively, justiciably, binding upon both him and the subordinate by virtue of the employment contract. Decision processes of this kind (as compared, for example, with the more trivial decisions of much research concerned with the throwing of dice), and the resulting objectively stated decisions, are no less independent and objective than is reading a thermometer or a barometer.

I believe that this last point will prove to apply to all derived measurement of properties of psychological and social things. Stated in general terms the proposition is as follows. The measurement and definition of these properties lie in the construction and use of objectively share-able social instruments (social procedures) which commit at least two individuals to joint, or common, or related purposive episodes (defined in terms of time of intention), and stated in such a manner as to be independently jus-ticiable in the case of disagreement either about the orig-inal intent or about whether the intent was achieved in the objectively agreed time.

It is this independent open justiciable quality of com-mitted agreement between people that makes nonsense of the idea that social entities are not directly observable like physical entities are. The process and the decision whereby a manager commits a subordinate to a given task in a given time—or to take an example from above, that of an agreement on a term of contract—are just as observable as a granite rock or as a process such as a rainstorm. It requires as part of the observation that we listen to what the people are saying to one another, agree-ing with one another. Listening to what they say and agree is what transforms their subjective mental pro-cesses into objective facts. And it is precisely this fea-ture—this necessary leaving in of stated perceptions and memories, and desires, and intentions, and social com-mitment—which makes the most objective possible type of measurement of human activity so human rather than cold and dehumanizing. It is the socially objectified hu-man purpose which allows for the measurement of pur-pose in terms of the time of intention, and for the mea-surement of subsequent achievement as against intention, in terms of the time actually taken.

RATING OF INDIVIDUAL PREFERENCES COMPARED WITH MEASUREMENT OF PROPERTIES

The process of the rating of individual preferences has been completely separated from that of the measurement of objectifiable properties. This separation was made first of all because it was felt to be the most useful, or the most realistic, or, to put it quite simply, the right thing to do. This step, however, poses a serious philosophical problem, a problem which has dogged the whole of our argument about measurement of properties: how can we know whether a phenomenon is an objectively constructed property of a given entity, or a particular person's attitude toward that entity or personal judgment about it? The particular approach adopted to the solution of this philosophical problem (whether or not this approach is made explicit or left implicitly rattling around) exerts a powerful influence upon the development of quantitative methods and concepts. In considering this problem the following formulation suggested itself.

The most commonly held view is that both properties and preferences are quantifiable by a common process called measurement. Underlying this view there are some unstated philosophical assumptions, the most important of which is that properties and preferences are fundamentally the same, because, or at least so it is argued, if you can assign transitively ordered numbering to any phenomena then the phenomena must be of the same kind.[11] It is this view I wish to question.

[11] N. R. Campbell, for example, considers length, price, and beauty all to be properties of the entity judged. The only distinction he makes is between those properties that can be dealt with by the scientist because they can be subject to agreed quantitative judgment (he puts length and price together), and those which cannot (beauty). As he puts it: "The . . . property, beauty, can certainly not be measured, unless we accept the view . . . that beauty is determined by the market value. . . . Beauty is not a property with which science can have any-

If we ask, for example, "How long, how valuable, and how beautiful are given entities, and where are they located?" our sense says that length is an objectively existing social construction about the entity beheld in the sense that it can be measured in a way that does not vary between observers, whereas value and beauty will vary with the preferences in the eye of each individual beholder. Preferences are more in the nature of properties of the observer than properties of the entity observed. They are a statement of the attitude toward the entity of each individual person judging it. Preferences by different people with respect to the value or utility of the same thing may range from one extreme to the other: from beautiful to ugly, good to bad, desirable to undesirable, depending upon the observer. As every economist and shopkeeper knows, one man's meat is another man's poison.

There is a difference between phenomena which are possessed by an entity in the sense of a socially shared objectively definable quality of it (properties), and those which are related to individually variable attitudes toward the entity. The problem is to define the nature of the existence and the location of these phenomena. The answer lies, I think, in the process of natural concatenation and the meaning of zero. Let me recall. In the case of the measurement of properties, we started with an entity in existence. That existence gave us our fundamental measure of property: the property of spatial length in the case of physical entities and the property of temporal length in the case of psychological and social entities. If we now subtract an amount of length (spatial or temporal, as the case may be) equal to the amount of

---

thing to do, because no agreement can be obtained for judgments concerning it; it could only become a matter for scientific investigation if a relation can be established between it and some property, such as price, concerning which agreement can be obtained" (1920, p. 268).

that property, we get both a zero measurement for the property and an entity which no longer exists. Property and entity disappear together.

Now let us examine the process of rating individual preference-based judgments about an entity. Here I am including values such as goodness, and esthetic judgments such as beauty, utility, and desirability, and the attitudes which lead to preference ratings and to choices. The entities may be material, or psychological, or social. The essence of such preference rating is that it is always individual and always relative, always comparative. There is no absolute scale. One entity is always more or less beautiful than another, more or less valuable, more or less preferred, desirable, good, satisfactory, or useful.[12] This feature leads to a central focus upon relative ordering relationships and ordinal or interval scaling. (See, for example, Lindley [1971]; Phillips [1974].)

Natural concatenation, however, cannot be carried out with such ratings. The reason for this limitation lies in that important number, zero. Zero under conditions of preference rating does not mean no entity. It refers only to a person's attitude toward the entity. The most that it can mean is no value, no interest, no beauty, no utility, unpreferred, a neutral or disinterested attitude as far as any given rater is concerned. It not only does not mean zero entity, it means a definitely existing entity, there to be valued, or rated, but not arousing any single sense of value common to everyone. Indeed, the value can become negative, and rating scales are, of course, frequently constructed in this way: the negative rating, quantified

[12] Ward Edwards emphasizes this point in his writings on multiattribute utility measurement (see, for example, Edwards and Guttentag [1975]).

in negative numbers, expressing ugliness, disutility, bad-ness, unsatisfactoriness, rejected rather than preferred.

We can now discover the meaning and location of pref-erences. Going through the same exercise as for meas-urement of properties, we start with an entity in existence. We can now rate the entity for particular attributes, by comparing it with other entities of the same type. We can then reduce the rating to zero (or even minus), but the entity does not disappear as it does in the case of entities and properties; it continues to exist as a zero- or minus-rated entity.

In short, an entity can be said to possess properties in the sense that entity and property coexist: zero prop-erty—zero entity. By contrast, entities and preferences about them may be said to be coincident but not coexis-tent: one is not absolutely dependent upon the other. Hence, zero preference—plenty of entity. Properties are measured on absolute-zero-based scales; preferences are rated on relative-zero-based, ordinal, interval, and ratio scales. Rating of preferences, however, can yield only or-dinal and interval scales. Such ratings cannot possibly yield ratio scaling, since there is no absolute zero: and if the data can be treated so as to derive a ratio scale, then it is because an objective property has been made explicit. And, be it noted, even the ordinal and interval scales obtained by preference rating are different from those obtained by measurement: they have neither absolute zero nor natural concatenation, at least one of which is present in the case of the ordinal and interval measure-ment of objective properties.[13]

[13] A brief study by Robyn Dawes, for example, illustrates the con-sequence of the failure to distinguish between scaling for the mea-surement of properties and scaling for the rating of preferences. He took five scales which had been constructed for the rating of various judgments in other studies—for example, ratings of authoritarianism, of the value of a police–community relations program, and of the

As against this analysis of a fundamental distinction between properties and attributes of entities, it might, I suppose, be argued that properties are themselves psychological attributions to objects, that they are merely the way human beings see their world. It should be obvious, however, that I am consistently referring to a phenomenal construction of the world, and in no way suggesting that the operational definition of properties by measurement somehow tells us about the nature of the noumenal world, about what is "really" out there. Entities, properties, and preferences are all aspects of the human construction of the world. This fact holds just as true for psychophysical measurement of color, of sones, of lumens, for which precise relationships are obtained between regularities in psychological responses to variations in the quantity of particular properties of a physical stimulus (Stevens, 1959).

It is essential, however, that we distinguish in that construction between phenomena that are objectively constructed and hence coexistent with particular entities

---

"attractiveness" of various Army jobs—and modified the questions so that they referred to estimates of the height of a number of people. He then demonstrated that these scales "gave a very reasonable estimate of height." He does not state, however, that height is an objectively definable property of a physical organism, and not an attributed value, and that the estimated scaling for height is based upon an absolute-zero which starts at the floor upon which the subjects are standing. Estimation of height is an estimate of a measure of a property: the estimates can be compared with a ratio-length measure; and zero height, no person! The values for which these rating scales were originally developed can be used only to compare the distribution and range of preference attributions made by a population of individuals using the scales; and a zero rating expresses only the relative indifference of the individual rater. The fact, therefore, that the scales when adapted for height measurement give reasonable estimates is not relevant with respect to their use for collecting information about the preference judgments which individuals attribute to things (Dawes, 1977, pp. 267–273).

and those which are individual opinions and merely coincident.

LEBESGUE AND MEASUREMENT MATHEMATICS

The foregoing argument receives support from the developments in measurement mathematics associated with Henri Lebesgue (1966). Lebesgue sets out three fundamental conditions for the definition of magnitudes assigned to bodies (1966, pp. 128–131).

(a) a magnitude G is said to be defined for the bodies belonging to a given family of bodies if, for each of them and for each position of each of them, a definite positive number can be assigned;
(b) if a body C is partitioned into a certain number of sub-bodies, $C_1, C_2, C_3, \ldots C_p$, and if for these bodies the magnitude G is g on the one hand and $g_1, g_2, g_3, \ldots g_p$, on the other, we must have
$$G = g_1 + g_2 + \ldots + g_p;$$
(c) the family of bodies for which a magnitude is defined must be sufficiently extensive for every body in the family to be reducible to a single point by successive reductions (without its leaving the family) in such a way that in the course of these reductions the magnitude decreases continuously from its original value to zero.[13]

---

[13] These propositions have been expressed mathematically in terms of "systematic methods of assigning a 'length' or measure of [subsets of the real line], and any such assignment should 'behave reasonably.' Experience defines this reasonable behavior as follows:

Let S be a collection of subsets of $[a, b]$ which is closed under countable unions, that is, if

$A_1, A_2, \ldots \varepsilon S$, then $\overset{\infty}{\underset{n=1}{\bigcirc}} A_n \varepsilon S$.

(i) A *set function* on S is a function which assigns to each set $S \varepsilon S$ a real number.

These conditions clarify the distinction between entities and their objective properties, and separate both from preference judgments about entities. Lebesgue distinguishes between two phenomena: first there are sets or families of bodies, and second there are the measured magnitudes of bodies composing the sets. Bodies are simply physical entities as used by Lebesgue: and he deals with the numbers of bodies in a set by enumeration.[14] Measured magnitude is the phrase used to describe properties: Lebesgue, in his examples, uses length, mass, vol-

---

(ii) A set function μ on S is called a *measure* if

   (a) $0 \leq \mu(A) \leq b - a$ for every $A \varepsilon S$,

   (b) $\mu(\phi) = 0$,

   (c) whenever $A \subset B_\infty$ and $A, B \varepsilon S$, then $\mu(A) \leq \mu(B)$ (monotonicity),

   (d) whenever $A = \cup A_n$, where $A_n \varepsilon S$ for $n = 1, 2 \ldots$ and
$$n = 1$$
$A_n \cap A_m = \phi$ for $n = m$, then
$$\mu(A) = \Sigma \, \mu(A_n)$$
$$n = 1$$

(countable additivity).

We will also require that subintervals of $[a, b]$ be in S, and the Lebesgue measure of an interval be equal to its ordinary length. Finally, we hope that every subset of $[a, b]$ will be in S, that is, we will be able to take the measure of any subset of $[a, b]$. However, we will see that this will be impossible if we wish to retain countable additivity (property (d) in the definition)" (Wilcox and Myers, 1978, pp. 15 and 16).

[14] Despite the fact that he defines measurement as all processes of assigning numbers to things, Campbell in practice also distinguishes measurement from enumeration and counting. He uses these terms to refer to the process of determining the numerosity of the members composing a system. These members are described as objects. He ties enumeration and counting to the identification of objects in a very fundamental way: "The division of our experience into individual òbjects is simply based on the conditions in which the conditions necessary for enumeration are found. What has been said about the division of a system into members, or individual objects, applies equally to the selection of the operation which is to be used to distinguish the objects in the process of counting" (Campbell, 1920, p. 298).

ume. That he does not concern himself with ratings of preferences can be shown by reference to the conditions.

The first condition would apply both to measurement of properties and to rating of preferences: the duration of a service contract (a measurable property) may be 4 years (say) and its value (a rated attribute) $10,000.

The second condition applies to property measurement, but does not necessarily apply to preference rating. If a 4-year contract is partitioned into a 3-year followed by a 1-year contract, then the partition of its measured magnitude of duration maps on to $4 = 3 + 1$. But it does not necessarily follow that the assessed, or rated, $10,000 value will divide into an assessment (rating) of $7,500 for the first part and an assessment of $2,500 for the second: the parts of the divided contract may have enhanced value, or diminished value, or no value at all.

The third condition also applies to property measurement but does not apply at all to preference ratings. A service contract is readily reducible by successive reductions to a mathematical point, in such a way that its intended length of time reduces continuously to zero; it is so reducible regardless of who does the reduction. But as far as value rating is concerned, a shortened contract may in fact increase in value to the point where completion in no time at all would be infinitely valuable; what actually happens will vary according to the particular person who is doing the valuation (the rating).

It may be noted that it is the combination of the second and the third conditions from which are derived the concatenative process and the absolute-zero baseline which were found to be critical for the quantification of properties, and for equal–ratio scaling. The absence of these conditions characterizes preference ratings, and precludes equal–ratio scaling of preferences.

In short, the Lebesgue conditions for the rigorous

mathematical definition of the measurement of magnitudes (the assignment of magnitudes to bodies) apply
clearly and systematically to the measurement of objective properties of human entities. These conditions thus
define such objective properties. It is equally clear that
the conditions do not apply to rating procedures for quan-
tifying preferences attributed by individuals to entities.
Such preferences require to be defined by other means—by
the definition of rating procedures.

Finally, it may be of interest to note how Lebesgue
himself fails to apply his conditions rigorously when he
turns briefly to examples using social entities. He states:
"The number of magnitudes is vast. As we have seen, it
includes numbers associated with geometry and physics
and also numbers having to do with economic questions,
such as the price of a piece of merchandise, the time
necessary to manufacture it, etc." (Lebesgue, 1966, p.
133).

The time necessary to manufacture a piece of merchandise is certainly a measured magnitude of the process. It will be self-evident that it conforms to all three
conditions of measurement. It will be equally evident,
however, that the price of a piece of merchandise does not
so conform. Price does not necessarily reduce as you reduce a piece of merchandise; different people will react
differently to such changes. Indeed, the price may increase with decrease in size if miniaturization is valued.
In fact, further consideration suggests that price is itself
a social entity associated with, or attaching to, the piece
of merchandise, and is not a measured magnitude. As an
entity, a price itself has a measurable magnitude, namely,
amount of money. As you reduce price by successive reductions to a point, the money quantity reduces continuously to zero. The recognition of social entities and their

measured magnitudes (or objective properties) requires special care.

Lebesgue's correct example—that of time necessary to manufacture a piece of merchandise—illustrates our general theme. This period of time is the measured time-span of achievement for the process. In order to get this measure, however, there must be a starting point as well as a completion point. The starting point is the point of intention, with an equally measurable time of intention. It is this latter measure which is the true beginning of mathematically rigorous measurement of human entities. Human purpose provides the foundation for the scientific study of human activity.

SUMMARY

In this chapter I have tried to demonstrate the importance of keeping purpose and intention in the analysis and measurement of human behavior, in two ways: first, in the clarification of the definition of psychological and social entities as categories of episode; and second, in the separation out of the objectively definable properties of such entities from the attributed preferences of individuals associated with them. The entities are quantifiable by assigning unity to each case and then using counting (enumeration) procedures. Objective properties of entities are definable and measurable by mapping on to an objective time yardstick marked out with a ratio–length scale. Preferences attributed to entities are definable and quantifiable by ordering personal judgments to ordinal or interval scales by rating procedures.

By taking intentional goal-directed activity and episodes as the starting point for the construction of a scientific study of social and psychological phenomena, it is possible to put the human sciences on precisely the same

294CREATIVITY AND WORK

footing with respect to measurement and quantification as the physical sciences. Paradoxically, the more "human," the more full of meaning, intention, desire, need, will, feeling, we keep our psychological and social sciences, the more quantitative and "scientific" they can become, in the sense both of the rigor and of the elegance of measurement.

REFERENCES

Brown, W., & Jaques, E. (1964), *Product Analysis Pricing*. London: William Heinemann Educational Books Ltd.
Campbell, N. R. (1920), *Foundations of Science: The Philosophy of Theory and Experiment* (formerly entitled *Physics, the Elements*). New York: Dover, 1957.
Coombs, C., Dawes, R., & Tversky, A. (1970), *Mathematical Psychology*. Englewood Cliffs, NJ: Prentice-Hall.
Dawes, R. M. (1977), Suppose we measured height with rating scales instead of rulers? *Appl. Psychol. Meas.*, 1:43–59.
Edwards, W., & Guttentag, M. (1975), Effective evaluation. In: *Evaluation and Experiment*, ed. C. A. Bennett & A. Lumsdaine. New York: Academic Press.
Hays, W. L. (1967), *Quantification in Psychology*. California: Brooks/Cole.
Jaques, E. (1976), *A General Theory of Bureaucracy*. Exeter, NH: Heinemann Educational Books Ltd.
Krantz, D. H., Luce, R. D., Suppes, P., & Tversky, A. (1971), *Foundations of Measurement*, Vol. 1. New York: Academic Press.
Lebesgue, H. (1966), Measure and magnitude. In: *Measure and the Integral*, trans. & ed. K. May. San Francisco: Holden-Day.
Lindley, D. (1971), *Making Decisions*. London: John Wiley.
Phillips, L. D. (1974), *Bayesian Statistics for Social Scientists*. New York: Cromwell.
——— (1980), *Generation Theory*. Working Paper 80-1. Uxbridge, Middlesex, UK: Brunel University Decision Analysis Unit.
Roberts, F. (1979), *Measurement Theory*, Vol. 4, *Encyclopedia of Mathematics and Its Applications*. Reading, MA: Addison-Wesley, Advanced Book Program.
Stevens, S. S. (1951), Mathematics, measurement and psychophysics. In: *Handbook of Experimental Psychology*, ed. S. S. Stevens. New York: John Wiley.
——— (1959), Measurement, psychophysics and utility. In: *Measurement: Definitions and Theories*, ed. C. W. Churchman & P. Ratooch. New York: John Wiley.

Wilcox, H. J., & Myers, D. L. (1978), *Introduction to Lebesgue Integration and Fourier Series*. Huntington, NY: Krieger.

Chapter 13

Death and the Midlife Crisis

In the course of the development of the individual there
are critical phases which have the character of change
points, or periods of rapid transition. Less familiar perhaps, though nonetheless real, are the crises which occur
around the age of thirty-five—which I shall term the
midlife crisis—and at full maturity around the age of
sixty-five. It is the midlife crisis with which I shall deal
in this paper.

When I say that the midlife crisis occurs around the
age of thirty-five, I mean that it takes place in the middle
thirties, that the process of transition runs on for some
years, and that the exact period will vary among individuals. The transition is often obscured in women by the
later onset of changes connected with the menopause. In
the case of men, the change has from time to time been
referred to as the male climacteric, because of the reduction in the intensity of sexual behavior which often occurs
at that time.

CRISIS IN GENIUS

I first became aware of this period as a critical stage in
development when I noticed a marked tendency toward
crisis in the creative work of great men in their middle

and late thirties. It is clearly expressed by Richard
Church in his autobiography *The Voyage Home*:

> There seems to be a biological reason for men and
> women, when they reach the middle thirties, finding
> themselves beset with misgivings, agonizing inquiries,
> and a loss of zest. Is it that state which the medieval
> schoolmen called *accidie*, the cardinal sin of spiritual
> sloth? I believe it is [1964, p. 139].

This crisis may express itself in three different ways:
the creative career may simply come to an end, either in
a drying-up of creative work, or in actual death; the creative capacity may begin to show and express itself for
the first time; or a decisive change in the quality and
content of creativeness may take place.

Perhaps the most striking phenomenon is what happens to the death rate among creative artists. I had got
the impression that the age of thirty-seven seemed to
figure pretty prominently in the death of individuals of
this category. This impression was upheld by taking a
random sample of some 310 painters, composers, poets,
writers, and sculptors, of undoubted greatness or of genius. The death rate shows a sudden jump between thirty-
five and thirty-nine, at which period it is much above the
normal death rate. The group includes Mozart, Raphael,
Chopin, Rimbaud, Purcell, Baudelaire, Watteau. There
is then a big drop below the normal death rate between
the ages of forty and forty-four, followed by a return to
the normal death rate pattern in the late forties. The
closer one keeps to genius in the sample, the more striking and clear-cut is this spiking of the death rate in midlife.

The change in creativity which occurs during this period can be seen in the lives of countless artists. Bach,
for example, was mainly an organist until his cantorship

at Leipzig at thirty-eight, at which time he began his
colossal achievements as a composer. Rossini's life falls
into two distinct periods: great creativity up to the age
of forty; and then seclusion and silence until his death
at the age of seventy-four. Racine had thirteen years of
continuous success culminating in *Phèdre* at the age of
thirty-eight; he then produced nothing for some twelve
years. The characteristic work of Goldsmith, Constable,
and Goya emerged between the ages of thirty-five and
thirty-eight. By the age of forty-three Ben Jonson had
produced all the plays worthy of his genius, although he
lived to be sixty-four. At thirty-three Gauguin gave up
his job in a bank, and by thirty-nine had established
himself in his creative career as a painter. Donatello's
work after thirty-nine is described by a critic as showing
a marked change in style, in which he departed from the
statuesque balance of his earlier work and turned to the
creation of an almost instantaneous expression of life.

Goethe, between the ages of thirty-seven and thirty-
nine, underwent a profound change in outlook, associated
with his trip to Italy. As many of his biographers have
pointed out, the importance of this journey and this period
in his life cannot be exaggerated. He himself regarded it
as the climax to his life. Never before had he gained such
complete understanding of his genius and mission as a
poet. His work then began to reflect the classical spirit
of Greek tragedy and of the Renaissance.

Michelangelo carried out a series of masterpieces until
he was forty: his "David" was finished at twenty-nine,
the decoration of the roof of the Sistine Chapel at thirty-
seven, and his "Moses" between thirty-seven and forty.
During the next fifteen years little is known of any artistic work. There was a creative lull until, at fifty-five,
he began to work on the great Medici monument and

then later on "The Last Judgment" and frescoes in the Pauline Chapel.

Let me make it clear that I am not suggesting that the careers of most creative persons either begin or end during the midlife crisis. There are few creative geniuses who live and work into maturity, in whom the quality of greatness cannot be discerned in early adulthood in the form either of created works or of the potential for creating them: Beethoven, Shakespeare, Goethe, Couperin, Ibsen, Balzac, Voltaire, Verdi, Handel, Goya, Dürer, to name but a very few at random. But there are equally few in whom a decisive change cannot be seen in the quality of their work—in whose work the effects of their having gone through a midlife crisis cannot be discerned. The reactions range all the way from severe and dramatic crisis, to a smoother and less troubled transition—just as reactions to the phase of adolescent crisis may range from severe disturbance and breakdown to relatively ordered readjustment to mental and sexual adulthood—but the effects of the change are there to be discerned. What then are the main features of this change?

There are two features which seem to me of outstanding importance. One of these has to do with the mode of work; the second has to do with the content of the work. Let me consider each of these in turn. I shall use the phrase "early adulthood" for the pre-midlife phase, and "mature adulthood" for the postmidlife phase.

CHANGE IN MODE OF WORK

I can best describe the change in mode of work which I have in mind by describing the extreme of its manifestation. The creativity of the twenties and the early thirties tends to be a hot-from-the-fire creativity. It is intense and spontaneous, and comes out ready-made. The spontaneous effusions of Mozart, Keats, Shelley, Rimbaud are the prototype. Most of the work seems to go on unconsciously. The conscious production is rapid, the pace of creation often being dictated by the limits of the artist's capacity physically to record the words or music he is expressing.

A vivid description of early-adult type of work is given in Gittings's biography of Keats:

> Keats all this year had been living on spiritual capital. He had used and spent every experience almost as soon as it had come into his possession, every sight, person, book, emotion or thought had been converted spontaneously into poetry. Could he or any other poet have lasted at such a rate? . . . He could write no more by these methods. He realized this himself when he wished to compose as he said "without fever." He could not keep this high pulse beating and endure [Gittings, 1954, p. 178].

By contrast, the creativity of the late thirties and after is a sculpted creativity. The inspiration may be hot and intense. The unconscious work is no less than before. But there is a big step beween the first effusion of inspiration and the finished created product. The inspiration itself may come more slowly. Even if there are sudden bursts of inspiration, they are only the beginning of the work process. The initial inspiration must first be externalized in its elemental state. Then begins the process of forming and fashioning the external product, by means of working and reworking the externalized material. I use the term *sculpting* because the nature of the sculptor's material—it is the sculptor working in stone of whom I am thinking—forces him into this kind of relationship with the product of his creative imagination. There occurs a process of interplay between unconscious intuitive work and inspiration, and the considered perception of the externally emergent creation and the reaction to it.

In her note "A Character Trait of Freud's," Riviere (1958) describes Freud's exhorting her in connection with some psychoanalytic idea which had occurred to her:

> Write it, write it, put it down in black and white . . . get it out, produce it, make something of it—*outside you*, that is; give it an existence independently of you [p. 146].

This externalizing process is part of the essence of work in mature adulthood, when, as in the case of Freud, the initially externalized material is not itself the end product, or nearly the end product, but is rather the starting point, the object of further working over, modification, elaboration, sometimes for periods of years.

In distinguishing between the precipitate creativity of early adulthood and the sculpted creativity of mature adulthood, I do not want to give the impression of drawing a hard and fast line between the two phases. There are of course times when a creative person in mature adulthood will be subject to bursts of inspiration and rapid-fire creative production. Equally, there will be found instances of mature and sculpted creative work done in early adulthood. The "David" of Michelangelo is, I think, the supreme example of the latter.

But the instances where work in early adulthood has the sculpted and worked-over quality are rare. Sometimes, as in scientific work, there may be the appearance of sculpted work. Young physicists in their twenties, for example, may produce startling discoveries, which are the result of continuous hard work and experimentation. But these discoveries result from the application of modern theories about the structure of matter—theories which themselves have been the product of the sculpted work of mature adulthood of such geniuses as Thomson and Einstein.

Equally, genuinely creative work in mature adulthood may sometimes not appear to be externally worked over and sculpted, and yet actually be so. What seems to be rapid and unworked-over creation is commonly the re-working of themes which have been worked upon before, or which may have been slowly emerging over the years in previous works. We need look no farther than the work of Freud for a prime example of this process of books written rapidly, which are nevertheless the coming to fruition of ideas which have been worked upon, fashioned, reformulated, left incomplete and full of loose ends, and then reformulated once again in a surging forward through the emergence of new ideas for overcoming pre-vious difficulties.

The reality of the distinction comes out in the fact that certain materials are more readily applicable to the precipitate creativity of early adulthood than are others. Thus, for example, musical composition, lyrical poetry, are much more amenable to rapid creative production than are sculpting in stone or painting in oils. It is note-worthy, therefore, that whereas there are very many poets and composers who achieve greatness in early adulthood—indeed in their early twenties or their late teens—there are very few sculptors or painters in oils who do so. With oil paint and stone, the working rela-tionship to the materials themselves is of importance, and demands that the creative process should go through the stage of initial externalization and working-over of the externalized product. The written word and musical notation do not of necessity have this same plastic ex-ternal objective quality. They can be sculpted and worked over, but they can also readily be treated merely as a vehicle for the immediate recording of unconsciously articulated products which are brought forward whole and complete—or nearly so.

QUALITY AND CONTENT OF CREATIVITY

The change in mode of work, then, between early and mature adulthood is a change from precipitate to sculpted creativity. Let me now consider for a moment the change in the quality and content of the creativity. The change I have in mind is the emergence of a tragic and philosophical content which then moves on to serenity in the creativity of mature adulthood, in contrast to a more characteristically lyrical and descriptive content to the work of early adulthood. This distinction is a commonly held one, and may perhaps be considered sufficiently self-evident to require little explication or argument. It is implied, of course, in my choice of the adjectives "early" and "mature" to qualify the two phases of adulthood which I am discussing.

The change may be seen in the more human, tragic and less fictitious and stage quality of Dickens's writing from *David Copperfield* (which he wrote at thirty-seven) onwards. It may be seen also in the transition in Shakespeare from the historical plays and comedies to the tragedies. When he was about thirty-one, in the midst of writing his lyrical comedies, he produced *Romeo and Juliet*. The great series of tragedies and Roman plays, however, began to appear a few years later; *Julius Caesar, Hamlet, Othello, King Lear*, and *Macbeth* are believed to have been written most probably between the ages of thirty-five and forty.

There are many familiar features of the change in question. Late adolescent and early adult idealism and optimism accompanied by split-off and projected hate, are given up and supplanted by a more contemplative pessimism. There is a shift from radical desire and impatience to a more reflective and tolerant conservatism. Beliefs in the inherent goodness of man are replaced by a recognition and acceptance of the fact that inherent goodness is accompanied by hate and destructive forces within, which contribute to man's own misery and tragedy. To the extent that hate, destruction, and death are found explicitly in early adult creativeness, they enter in the form of the satanic or the macabre, as in Poe and in Baudelaire, and not as worked-through and resolved anxieties.

The spirit of early adult creativeness is summed up in Shelley's *Prometheus Unbound*. Shelley's wife suggests that a feature of his view of humanity is that evil is not inherent in human nature; he believed, with passion, that all that was necessary was for mankind to will that evil should disappear and there would be none.

This early adult idealism is built upon the use of unconscious denial and manic defenses as normal processes of defense against two fundamental features of human life—the inevitableness of eventual death, and the existence of hate and destructive impulses inside each person. I shall try to show that the explicit recognition of these two features, and the bringing of them into focus, is the quintessence of successful weathering of the midlife crisis and the achievement of mature adulthood.

It is when death and human destructiveness—that is to say, both death and the death instinct—are taken into account, that the quality and content of creativity change to the tragic, reflective, and philosophical. The depressive position must be worked through once again, at a qualitatively different level. The misery and despair of suffering and chaos unconsciously brought about by oneself are encountered and must be surmounted for life to be endured, and for creativity to continue. Nemesis is the key, and tragedy the theme, of its recognition.

The successful outcome of mature creative work lies thus in constructive resignation both to the imperfections of men and to shortcomings in one's own work. It is this constructive resignation that then imparts serenity to life and work.

THE DIVINE COMEDY

I have taken these examples from creative genius because I believe the essence of the midlife crisis is revealed in its most full and rounded form in the lives of the great. It will have become manifest that the crisis is a depressive crisis, in contrast to the adolescent crisis, which tends to be a paranoid–schizoid one. In adolescence, the predominant outcome of serious breakdown is schizophrenic illness; in midlife the predominant outcome is depression, or the consequences of defense against depressive anxiety as reflected in manic defenses, hypochondriasis, obsessional mechanisms, or superficiality and character deterioration. Working through the midlife crisis calls for a reworking through of the infantile depression, but with mature insight into death and destructive impulses to be taken into account.

This theme of working through depression is magnificently expressed in *The Divine Comedy*. This masterpiece of all time was begun by Dante following his banishment from Florence at the age of thirty-seven. In the opening stanzas he creates his setting in words of great power and tremendous psychological depth. He begins:

In the middle of the journey of our life, I came to myself within a dark wood where the straight way was lost.

Ah, how hard it is to tell of that wood, savage and harsh
and dense, the thought of which renews my fear. So
bitter is it that death is hardly more [1946a, p. 61, lines
1–10].

These words have been variously interpreted; for example, as an allegorical reference to the entrance to hell, or
as a reflection of the poet's state of mind on being forced
into exile, homeless and hungry for justice. They may,
however, be interpreted at a deeper level as the opening
scene of a vivid and perfect description of the emotional
crisis of the midlife phase, a crisis which would have
gripped the mind and soul of the poet whatever his religious outlook, or however settled or unsettled his external affairs. The evidence for this conclusion exists in
the fact that during the years of his early thirties which
preceded his exile, he had already begun his transformation from the idyllic outlook of the *Vita Nuova* (age
twenty-seven–twenty-nine) through a conversion to "philosophy" which he allegorized in the *Convivio* written
when he was between thirty-six and thirty-eight years
of age.

Even taken quite literally, *The Divine Comedy* is a
description of the poet's first full and worked-through
conscious encounter with death. He is led through hell
and purgatory by his master Virgil, eventually to find
his own way, guided by his beloved Beatrice, into para-
dise. His final rapturous and mystical encounter with the
being of God, represented to him in strange and abstract
terms, was not mere rapture, not simply a being overwhelmed by a mystical oceanic feeling. It was a much
more highly organized experience. It was expressly a vision of supreme love and knowledge, with control of impulse and of will, which promulgates the mature life of
greater ease and contemplation which follows upon the

working-through of primitive anxiety and guilt, and the return to the primal good object.

Dante explicitly connects his experience of greater mental integration, and the overcoming of confusion, with the early infantile relation to the primal good object. As he nears the end of the 33rd Canto of "Paradiso," the climax of his whole grand scheme, he explains:

> Now my speech will come more short even of what I remember than an infant's who yet bathes his tongue at the breast [1946b, p. 482, lines 106–108].

But the relationship with the primal good object is one in which reparation has been made, "Purgatorio" has been traversed, loving impulses have come into the ascendant, and the cruelty and harshness of the superego expressed in the inferno have been relieved. Bitterness has given way to composure.

In Dante, the result of this deep resolution is not the reinforcing of manic defense and denial which characterizes mystical experience fused with magic omnipotence; but rather the giving up of manic defense, and consequent strengthening of character and resolve, under the dominion of love. As Croce (1922) has observed:

> What is not found in the "Paradiso," for it is foreign to the spirit of Dante, is flight from the world, absolute refuge in God, asceticism. He does not seek to fly from the world, but to instruct it, correct it, and reform it ... he knew the world and its doings and passions [p. 279].

AWARENESS OF PERSONAL DEATH

Although I have thus far taken my examples from the extremes of genius, my main theme is that the midlife crisis is a reaction which not only occurs in creative genius, but manifests itself in some form in everyone. What then is the psychological nature of this reaction to the midlife situation, and how is it to be explained?

The simple fact of the situation is the arrival at the midpoint of life. What is simple from the point of view of chronology, however, is not simple psychologically. The individual has stopped growing up, and has begun to grow old. A new set of external circumstances has to be met. The first phase of adult life has been lived. Family and occupation have become established (or ought to have become established unless the individual's adjustment has gone seriously awry); parents have grown old, and children are at the threshold of adulthood. Youth and childhood are past and gone, and demand to be mourned. The achievement of mature and independent adulthood presents itself as the main psychological task. The paradox is that of entering the prime of life, the stage of fulfillment, but at the same time the prime and fulfillment are dated. Death lies beyond.

I believe, and shall try to demonstrate, that it is this fact of the entry upon the psychological scene of the reality and inevitability of one's own eventual personal death that is the central and crucial feature of the midlife phase—the feature which precipitates the critical nature of the period. Death—at the conscious level—instead of being a general conception, or an event experienced in terms of the loss of someone else, becomes a personal matter, one's own death, one's own real and actual mortality. As Freud (1915) has so accurately described the matter:

We were prepared to maintain that death was the necessary outcome of life. . . . In reality, however, we were accustomed to behave as if it were otherwise. We displayed an unmistakable tendency to "shelve" death, to eliminate it from life. We tried to hush it up. . . . That is our own death, of course. . . . No one believes in his own death. . . . In the unconscious everyone is convinced of his own immortality [p. 88].

This attitude toward life and death, written by Freud in another context, aptly expresses the situation which we all encounter in midlife. The reality of one's own personal death forces itself upon our attention and can no longer so readily be shelved. A thirty-six-year-old patient, who had been in analysis for seven years and was in the course of working through a deep depressive reaction which heralded the final phase of his analysis some eighteen months later, expressed the matter with great clarity. "Up till now," he said, "life has seemed an endless upward slope, with nothing but the distant horizon in view. Now suddenly I seem to have reached the crest of the hill, and there stretching ahead is the downward slope with the end of the road in sight—far enough away it's true—but there is death observably present at the end."

From that point on this patient's plans and ambitions took on a different hue. For the first time in his life he saw his future as circumscribed. He began his adjustment to the fact that he would not be able to accomplish in the span of a single lifetime everything he had desired to do. He could achieve only a finite amount. Much would have to remain unfinished and unrealized.

This perspective on the finitude of life was accompanied by a greater solidity and robustness in his outlook, and introduced a new quality of earthly resignation. It reflected a diminishing of his unconscious wish for immortality. Such ideas are commonly lived out in terms of denial of mourning and death, or in terms of ideas of immortality, from notions of reincarnation and life after death, to notions of longevity like those expressed by the successful twenty-eight-year-old novelist who writes in his diary, "I shall be the most serious of men, and I shall live longer than any man."

UNCONSCIOUS MEANING OF DEATH

How each one reacts to the midlife encounter with the reality of his own eventual death—whether he can face this reality, or whether he denies it—will be markedly influenced by his infantile unconscious relation to death—a relationship which depends upon the stage and nature of the working through of the infantile depressive position, as Melanie Klein discovered and vividly described (1940, 1955). Let me paraphrase her conclusions.

The infant's relation with life and death occurs in the setting of his survival being dependent on his external objects, and on the balance of power of the life and death instincts which qualify his perception of those objects and his capacity to depend upon them and use them. In the depressive position in infancy, under conditions of prevailing love, the good and bad objects can in some measure be synthesized, the ego becomes more integrated, and hope for the reestablishment of the good object is experienced; the accompanying overcoming of grief and regaining of security is the infantile equivalent of the notion of life.

Under conditions of prevailing persecution, however, the working through of the depressive position will be to a greater or lesser extent inhibited; reparation and synthesis fail; and the inner world is unconsciously felt to contain the persecuting and annihilating devoured and destroyed bad breast, the ego itself feeling in bits. The chaotic internal situation thus experienced is the infantile equivalent of the notion of death.

Ideas of immortality arise as a response to these anxieties, and as a defense against them. Unconscious fantasies of immortality are the counterpart of the infantile fantasies of the indestructible and hence immortal aspect of the idealized and bountiful primal object. These fantasies are equally as persecuting as the chaotic internal situation they are calculated to mitigate. They contain omnipotent sadistic triumph, and increase guilt and persecution as a result. And they lead to feelings of intolerable helplessness through dependence upon the perfect object which becomes demanding of an equal perfection in behavior.

Does the unconscious, then, have a conception of death? The views of Melanie Klein and those of Freud may seem not to correspond. Klein assumes an unconscious awareness of death. Freud assumes that the unconscious rejects all such awareness. Neither of these views, taken at face value, is likely to prove correct. Nor would I expect that either of their authors would hold to a literal interpretation of their views. The unconscious is not aware of death per se. But there are unconscious experiences akin to those which later appear in consciousness as notions of death. Let me illustrate such experiences.

A forty-seven-year-old woman patient, suffering from claustrophobia and a variety of severe psychosomatic illnesses, recounted a dream in which she was lying in a coffin. She had been sliced into small chunks, and was dead. But there was a spiderweb-thin thread of nerve running through every chunk and connected to her brain. As a result she could experience everything. She knew she was dead. She could not move or make any sound. She could only lie in the claustrophobic dark and silence of the coffin.

I have selected this particular dream because I think

it typifies the unconscious fear and experience of death. It is not in fact death in the sense in which consciously we think about it, but an unconscious fantasy of immobilization and helplessness, in which the self is subject to violent fragmentation, while yet retaining the capacity to experience the persecution and torment to which it is being subjected. When these fantasies of suspended persecution and torture are of pathological intensity, they are characteristic of many mental conditions: catatonic states, stupors, phobias, obsessions, frozen anxiety, simple depression.

A CASE OF DENIAL OF DEATH

In the early adult phase, before the midlife encounter with death, the full-scale reworking-through of the depressive position does not as yet necessarily arise as a part of normal development. It can be postponed. It is not a pressing issue. It can be put to one side, until circumstances demand more forcibly that it be faced.

In the ordinary course of events, life is full and active. Physiologically, full potency has been reached, and activity—social, physical, economic, sexual—is to the fore. It is a time for doing, and the doing is flavored and supported to a greater or lesser degree—depending on the emotional adjustment of the individual—by the activity and denial as part of the manic defense.

The early adult phase is one, therefore, in which successful activity can in fact obscure or conceal the operation of strong manic defenses. But the depressive anxiety that is thus warded off will be encountered in due course. The midlife crisis thrusts it forward with great intensity, and it can no longer be pushed aside if life is not to be impoverished.

This relationship between adjustment based upon activity in the early adult phase, and its failure in midlife if the infantile depressive position is not unconsciously (or consciously, in analysis) worked through again, may be illustrated in the case of a patient, Mr. N, who had led a successful life by everyday standards up to the time he came into analysis. He was an active man, a "doer." He had been successful in his career through intelligent application and hard work, was married with three children, had many good friends, and all seemed to be going very well.

The idealized content of this picture had been maintained by an active carrying on of life, without allowing time for reflection. His view was that he had not come to analysis for himself, but rather for a kind of tutorial purpose—he would bring his case history to me and we would have a clinical seminar in which we would conduct a psychoanalytic evaluation of the case material he had presented.

As might be expected, Mr. N had great difficulty in coping with ambivalence. He was unconsciously frightened of any resentment, envy, jealousy, or other hostile feelings toward me, maintaining an attitude of idealized love for me and tolerant good nature toward every attempt on my part to analyze the impulses of destructiveness, and the feelings of persecution which he was counteracting by this idealization.

When we finally did break through this inability to cope with ambivalence—indeed a pretty complete unfamiliarity with the experience—it emerged that, in all his relationships, his idealization was inevitably followed by disappointment—a disappointment arising out of failure to get the quality of love he was greedily expecting in return, and nursed by the envy of those whom he idealized.

It was out of the analysis of material of this kind that

we were able to get at the reflection in the analysis of
his early adult mode of adjustment. He admitted that he
was ill, and that unconscious awareness of his illness
undoubtedly was the main reason for his seeking analysis. Being active, and being overconcerned for others
were soporifics to which he had become addicted. Indeed,
he confessed, he had resented my analysis taking this
defensive addiction away from him. He had secretly en-
tertained ideas of stopping his analysis "because all this
thinking about myself, instead of doing things, is no good.
Now I realize that I have been piling up my rage against
you inside myself, like I've done with everyone else."

Thus it was that during the first year of his analysis,
the patient lived out many of the techniques which had
characterized his early adult adjustment. It was with the
onset of the Christmas holiday that the unconscious depressive anxiety, which was the main cause of his disturbance in midlife, came out in full force. It is this
material that illustrates the importance of the depressive
position and unconscious feelings about death in relation
to the midlife crisis.

He had shown definite signs before the holiday of feelings of being abandoned, saying that not only would he
not see me, but his friends were to be away as well. Three
days before the end of the holiday, he telephoned me and,
in a depressed and tearful voice, asked if he could come
to see me. I arranged a session that same evening.

When he came to see me, he was at first afraid to lie
on the couch. He said that he wanted just to talk to me,
to be comforted and reassured. He then proceeded to tell
me how, from the beginning of the holiday, a black gloom
had settled upon him. He yearned for his mother to be
alive, so that he could be with her and be held and loved
by her. "I just felt completely deserted and lost," he said.
"I sat for hour after hour, uanble to move or to do any

work. I wanted to die. My thoughts were filled with su-
icide. Then I became terrified of my state of mind. That's
why I phoned you. I just had never conceived it as even
remotely possible that I could lose my self-control like
this." Things were made absolutely unbearable, he then
explained, when one of his children had become nearly
murderously aggressive toward his wife a few days before. His world seemed to have gone to pieces.

This material, and other associations, suggested that
his wife stood for the bad aspect of his mother, and his
son for the sadistic murderous part of himself. In his fear
of dying, he was reexperiencing his own unconscious fantasies of tearing his mother to pieces, and he then felt
abandoned and lost. As I interpreted on these lines, he
interjected that the worst thing was the feeling of having
gone to pieces himself. "I can't stand it," he said, "I feel
as though I'm going to die."

I then recalled to him a dream he had had just before
the holiday, that we had not had time to analyze, and
which contained material of importance in the understanding of his infantile perception of being dead. In this
dream he was a small boy sitting crying on the curb in
his home town. He had dropped a bottle of milk. It lay
in jagged shattered bits in the gutter. The fresh good milk
ran away, dirtied by contact with the muck in the gutter.
One of his associations to the dream was that he had
broken the bottle by his own ineptness. It was no use
moaning and crying over the spilt milk, since it was himself, after all, who had caused the damage.

I related his dream to his feeling of being abandoned
by me. I was the bottle of milk—containing good
milk—which he destroyed in his murderous rage because
I abandoned him and went dry. He unconsciously felt the
Christmas holiday as losing me, as he felt he had lost his
mother and the good breast, because of his ineptness—his

violence and lack of control—and his spoiling me internally with his anal muck. He then felt internally persecuted and torn to pieces by the jagged bits of the bottle, representing the breast, myself, and the analysis; as Klein (1955) has expressed it, "the breast taken in with hatred becomes the representative of the death instinct within" (p. 313).

I would conclude that he had unconsciously attempted to avoid depression by paranoid–schizoid techniques of splitting and deflecting his murderous impulses away from me, through his son against his wife. These techniques had now begun to fail, however, because of previous analytical work with respect to his splitting and denial. Whereas he had been able to deny what in fact turned out to be a pretty bad situation in his home, by perceiving it merely as the product of his own projections, he now became filled with guilt, anxiety, and despair, as he began to appreciate more that in reality the relationships at home were genuinely intolerable and dangerous, and were not just a projection of his own internal chaos and confusion.

During the succeeding months, we were able to elaborate more fully his attitude toward death as an experience of going to pieces.

A connection between his phobic attitude to death and his escape into activity was manifested, for instance, in his recalling one day a slogan that had always meant so much to him—"Do or die." But now it came to him that he had always used his own personal abbreviation of the slogan—simply "Do." The possibility of dying just did not consciously exist for him.

On one occasion he demonstrated at first hand how his fear of death had caused him always to retreat from mourning. A friend of his died. The patient was the strong and efficient one, who made all the necessary arrangements, while friends and family stood about helplessly, bathed in tears and paralyzed with sorrow. He experienced no feeling—just clearheadedness and a sense of action for the arrangements which had to be made. He had always been the same, had done the same when his father and his mother had died. More than that, however, when I interpreted his warding off of depression by means of denial of feeling and refuge in action, he recalled an event which revealed the unconscious chaos and confusion stirred within him by death. He remembered how, when a cousin of his had suddenly collapsed and died a few years before, he had run back and forth from the body to the telephone to call for a doctor, oblivious of the fact that a small group of people had gathered about the body, and not realizing that everyone but himself was perfectly aware that his cousin was quite dead, and had been for some time before he arrived upon the scene.

The chaos and confusion in the patient in connection with death I would ascribe to his unconscious infantile fantasies equivalent to death—the fantasies of the destroyed and persecuting breast, and of his ego being cut to pieces.

Mainly, I think, because of the love he got from his father, probably reinforcing his own innate good impulses and what he has had described to him as good breast-feeding in the first five weeks with his mother, he had been able to achieve a partial working through of the infantile depressive position, and to develop his good intellectual capacities. The partial character of his working through was shown in the extent of his manic denial and activity, and his excessive use of splitting, introjection and projection, and projective and introjective identification.

During the period of early adulthood—the twenties and early thirties—the paranoid–schizoid and manic defense techniques were sufficiently effective. By means of his apparent general success and obsessional generosity, he was able to live out the role of the good mother established within, to nurture the good part of himself projected into others, to deny the real situation of envy and greed and destructiveness expressed by him as his noxiousness, and to deny the real impoverishment of his emotional life, and lack of genuine love and affection in his behavior as both husband and father.

With the onset of mature adulthood in his midthirties, his defensive techniques began to lose their potency. He had lost his youth, and the prospect of middle age and of eventual death stimulated a repetition and a reworking through of the infantile depressive position. The unconscious feelings of persecution and annihilation which death represented to him were reawakened.

He had lost his youth. And with both his parents dead, nobody now stood between himself and the grave. On the contrary, he had become the barrier between his children and their perception of death. Acceptance of these facts required constructive resignation and detachment. Unconsciously such an outlook requires the capacity to maintain the internal good object, and to achieve a resigned attitude to shortcomings and destructive impulses in oneself, and imperfections in the internal good object. My patient's unconscious fantasies of intolerable noxiousness, his anxieties of having polluted and destroyed his good primal object so that he was lost and abandoned and belonged nowhere, and his unconscious fantasies of the badness of his internalized mother as well as his father, precluded such detachment and resignation. The psychological defenses which had supported his adjustment in early adult life—an adjustment of a limited kind, of course, with a great core of emotional impoverishment—failed him at the midlife period when, to the persecutory world in which he unconsciously lived, were added his anxieties about impending middle and old age, and death. If he had had a less well-established good internal object, and had been innately less constructive and loving, he might have continued his mature adult life along lines similar to his early adult type of adjustment; but if he had, I think his midlife crisis would have been the beginning of a deterioration in his character, and bouts of depression and psychosomatic illness, due to the depth and chronicity of his denial and self-deception, and his distorted view of external reality.

As it has worked out, however, the positive factors in his personality makeup enabled him to utilize his analysis, for which he developed a deep sense of value and appreciation. The overcoming of splitting and fragmentation first began to show in a session in which, as out of nowhere, he saw two jagged edged right-angled triangles. They moved together, and joined to make a perfect square. I recalled the dream with the broken bits of bottle to him. He replied, "It's odd you should mention that; I was just thinking of it. It feels like the bits of glass are coming together."

EVASION OF AWARENESS OF DEATH

One case history does not of course prove a general thesis. It can only illustrate a theme, and the theme in this instance is the notion that the circumstances met by this patient at the midlife phase are representative of a general pattern of psychological change at this stage of life. The extent to which these changes are tied up with physiological changes is a question I am not able to tackle. One can readily conjecture, however, that the connection must be an important one—libido, the life-creating impulse, represented in sexual drive, is diminishing, and the death instinct is coming relatively more into the ascendant.

The sense of the agedness of parents, coupled with the maturing of children into adults, contributes strongly to the sense of aging—the sense that it is one's own turn next to grow old and die. This feeling about the age of parents is very strong—even in patients whose parents died years before there is the awareness at the midlife period that their parents would then have been reaching old age.

In the early adult phase of life, contemplativeness, detachment, and resignation are not essential components of pleasure, enjoyment, and success. Manically determined activity and warding off of depression may therefore—as in the case of Mr. N—lead to a limited success and pleasure. Splitting and projection techniques can find expression in what are regarded as perfectly normal patterns of passionate support for idealized causes, and equally passionate opposition to whatever may be felt as bad or reactionary.

With the awareness of the onset of the last half of life, unconscious depressive anxieties are aroused, and the repetition and continuation of the working through of the infantile depressive position are required. Just as in infancy—to quote Klein again (1940, p. 314)—"satisfactory relations to people depend upon the infant's having succeeded against the chaos inside him (the depressive position) and having securely established his 'good' internal objects," so in midlife the establishment of a satisfactory adjustment to the conscious contemplation of one's own death depends upon the same process, for otherwise death itself is equated with the depressive chaos, confusion, and persecution, as it was in infancy.

When the prevailing balance between love and hate tends more toward the side of hate, when there is instinc-

tual defusion, there is an overspill of destructiveness in
any or all of its various forms—self-destruction, envy,
grandiose omnipotence, cruelty, narcissism, greed—and
the world is seen as having these persecuting qualities
as well. Love and hate are split apart; destruction is no
longer mitigated by tenderness. There is little or no pro-
tection from catastrophic unconscious fantasies of annihilating one's good objects. Reparation and sublimation,
the processes which underlie creativeness, are inhibited
and fail. And in the deep unconscious world there is a
gruesome sense of invasion and habitation by the psychic
objects which have been annihilated.

In primitive terms, the process of sculpting is experienced partly as a projective identification, in which the
fear of dying is split off and projected into the created
object (representing the creative breast). Under the dominance of destructiveness the created object, like the
breast, is felt to:

> [R]emove the good or valuable element in the fear of
> dying, and to force the worthless residue back into the
> infant. The infant who started with a fear that he was
> dying ends up by containing a nameless dread [Bion,
> 1962, p. 84].

The conception of death is denuded of its meaning, and
the process of sculpted creativity is stopped. It is the experience of a patient who, having created a work of art
by spontaneous effusion, found that "it goes dead on me;
I don't want to have anything more to do with it; I can
never work on it further once it is outside, so I can never
refine it; it completely loses its meaning for me—it's like
a strange and foreign thing that has nothing to do with
me."

The ensuing inner chaos and despair is unconsciously

fantasied in terms akin to an inferno: "*I came to myself within a dark wood . . . savage and harsh and dense.*" If this state of mind is not surmounted, hate and death must be denied, pushed aside, warded off, rejected. They are replaced by unconscious fantasies of omnipotence, magic immortality, religious mysticism, the counterpart of infant fantasies of being indestructible and under the protective care of some idealized and bountiful figure.

A person who reaches midlife, either without having successfully established himself in marital and occupational life, or having established himself by means of manic activity and denial with consequent emotional impoverishment, is badly prepared for meeting the demands of middle age, and getting enjoyment out of his maturity. In such cases, the midlife crisis, and the adult encounter with the conception of life to be lived in the setting of an approaching personal death, will likely be experienced as a period of psychological disturbance and depressive breakdown. Or breakdown may be avoided by means of a strengthening of manic defenses, with a warding off of depression and persecution about aging and death, but with an accumulation of persecutory anxiety to be faced when the inevitability of aging and death eventually demands recognition.

The compulsive attempts, in many men and women reaching middle age, to remain young, the hypochondriacal concern over health and appearance, the emergence of sexual promiscuity in order to prove youth and potency, the hollowness and lack of genuine enjoyment of life, and the frequency of religious concern, are familiar patterns. They are attempts at a race against time. And in addition to the impoverishment of emotional life contained in the foregoing activities, real character deterioration is always possible. Retreat from psychic reality encourages intellectual dishonesty, and a weakening of moral fiber and of courage. Increase in arrogance, and ruthlessness concealing pangs of envy—or self-effacing humbleness and weakness concealing fantasies of omnipotence—are symptomatic of such change.

These defensive fantasies are equally as persecuting, however, as the chaotic and hopeless internal situation they are meant to mitigate. They lead to attempts at easy success, at a continuation on a false note of the early adult lyricism and precipitate creation—that is, creation which, by avoiding contemplation, now seeks not to express but to avoid contact with the infantile experience of hate and of death. Instead of creative enhancement by the introduction of the genuinely tragic, there is emotional impoverishment—a recoil away from creative development. As Freud incisively remarked: "Life loses in interest, when the highest stake in the game, life itself, may not be risked." Here is the Achilles heel of much young genius.

WORKING THROUGH THE DEPRESSIVE POSITION

When, by contrast, the prevailing balance between love and hate is on the side of love, there is instinctual fusion, in which hate can be mitigated by love, and the midlife encounter with death and hate takes on a different hue. Revived are the deep unconscious memories of hate, not denied but mitigated by love; of death and destruction mitigated by reparation and the will to life; of good things injured and damaged by hate, revived again and healed by loving grief; of spoiling envy mitigated by admiration and by gratitude; of confidence and hope, not through denial, but through the deep inner sense that the torment of grief and loss, of guilt and persecution, can be endured and overcome if faced by loving reparation.

Under constructive circumstances, the created object

in midlife is experienced unconsciously in terms of the good breast which would in Bion's (1962) terms:

> [M]oderate the fear component in the fear of dying that had been projected into it and the infant in due course would re-introject a now tolerable and consequently growth stimulating part of its personality [p. 116].

In the sculpting mode of work the externally created object, instead of being experienced as having impoverished the personality, is unconsciously reintrojected, and stimulates further unconscious creativeness. The created object is experienced as life-giving. The transformation of the fear component in the fear of dying into a constructive experience is forwarded. The thought of death can be carried in thinking, and not predominantly in projective identification, so that the conception of death can begin to find its conscious realization. The reality-testing of death can be carried out in thinking, separated partly from the process of creating an external object. At the same time the continuing partial identification of the creative sculpting with the projection and reintrojection of the fear of dying gives a stimulus to the sculpting process because of its success in forwarding the working through of the infantile projective identification with a good breast.

Thus in midlife we are able to encounter the onset of the tragedy of personal death with the sense of grief appropriate to it. We can live with it, without an overwhelming sense of persecution. The infantile depressive position can be further worked through unconsciously, supported by the greater strength of reality-testing available to the nearly mature individual. In so reworking through the depressive position, we unconsciously regain the primitive sense of wholeness—of the goodness of our-

selves and of our objects—a goodness which is sufficient
but not idealized, not subject to hollow perfection. The
consequent feeling of limited but reliable security is the
equivalent of the infantile notion of life.

These more balanced conditions do not, however, pre-
suppose an easy passage through the midlife crisis. It is
essentially a period of purgatory—of anguish and depression. So speaks Virgil:

> Down to Avernus the descent is light. But thence thy
> journey to retrace, there lies the labour, there the
> mighty toil by few achieved [1953, lines 126–127].

Working through again the infantile experience of loss
and of grief gives an increase in confidence in one's capacity to love and mourn what has been lost and what
is past, rather than to hate and feel persecuted by it. We
can begin to mourn our own eventual death. Creativeness
takes on new depths and shades of feeling. There is the
possibility, however, of furthering the resolution of the
depressive position at a much deeper level. Such a working through is possible if the primal object is sufficiently
well established in its own right and neither excessively
idealized nor devalued. Under such circumstances there
is a minimum of infantile dependence upon the good object, and a detachment which allows confidence and hope
to be established, security in the preservation and development of the ego, a capacity to tolerate one's shortcomings and destructiveness, and withal, the possibility
of enjoyment of mature adult life and old age.

Given such an internal situation, the last half of life
can be lived with conscious knowledge of eventual death,
and acceptance of this knowledge, as an integral part of
living. Mourning for the dead self can begin, alongside
the mourning and reestablishment of the lost objects and

the lost childhood and youth. The sense of life's continuity may be strengthened. The gain is in the deepening of awareness, understanding, and self-realization. Genuine values can be cultivated—of wisdom, fortitude, and courage, deeper capacity for love and affection and human insight, and hopefulness and enjoyment—qualities whose genuineness stems from integration based upon the more immediate and self-conscious awareness and acceptance not only of one's own shortcomings but of one's destructive impulses, and from the greater capacity for sublimation which accompanies true resignation and detachment.

SCULPTED CREATIVITY

Out of the working through of the depressive position, there is further strengthening of the capacity to accept and tolerate conflict and ambivalence. One's work need no longer be experienced as perfect. It can be worked and reworked, but it will be accepted as having shortcomings. The sculpting process can be carried on far enough so that the work is good enough. There is no need for obsessional attempts at perfection, because inevitable imperfection is no longer felt as bitter persecuting failure. Out of this mature resignation comes the serenity in the work of genius, true serenity, serenity which transcends imperfection by accepting it.

Because of the greater integration within the internal world, and a deepening of the sense of reality, a freer interaction can occur between the internal and the external worlds. Sculpted creativity expresses this freedom with its flow of inspiration from inside to outside and back, constantly repeated, again, and yet again. There is a quality of depth in mature creativity which stems from constructive resignation and detachment. Death is not infantile persecution and chaos. Life and the world go on, and we can live on in our children, our loved objects, our works, if not in immortality.

The sculpting process in creativity is facilitated because the preparation for the final phase in reality-testing has begun—the reality-testing of the end of life. For everyone, the oncoming years of the forties are the years when new starts are coming to an end. This feeling can be observed to arise in a particularly poignant way by the midforties. This sense of there being no more changing is anticipated in the midlife crisis. What is begun has to be finished. Important things that the individual would have liked to achieve, would have desired to become, would have longed to have, will not be realized. The awareness of oncoming frustration is especially intense. That is why, for example, the issue of resignation is of such importance. It is resignation in the sense of conscious and unconscious acceptance of inevitable frustration on the grand scale of life as a whole.

This reality-testing is the more severe the greater is the creative ability of the individual, for the time scale of creative work increases dramatically with ability. Thus the experience is particularly painful in genius, capable of achieving vastly more than it is possible to achieve in the remaining years, and therefore frustrated by the immense vision of things to be done which will not be done. And because the route forward has become a cul-de-sac, attention begins its Proustian process of turning to the past, working it over consciously in the present, and weaving it into the concretely limited future. This consonance of past and present is a feature of much mature adult sculpting work.

The positive creativeness and the tone of serenity which accompany the successful endurance of this frustration are characteristic of the mature production of Beethoven, Goethe, Virgil, Dante, and other giants. It is the spirit of the "Paradiso," which ends in words of strong and quiet confidence:

But now my desire and will, like a wheel that spins with even motion, were revolved by the Love that moves the sun and other stars [1946c, p. 484, lines 143–145].

It is this spirit, on a smaller scale, which overcomes the crisis of middle life, and lives through to the enjoyment of mature creativeness and work in full awareness of death which lies beyond—resigned but not defeated. It is a spirit that is one criterion of the successful working through of the depressive position in psychoanalysis.

REFERENCES

Bion, W. (1962), *Learning from Experience*. New York: Basic Books.
Church, R. (1964), *The Voyage Home*. London: Heinemann.
Croce, B. (1922), *Aesthetic: As Science of Expression and General Linguistic*, trans. D. Austies. London: Macmillan.
Dante (1946a), *The Divine Comedy*, trans. J. D. Sinclair, Vol. 1. London: Bodley Head, p. 62, lines 1–100.
——— (1946b), *The Divine Comedy*, trans. J. D. Sinclair, Vol. 3. London: Bodley Head, p. 482, lines 106–108.
——— (1946c), *The Divine Comedy*, trans. J. D. Sinclair, Vol. 3. London: Bodley Head, p. 484, lines 143–145.
Freud, S. (1915), Thoughts for the times on war and death. *Standard Edition*, 14:273–302. London: Hogarth Press, 1957.
Gittings, R. (1954), *John Keats*. London: Heinemann.
Klein, M. (1935), A contribution to the psychogenesis of manic-depressive states. In: *Contributions to Psycho-Analysis*. London: Hogarth Press, 1948.
——— (1940), Mourning and its relation to manic-depressive states. In: *Contributions to Psycho-Analysis*. London: Hogarth Press, 1968.
——— (1955), On identification. In: *New Directions in Psycho-Analysis*. New York: Basic Books.
Riviere, J. (1958), A character trait of Freud's. In: *Psycho-Analysis and Contemporary Thought*, ed. J. D. Sutherland. London: Hogarth Press.
Virgil (1953), *Aeniad*, trans. E. V. Rieu. London: Penguin, Book VI, lines 126–127.

Chapter 14

Disturbances in the Capacity to Work

In its most general sense, work as conceived by Freud (1911) (and I am here concerned with work in the psychological sense only) is the mental energy or effort expended in striving to reach a goal or objective by means of the operation of the reality principle, and in the face of the demands of the pleasure principle.[1] If we examine this activity closely, however, a number of important features claim our attention.

The operation of the reality principle leads to delayed rather than immediate gratification. It requires the exercise of discretion (in the sense of judgment, and not the social sense of being discreet) in determining which courses of action will eventually lead to the best result. Discrimination and judgment must be used, and decisions made. Decision contains the uncertainty of the wisdom of the choice, and calls for the capacity to tolerate uncertainty while awaiting the final outcome, and possible failure.

Revised and expanded version of a paper read at the 21st International Congress of Psycho-Analysis, July 1959.
[1] This conception of work is followed by most psychoanalytical writers on the subject, as for example Hendrick (1943), Oberndorf (1951), and Lantos (1952).

This uncertainty, however, it must be noted, has a special quality. The use of discretion depends upon unconscious as well as conscious mental functioning—the capacity for synthesis of unconscious ideas and intuitions and bringing them into consciousness. We may not be surprised to find, therefore, that at the core of this uncertainty lies anxiety—the anxiety aroused by having to depend for success upon the coherence and availability of unconscious mental life.

I was able to confirm this conclusion in social-analytic work in industry which I have reported elsewhere (1956). In the course of these studies, two major components of work were separated: first, the prescribed limits—laws, customs, resources, instructions, rules and regulations, and material limitations—which allow no room for discretion but set the frame within which discretion is exercised; and second, the discretionary content, comprising all those aspects in which discretion and choice have to be exercised. The force of this distinction was brought home to me when it became clear that what is experienced as psychic effort in work—the intensity or weight of responsibility—is entirely concerned with the discretionary content of work. To conform to rules and regulations and other prescribed aspects of work requires knowledge; you either know or you do not; but it does not require the psychic effort of discretion and decision, with its attendant stirring of anxiety.

I was able to demonstrate that weight or level of responsibility is objectively measurable in terms of the maximum spans of time during which discretion must be exercised by a person on his own account. The longer the span of time, the more the unconscious material that must be made conscious, and the longer must uncertainty about the final outcome and the anxiety about one's judgment and discretion be tolerated. In short, the longer the path toward gratification chosen in accord with the reality principle, the greater is the experience of psychic effort or work.

We are led then to the following definition of work, and formulation of the capacity to work. *Work* is the exercise of discretion within externally prescribed limits to achieve an object which can be reality-tested, while maintaining a continuous working through of the attendant anxiety. The *capacity to work* depends upon the coherence of the unconscious, and upon the integration and strength of the ego and its capacity, in the face of anxiety and uncertainty, to sustain its functions, to maintain the reality principle, and to exert pressure to make the unconscious conscious.

THE MAIN COMPONENTS IN MENTAL ACTIVITY

Work is never a simple process of striving toward an external objective. Combined in any act of work there is always a relation to the objective perceived as symbol. In order to advance our analysis, I shall have to digress for a moment to establish a few conceptions and terms in connection with perception and symbol formation.

The perception of an object is determined by the interplay of the requisite content of the percept with two types of symbolic content which have been variously designated; for example, by Segal (1957) as symbols and symbolic equations, and by Jones (1958) as symbols and true symbols. Whatever the terms used for the two types of symbolic content—and many writers, including Milner (1952) and Rycroft (1956), have emphasized the importance of the distinction—the central factor is that stressed by Klein (1930) (and elaborated by Segal); namely, the degree of concreteness of the symbol, and the extent to which it coexists with the object or engulfs it. The degree of concreteness in turn depends upon the intensity and character of the splitting process which underlies the symbol formation. It is consistent with recent developments in Klein's conception of the paranoid–schizoid position (and indeed with unstated assumptions in her earlier work) to assume that it is when violent splitting with fragmentation of the object and the self is predominant that concrete rather than plastic symbol formation occurs. I propose to show that this assumption is useful and necessary not only in considering the problem of work, but in considering all mental processes, especially the fundamental process of perception, and shall use the following terms and schema.

The perception of an object is determined by the interconnection of:

1. The requisite content of the perception, resulting in a mental percept of the object itself;
2. The symbolic content, in which the object is modified by projective identification, split-off parts of the self and internal objects being unconsciously perceived as in the external object or connected with it, and the object introjected in the modified form;
3. What I propose to term the *concretive content*, in which the object is modified by the explosive projection into it of violently split and fragmented internal objects and parts of the self, loses its own identity and becomes a concrete symbol (or, in Segal's terms, a symbolic equation); it is then violently introjected and experienced internally in concrete corporeal form in a split-off and fragmented state within the body ego.[2]

---

[2] This conception of concretism is connected with phenomena similar to those described by Goldstein (Goldstein and Scheerer, 1939)

This distinction between ordinary projection and introjection and the more concrete processes of violent projection and introjection is one consistently made by Klein in her earlier papers, in which she frequently uses the terms *expulsion* and *incorporation* to refer to the more violent processes. Bion, in his papers on hallucinosis (e.g., Bion, 1958), emphasizes the distinction, and retains these earlier terms.

Developmentally, violent splitting with fragmentation is associated with the earliest phases of the paranoid–schizoid position, when the rudimentary ego is under the impact of intense destructive impulses and instinctual defusion. At this stage, ordinary splitting fails as an ego defense because of the intensity of the anxiety aroused by the split-off persecuting primal object, and from the dangers of destroying the idealized split-off good object. As Klein (1958) has shown, both aspects of the split primal object become experienced as persecutory, and contribute to the remorseless quality of the primitive superego.

Symbol formation with lessened concretism becomes possible at the transition stage between the paranoid –schizoid and depressive positions. The ego, with greater integration, is more able to contend with persecutory anxiety by means of less violent splitting and with lessened fragmentation. There results a growing confidence in the capacity to sustain the good objects split-off and segregated from the bad ones. The ensuing capacity to reduce anxiety by formation of symbols (Klein, 1930) in turn

---

under the heading of concrete as against abstract thinking, and by Piaget (1953) under the heading of syncretism. I believe that the processes of violent splitting and fragmentation, followed by explosive projection and violent introjection, with the accompanying very concrete forms of identification, offer an explanation of the dynamics of the phenomena observed by Goldstein in his patients with brain damage, and by Piaget in young children.

facilitates the onset of the depressive position. Contact
with reality is strengthened, greater reality in perception
comes to the fore, and a whole range of defenses becomes
available, especially reparation and sublimation and a
more fully developed use of symbol formation (Segal,
1957). Davidson (1959) has given a graphic account of
this process in his clinical description of the treatment
of a patient suffering from schizophrenia with mutism.
In passing, I would suggest that it is precisely because
symbol formation is always based upon some splitting
that symbols tend toward being normative in mode—either
good or bad.

In separating out three main components of perceptual processes, and indeed of all mental activity—the requisite, symbolic, and concretive—I am doing so for the
purpose of analysis only, and not to suggest that there
are objective ego activities separated from symbolic and
concrete contents and the conflicts and anxieties from
which they arise. It is precisely the coexistence and interconnection of these components of mental activity
which I wish to demonstrate in work: the relative quantity, balance, and content of the three components determining the degree of realism, the creativeness, the
energy, and the direction in work, as well as the extent
to which that work contributes to advances in psychic
integration. The present formulation thus differs from
that of Hartmann (1938) who, in defining what he terms
the *conflict-free ego sphere*, writes of "that ensemble of
functions which at any given time exert their effects outside the region of mental conflicts" (p. 187). In contrast
to Hartmann, I believe that the path from psychoanalysis
to a general psychology cannot be traversed without taking into account the fundamental role of conflict in all
mental functioning—a view which I hope may be supported by the present chapter. In particular, I think that

the understanding of normal psychological processes will be enhanced by teasing out from within them, and elaborating, the various types of splitting processes employed by the ego in dealing with conflict, and the vicissitudes of the resulting splits and fragmentations of the ego, objects, and impulses—a point frequently stressed by Klein.

THE PROCESS OF WORK

I now wish to turn to the process of work itself. Six main stages may be recognized:

1. the achievement of a particular objective is undertaken, and a *relationship is established with the objective*;
2. an *appropriate quantity of the mental apparatus must be allocated* to the task;
3. an *integrative reticulum* must be constructed and elaborated, within which the work is organized;
4. concentration upon the task, teasing out the contents of those areas of the mind occupied upon it, and a scrutiny and searching for elements which will help in solving the problem; a process I shall designate by the terms *lysis* and *scanning*;
5. *gathering, linking*, and *synthesis* of the elements which fit;
6. *decision*, by which is designated a taking of action with significant committal of resources.

The processes I shall describe will refer throughout to the interplay of mental events between the conscious and unconscious areas of the mind. Although the focus of emphasis oscillates continually between the conscious and the unconscious—each one alternately becoming figure and then ground—neither the one nor the other process is ever inactive.

I shall outline the six stages of work sequence for
purposes of presentation. In reality the various stages
interact. The first integrative reticulum may be tenta-
tive—a hypothesis, or a mere hunch or feeling. Insufficient, or too much, mental capacity may be allocated. As
lysis and synthesis proceed, and knowledge is collected,
the integrative reticulum may be modified, and more or
less mental capacity allocated; the libidinal relationship
with the objective may be altered—ambivalence and the
intensity of libidinal investment increasing or decreasing
as the task and its difficulties are encountered and experienced.

Moreover, as lysis and linking proceed, trials may be
essayed in external reality, but without extensive committal of resources, the knowledge and intuitions built
up from these trials being fed back into the elements
available for linking.

RELATION WITH THE OBJECTIVE

An objective is an object-to-be—one which has to be
brought into being, to be created. The objective may be
worked for because of inner need and compulsion, for the
personal satisfaction to be derived regardless of other
gain. It may be an allocated task constituting part of a
person's employment.

The amount of energy mustered for a task will depend
upon both the desire to achieve the objective and obtain
the attendant reward, and the symbolic meaning of the
objective and attendant psychic gratification. Work is
most satisfying when both these elements are consistent
with each other, and relatively undisturbed by concretism.

If the depressive position has been sufficiently worked
through, the symbolic content of work will be connected

mainly with reparation. The analytic literature contains many instances, for example, where the objective represents the creation of a baby and giving birth to it. At a deeper level is symbolized the reparation, restoring, and recreation of the primal good object, and revival of good impulses and good parts of the self. The objective in work is nicely suited for such a symbol, since it exists only as a partial schema requiring to be completed and brought to life by loving care and work. At the same time as the objective is symbolically identified with the good object undergoing reparation and restoration, the bad objects and bad impulses and parts of the self are symbolically identified with obstacles in the way of the work. The more the reality content of the work is consistent with the unconscious symbolic reparative activities, the greater will be the love for the task.

If the discrepancy between the reality and symbolic aspects is too great, lack of interest or hatred is aroused, and loss of incentive ensues. This hatred may be intensified by violent splitting and fragmentation, the incomplete objective being concretely introjected and identified with destroyed and persecuting internal objects. The objective itself then becomes increasingly persecutory through violent projection and concrete symbol formation. Moreover, the intensity of the concretism will determine the extent to which "putting oneself into the job" becomes a matter of strong positive motivation and sound effort, or of confusion and inhibition. The negative effect is produced by the unconscious experience of losing parts of the self and internal objects into the task concretely perceived, combined with the experience of getting parts of the job lost inside oneself—in the same manner, for example, as when genital sexuality is inhibited by urethral and anal sadism. Fears of failure are then intensified through unconscious fears of uncontrolled destructive impulses.

ALLOCATION OF MENTAL CAPACITY

The amount of mental capacity allocated (i.e., the amount of occupation with the task) will be determined by the judgment of the size of the task, given greater or lesser effect by the intensity of libidinal involvement and the amount of ambivalence. The accuracy of the judgment of size of task will be influenced by knowledge of that type of work. It will be distorted by violent splitting and fragmentation. The stronger the love for the real and the symbolic objective, the greater the psychic energy that will be made available for the task.

The allocation of mental capacity requires a genuine act of mental investment. More, it requires the segregation of the invested area from interference by other mental activities. It is an allocation in time as well as in amount. The intensity of absorption in the task is at stake. It is an estimate, and one which may require subsequent revision. The greater the time framework, ordinarily the greater is the area of the mental apparatus that is brought into play. To be preoccupied with other things means just what the word implies: so much of the mental apparatus has already been allocated that not enough is available for the task at hand. Segregation breaks down, and concentration on the task is disturbed. Capacity to work is impaired in neurosis by the absorption of mental capacity in internal conflict, which leaves relatively little capacity available for any other work.

INTEGRATIVE RETICULUM

The integrative reticulum is the mental schema of the completed object and the means of creating it, organized in such a manner that the gaps both in the mental picture of the object and in the methods of creating it are established. Consciously, it is a combination of any or all of concepts, theories, hypotheses, and working notions or hunches. Unconsciously, it is a constellation of ideas-in-feeling, memories-in-feeling, fantasies, and internal objects—brought together and synthesized to the extent necessary to direct behavior, even if not sufficiently to become conscious.

The creation of an adequate reticulum requires sufficient ego-strength to achieve the necessary intensity of concentration upon the task. If ambivalence about the task is low, and if there is not excessive splitting of the conscious from the unconscious parts of the mind, then the greater the ego-strength and the greater the conscious mental concentration and effort applied to the task, the greater will be the concentration upon the task in the unconscious mind. That is to say, conscious mental effort has a continuous effect upon the mobilizing of unconscious mental activity and effort, and upon the content and direction of that activity.

Conversely, the strength of the ego-activity mobilized for the task, the capacity to concentrate upon the objective, and the coherence and synthesizing power of the resulting reticulum, depend in large measure upon the coherence in the organization of the unconscious mental processes. The degree of coherence in the unconscious is associated with the dominance of loving impulses over destructiveness, and the intactness of internal good objects—these conditions reducing the dependence of the ego upon violent splitting. When, however, there is insufficient coherence and violent splitting and fragmentation occur, a satisfactory integrative reticulum cannot be established. Indeed a schema of the objective constructed under such conditions will itself be split and fragmented and will thus facilitate further splitting and fragmentation: it acts as a disintegrating rather than an integrative reticulum inducing confusion and disorganization in work.

The assumption of unconscious influences upon conscious mental processes requires no elaboration. The two assumptions, however, that of coherent structure and function in unconscious processes, and that of conscious effort in influencing the intensity, coherence, direction, and content of unconscious activity, may warrant a brief comment. The validity of these assumptions may be simply demonstrated. The successful accomplishment of any task requires the exercise of some or all of the functions which we describe as touch, or feel, or sense, or intuition, or insight. These functions are exercised in the main unconsciously, and are not simply preconscious. They can be brought into play by conscious orientation toward a particular task. Once set going, they may operate, for instance, during sleep, throwing up a result that is consciously available, but without the problem-solving activities themselves becoming conscious. Such activities demand the assumption of coherence and dynamic organization in the unconscious, intimately connected with conscious activities.

LYSIS AND SCANNING

By lysis, I refer to the process of separating and teasing out the contents of those areas of the mind occupied in the task—the products of conscious knowledge and of unconscious fantasies and feelings, awareness through experience, and intuition. By scanning, I refer to the process of mentally looking over and considering the teased-out materials. Both lysis and scanning are concerned with making the unconscious conscious.

Lysis and scanning require the capacity to loosen the elements organized within other sets of ideas, so that many relevant elements may be abstracted and used in the new context; for example, certain ideas in a book, or the unconscious memory of a particular feature of the behavior of another person, or of one's own childhood. At the same time the integrative reticulum itself must be loosened and prepared for the linking of new elements, the reticulum possibly needing to be modified in the process. Scanning may be external as well as internal. When insufficient material is discerned in the conscious and sensed in the unconscious mind, new information is sought in the outside world, by search and by research. When libidinal investment in the work is high, so are curiosity and the need for truth—and the desire to discover and use such knowledge as already exists—so that the work of others is prized and valued.

If the ego-strength is sufficient, the concentration of mental effort on the task within the frame of the integrative reticulum results in the loosening out and mobilization of thoughts and ideas relevant to the task. These elements do not come only from the conscious ego. If the unconscious ego is sufficiently oriented toward the task, it will be influenced into throwing forth elements associated with gaps in the reticulum. The more coherent is the organization of the unconscious ego, the greater is the influence upon it of the exertion of conscious mental concentration and effort; and the greater will be the release of elements from the unconscious to be made available for scanning and for possible use in achieving the objective.

In lysis and scanning, if the mental process is plastic, elements of thought are made available for synthesis within other thought processes, without destroying their mental context. At the symbolic level, this process goes on by means of a wide range of possible splits and fusions, but with the good and bad aspects of the splitting maintained intact. To the extent, however, that persecutory anxiety, violent splitting, and the ensuing concretism are at work, lysis and scanning are inhibited or lead to confusion, because lysis is experienced as fragmentation and disintegration. The mental process is concrete and inflexible, the bits and particles are not available for synthesis, and the integrative reticulum becomes unmodifiable.

GATHERING, LINKING, AND SYNTHESIS

As the process of lysis and scanning proceeds, those elements which fit together and into the schema are gathered together. The question of what constitutes fittingness is of the greatest importance, and warrants a separate treatment beyond the scope of the present chapter.[3] The loosened elements are mentally tried out for fit into gaps in the reticulum, and those which fit are retained. The sensation is that of insight, of notions which click.

The gathering together of these elements, and their linking within the integrative reticulum constitutes the act of synthesis. To gather, meaning to draw together into a heap, comes from the same root as the word *good*.[4] Linguistically, then, there is reason to connect the creative gathering and synthesizing processes in work, with the unconscious experience of establishing the good object.

Where the apposition and fit are *unconsciously* made, the sensation of insight is one of "feel"—something clicks,

---

[3] It is a question which takes us, for example, into the role of insight and of trial-and-error in learning and in problem solving.

[4] Both are from the Indo-European root "gad," which means fit or suitable.

but it is not quite clear what. It is the feeling that one could *do* it oneself, or *demonstrate* how to do it, but yet not be able to explain how. Effort and study are required to bring the experience into the preconscious by discovering verbal images which correspond to it, and thus to bring the elements forth into consciousness, as Freud (1923) has described in *The Ego and the Id*. The existence of a coherent integrative reticulum spanning the conscious and the unconscious ego acts as a powerful agent enabling the unconscious thus to be made conscious. The necessary act of attending to the task is experienced as mental strain.

When concretism is strong, however, linked objects are experienced as persecuting, the act of synthesis—as shown by Bion in another context (1959)—representing the unconscious internal reenactment of the primal scene. The mental processes in work are therefore attacked, and the integrative reticulum subjected to tearing and destructive annihilation. The effect of the erotization of work is thus influenced by the strength of concretism: if concretism is weak, symbolic erotization of the objective in work may facilitate the work and reinforce sublimation; if it is strong, work is disturbed and sublimation is inhibited because of the concreteness of the erotization.

DECISION AND ACTION

When the mental process has proceeded sufficiently far, or when time begins to run out, the moment of decision and committal is reached. By the term *decision*, I wish to designate the taking of action to create the object in whole or in part, with a significant committal of resources, so that if the discretion and judgment exercised have been adequate, success will be achieved, but if they have been inadequate, failure will be experienced with wastage of the resources committed.

By decision, therefore, I mean what the term implies—"decaedere," a cutting apart—an act from which there is no turning back. It is the point at which a person's confidence in his mental capacity is put on trial, for the consequence of an act of decision is reality-testing. The results of the decision have to be faced. It is the moment when anxieties about the task are mobilized to the very greatest extent.

If, therefore, there is much violent splitting with fragmentation, catastrophe is unconsciously anticipated. This fear of catastrophe is of the paranoid–schizoid type. It is the fear of self-inflicted failure through self-imposed stupidity and self-deception which occur whenever violent splitting and fragmentation, with their attendant confusion, are at work. It leads, following actual failure, to self-recrimination of the "if only I had done so-and-so" type: and defense against this self-castigation by projection of the blame only intensifies persecutory anxiety, and in no way repairs the damage. The potency of the destructive impulses is experienced as immediately present. Consequently, irreality and a retreat to the pleasure principle result. Evasion of reality-testing may be achieved by obsessional indecisiveness and paralysis of action or, equally, by careless and grandiose "decisiveness" based upon magically omnipotent fantasies and offhand disregard of the result.

If, however, the objective in work is successfully achieved in reality, then reparation is reinforced, the bad objects and impulses are diminished by identification with the obstacles that have been overcome, and splitting is lessened. Integration in the ego is advanced, and the operation of the reality principle is strengthened.

But perhaps most important is the fate of the concrete

components of the mental processes involved in the work. The very fact that a decision was made requires that some of the energy bound in maintaining the fragmentation is released, and with it some of the anxiety that had been tied up in the fixed and concrete symbolism. But the success of the objective work combined with the processes of symbol formation in creating an object in external reality, and reparation internally, mitigates hate and diminishes persecutory anxiety, increases the capacity to tolerate depressive anxiety and loss, and hence diminishes the need for violent splitting and fragmentation. Additional symbol formation occurs. And with the release and experience of anxiety there is relief as well, because of the experience, no matter how slight, of the capacity to tolerate that anxiety without disintegration, and to be creative in spite of it. I shall not, however, elaborate this point further. For Klein (1940) has shown in detail in her paper on "Mourning and Its Relation to the Manic-Depressive States" how every experience of overcoming obstacles and anxiety—and this applies strongly in work—leads to a furthering of the working through of the infantile depressive position, and a step forward in maturity and in the capacity for sublimation.

A NOTE ON THE ROLE OF THE SUPEREGO IN WORK

My omission of any reference to the role of the superego in work is no measure of its importance; for example, if it is not excessively persecutory, it plays a constructive role in facilitating sublimation, and forwarding work. But it is a subject which I cannot pursue on this occasion, other than to touch briefly upon one point.

When the superego develops in a setting of violent splitting and fragmentation it becomes harsh and per-

secuting in its relation to the ego, and is experienced as
severely restrictive. Klein has elaborated this theme in
her paper "On the Development of Mental Functioning"
(1958). This circumstance is revived in work when concretism is strong. The prescribed limits—the rules and
regulations—within which the work is to be carried out
are experienced as persecuting. And, equally serious,
knowledge itself becomes experienced as persecutory, because one of the important effects of knowledge is to re-
strict and limit the ego's field of choice of action, in the
same way as does the superego. Unconsciously, then,
knowledge is hated and is rejected, commonly by its being
fragmented and repressed. The ensuing resentment against
work is readily illustrated in the behavior of delinquents
and borderline psychotics who react to the demands of
conforming to the prescribed content of work and the
knowledge to be exercised, by omnipotence, carelessness,
and hostile negligence. Equally familiar is the reaction
formation of concrete acceptance of the knowledge one
knows and overdependence upon it, with resentment
against new knowledge which threatens existing conceptions, theories, and frames of reference.

PSYCHOANALYSIS AT WORK

We may illustrate these processes and the effects of concretism under ordinary everyday conditions, by a brief
reference to work which we all know—that of psychoan-
alyzing a patient. The love and energy with which we
pursue the treatment is dependent upon the consistency
between the conscious objective of mental healing and
the content and strength of our unconscious symbolical
reparative drive. We must have undergone sufficient personal analysis to enable us to allocate the requisite mental capacity to the task without interference from other

preoccupations—especially unconscious anxieties—which might distract our attention and weaken our concentration upon the patient's unconscious mind. In listening to our patients, we each use an integrative reticulum, built up from an amalgam of previous material from the patient, and from the particular theories, concepts, and working notions we employ. This integrative reticulum determines our mental set or attitude and hence influences both the direction of our attention and the weight we place upon various aspects of the material that is forthcoming. It thus influences to an important extent what we each actually observe in our patients.

The clarity of our understanding of our patients will, moreover, depend upon the interaction between our objective perception of the patient and the exploration of the patient by projective and introjective identification through which we symbolically experience what it would be like if we were the patient, and if the patient were ourselves. It is likely, however, that the concretive content of the experience will always interfere with this symbolic process to a certain extent, the consequence being that one unconsciously feels oneself to be lost in the patient, and the patient confused inside oneself. This type of concrete projective and introjective identification occurs in countertransference. If concretism is strong, our relationship with the patient may be distorted and disturbed.

The state of mind in lysis and scanning can be illustrated in the free-floating attention necessary for psychoanalytic interpretation. It is free-floating only in the limited sense of being free within a previously established integrative reticulum of analytic theory and of knowledge about the patient. Lysis and scanning occur within this scheme, elements of the patient's associations and behavior being scrutinized and picked over in our search for what to interpret—the integrative reticulum acting as a kind of sieve. Then, by virtue of our own conscious and unconscious mental activity, various elements become linked in our minds, and a potential interpretation is gradually gathered up and consciously formed. At the same time, our sense of timing and tone and verbal formulation remains largely unconscious.

The moment of decision is that point when, having gathered together the material which we consider relevant to an interpretation, we not only feel that the time has come to make an interpretation, but we actually make it—we say it to the patient—we commit ourselves. Having done so, we must then face in reality the effects and consequences of our interpretation.

It is probably the case that psychoanalytic work calls for more continuous concentration and mental work than any other. This fact, plus the fact that one's own anxieties are always subject to being aroused by those of the patient, makes us as analysts more readily vulnerable to disturbances in work by concretism. For instance, concentration might flag and attention wander, or the necessary continuous attention to minute detail in following the patient's associations might provoke a certain amount of confusion. In more extreme form, linking may be inhibited, and interpretation may be experienced as dangerous. Decisiveness in interpretation could be impaired.

A CLINICAL ILLUSTRATION

I wish now to present some clinical material from the analysis of a patient who suffered a schizophrenic breakdown, and who in his fifth year of analysis was just getting back to work. I have chosen this case because it magnifies and highlights the effects of concretism by showing its operation in the setting of a large amount of violent splitting and fragmentation.

The patient, a twenty-eight-year-old man, had worked as a script writer. The interaction of the various phases in work which I have described may be illustrated by material from a number of sessions at a time when he was trying to write a script for television. He came to one session in a half-triumphant half-despairing frame of mind. He thought he had written an excellent talk, but was convinced no one would buy it. "If they did," he boasted triumphantly, "I would show them; I'd capture the audience!"

His attitude struck me as very similar to that of the previous day, when (as on some other occasions) we had analyzed how he had attempted omnipotently to capture me with his talk, so as to get me to do exactly as he pleased—to analyze him, give him insulin treatment, let him stay with me in my house, sleep with my wife, and take over my friends and social life. I interpreted to him, therefore, that he wanted to use television to enter the homes of people and control them with his talk.

He roared with laughter at this connection, and gurgled with triumphant glee, "I'd tell them! I'd get into millions of homes at once. The bastards—I'd shit all over them!"

In the light of his associations and previous material, I was able to interpret to him that the TV audience represented to him his own internal family broken into millions of bits—whom he projected into the viewing families. He was then able to gain control over them by gaining omnipotent control over the television, and entering into their homes. The entry was a forced entry, with his faeces, in which he greedily possessed and controlled everything—food, comfort, and parental sexuality. At a deeper level, it was unconsciously a forced entry into his mother's breast and body.

The producers who would turn down his program were unconsciously his father who was envious of his potency, and who would try to prevent him from forcing entry into his mother and taking control of her. The persons who were libeled in the talk and whom he sought to destroy by so doing, represented his own sadistic and destructive superego; and it was this superego that was fragmented and projected into me and attacked, so that he felt me to be on their side and against him.

When he tried to write, therefore, he had neither a unified objective nor a coherent integrative reticulum. He was literally all over the place. He admitted that those passages of his talk which contained the more persecuted and libelous material tended to be badly written and confused—*garbled* was the term he used. In effect, he could be said to be using a disintegrative framework rather than an integrative one for parts of his writing—attempting to smash his material in bits to disturb and confuse the fragmented internal objects and parts of himself projected into his audience rather than to satisfy that audience.

Under these conditions, the process of lysis was severely interfered with. He explained how, as he tried to write, he could not sort out his ideas. As he tried to find just the right words, the words and ideas seemed to break up in his mind. He could not think in words. He could only spell. A cat was not a cat, but a C–A–T. But even worse, he could not spell correctly, could not get the letters back together into words. Then he felt people laughing at him—his audience, producers, friends jeered and triumphed at his impotence.

Linking and synthesis became impossible for him at such a time, because he experienced himself so concretely inside the job standing for his mother's body. To link only increased his persecutory anxiety, because, for example, it was experienced as a bringing together of the cruel and sadistic penis with the already dangerous contents of his mother's body. Moreover, if he tried to look outside for additional information or knowledge, he became so utterly consumed by envy that he went almost blind with rage. On one occasion, he read a few pages of a favorite author to get just the right style for something he was writing. He then found himself unable to write. In his session on the same day, his associations took us to his unconscious envious and greedy eating of the words on the page—literally "tearing them out of context"—and then feeling terrified and dominated by them internally, with the fear that they would appear in spoilt but recognizable form in his own writing. The simultaneous idealization and incorporation of the other author and her work partly made matters worse by increasing his own feelings of inferiority, hopelessness, and despair.

Under these conditions, decision became terrifying and he would retire to bed, sometimes for days on end, and retreat into magical fantasies in which he believed for the time being that he was sorting out all his difficulties.

WORKING CAPACITY AND CONFIDENCE

I should like finally to return to an earlier theme—that weight or heaviness of responsibility is connected with the length of time a person must exercise discretion on his own account. The longer the time-span the longer must the anxiety of uncertainty be faced—anxiety without which work cannot be said to have been done. The ability to maintain a continuous working through of that anxiety, and to go on exercising discretion and making decisions, demands that the requisite and symbolic con-

tents of the mental processes involved in work must pre-
dominate over the concretive processes—a state of affairs
requiring the dominance of love over hate. It is these
conditions which lead to confidence in one's own judgment
and capacities. They reduce persecutory anxiety and violent splitting. They provide an unconscious sense of well-
being and ease, and faith in the ability to restore and
nurture the internal good objects. These feelings lie at
the root of confidence in one's own creative impulses and
sublimations and capacity to tolerate anxiety and uncertainty.

To the extent that these conditions are not fulfilled,
confidence in work, and the capacity to do it, are diminished. Uncertainty replaces confidence, and increases
anxiety and confusion. The longer the time-span of the
discretion to be exercised, the greater will be the piling
up of anxiety and uncertainty. Under these conditions
the processes of sublimation tend to be reversed. Plastic
symbol formations break down and become increasingly
fragmented and concretive in order to bind defused instinctual energy and to diminish persecutory anxiety. I
believe that these are the basic processes underlying disturbed work.

This description applies equally to neurotic flight into
excessive work. Such flight generally contains as a dominant feature the splitting-off and fragmentation of a part
of the work field with the result that the work tends to
be soulless and lacking in humanity. The internal reflection of this work is a splitting-off and fragmentation
of parts of the mind, so that psychic processes which
might enrich the work-process are not available, and sublimation is inhibited. One of the paradoxical results of
making a "success" of such work is that concretism and
fragmentation are thus reinforced, and an impoverishment of personality occurs.

Processes of disintegration and concretism are always present to some extent in the unconscious, and they are reinforced by the failure and anxiety they induce. These processes require constantly to be reversed, and daily work is one of the means by which this reversal occurs. Working—and especially working for a living—is therefore a fundamental activity in a person's testing and strengthening of his sanity.

ETYMOLOGICAL APPENDIX

A number of the psychological processes described above can be illustrated in the metaphoric content of the language of work which symbolizes these processes and the accompanying sensations, in concrete terms.

1. *Lysis* ("lysis"—to loosen) is the root of analysis, to loosen apart. This notion of a loosening and separating out of mental elements at this stage in work occurs in many words connected with it: *discern, discriminate*, and *discretion* (all from "dis-cernere," to separate apart). The term *skill* has the same reference (from "skijl," to divide or separate), relating it to the ability to tease out and discern; so also have the words connected with solving a problem, *solve, resolve, solution* (from "se-luere," to loosen apart, "luere" being the Latin equivalent of the Greek "lysis").

The loosening in the above sense is linguistically to be contrasted with fragmentation ("frangere," to fracture or break) which expresses a sharp and conclusive breaking apart.

As against words having to do with discretion and choice, *knowledge* ("gignoskein," a reduplicated form) has the meaning of being able automatically to reproduce previously established data without the anxiety of choice.

2. *Scanning* (from "scandere," to climb or ascend) has

the sense of rising above the loosened elements in the mind and examining them from on high. *Search* and *research* ("circare," to circle about) and *concentrate* ("concentre," center together) express the sense of mentally circling about the loosened elements, and bringing relevant ones together.

The mental circling about from above accords with the concept of a *plan* ("planus," a plain or plateau), that is, a clear area at the surface of the mind from which the elements below can be perceived, and on to which they can be raised. A *hypothesis* ("hypo-thesis," place below) is a construction placed among the elements in the deeper layers of the mind to help in sorting out those which are to be raised to the surface plain. The conception of *relevance* ("re-levare," to raise again) expresses this sense of lifting or raising up and out.

To concentrate gives additional information if we take it back to its Greek root ("kentron," a spike, goad, prick, center) which carries the sense of goading or pricking together. This meaning falls into line with the act of *distinguishing* various elements ("dis-stinguere," to prick apart, or to separate by marking with a prick), as though in the process of lysis, those mental elements which on loosening appear to be relevant are mentally marked for synthesis. In line with this conception is the verbal root of *disappointment* ("dis-ad-punctare," against marking by a prick), in which the process of mental marking of elements is frustrated and leads to failure.

3. *Gathering* and *good* are connected in that both derive from the Indo-European root "gad," meaning fit or suitable; that which is good is that which comprises good and suitable parts gathered together into one whole. The *art* of bringing relevant material together ("ars," fit) is that of the act of fitting. This notion of fitting or fixing elements together appears in many of the terms related

to this phase of work: making connections ("connectere," to bind or knit together), bringing into *context* ("con-texere," to weave together) and *synthesizing* ("syn-thesis," place together).

The *exertion* necessary ("ex-serere," to fasten or bind out) has to do with the putting together in such a manner as to get it out into active use; that is, into consciousness and then into use in reality, or to force it out ("ex-fortis," effort), by means of *effort*.

As against these words associated with a putting or weaving or binding together in an organized form, *confusion* ("con-fundere," to pour together) has the sense of mental elements running together in an unorganized fashion, without patterning or plan.

4. These processes of analysis and synthesis (loosening and bringing together) of the contents of thought are accompanied by differentiation and integration of the mental apparatus itself. The *differentiation* ("dis-ferre," to carry apart) has to do with the capacity to bring different parts of the mental apparatus and different mental processes into play, without destroying mental integration. *Integration* ("integrare," renew, heal, or repair, which in turn is from "in-tangere," untouch, unharm) carries this metaphoric sense of undestroyed or left intact even though differentiated; the deeper psychological significance of this emerges in the fact that "intangere" (Indo-European root "dak," to bite or tear, from whence, e.g., the Greek "dakos," animal of which the bite is dangerous) refers also to unharmed by eating, or untasted, an unconscious etymological connection between mental integration and being undamaged by oral sadism.

5. The use of *decision* in the active sense of committed to action is given by its root ("de-caedere," to cut apart). The essence of a decision is that once it is taken, the

person is cut off from the other courses of action he might have taken.

6. The relating of the sensation of *failure* in work to psychic mechanisms of self-deception is consistent with its derivation ("fallere," to be deceived—and deceive deriving from "de-cipere," to take by causing to fall into a trap); in effect, the internal objects and split-off mental processes are trapped or ensnared as a defense against destructive impulses and persecutory anxiety. *Frustration* ("frustrari," to disappoint, and "frustrus," deceitful) carries a similar connotation of being disappointed through deceit. That is, frustration and failure caused by a person's own inability are experienced in terms of paranoid feelings of being deceitfully treated, a projection of the cunning and deceit characteristic of paranoid–schizoid defenses which frequently contribute to failure.

REFERENCES

Bion, W. R. (1958), On hallucination. *Internat. J. Psycho-Anal.*, 39:341–349.
––––– (1959), Attacks on linking. *Internat. J. Psycho-Anal.*, 40:144–150.
Davidson, S. S. (1959), On catatonic stupor and catatonic excitement. Paper presented to British Psycho-Analytic Society, April 29.
Freud, S. (1911), Formulations on the two principles of mental functioning. *Standard Edition*, 12:218–226. London: Hogarth Press, 1961.
––––– (1923), The ego and the id. *Standard Edition*, 19:13–63. London: Hogarth Press, 1961.
Goldstein, K., & Scheerer, G. (1939), *The Organism*. New York: American Book Co.
Hartmann, H. (1938), *Ego Psychology and the Problem of Adaptation*. New York: International Universities Press, 1958.
Hendrick, I. (1943), Work and the pleasure principle. *Psychoanal. Quart.*, 19:198–209.
Jaques, E. (1956), *Measurement of Responsibility*. Cambridge, MA: Harvard University Press.
Jones, E. (1958), The theory of symbolism. In: *Papers on Psycho-Analysis*. Baltimore: William Wood.

Klein, M. (1930), On the importance of symbol formation in the development of the ego. In: *Collected Writings*, Vol. 3. New York: McGraw-Hill, 1977.

—— (1940), Mourning and its relation to the manic-depressive states. In: *Collected Writings*, Vol. 3. New York: McGraw-Hill, 1977.

—— (1958), On the development of mental functioning. In: *Collected Writings*, Vol. 3. New York: McGraw-Hill, 1977.

Lantos, B. (1952), Metapsychological considerations on the concept of work. *Internat. J. Psycho-Anal.*, 33:114–117.

Milner, M. (1952), Aspects of symbolism in comprehension of the not-self. *Internat. J. Psycho-Anal.*, 33:117–123.

Oberndorf, C. P. (1951), The psychopathology of work. In: *Bull. Menn. Clin.*, 196–206.

Piaget, J. (1953), *The Origin of Intelligence in the Child.* London: Routledge & Kegan Paul.

Rycroft, C. (1956), Symbolism and its relation to primary and secondary processes. *Internat. J. Psycho-Anal.*, 37:167–174.

Segal, H. (1957), Notes on symbol formation. *Internat. J. Psycho-Anal.*, 38:268–278.

Chapter 15

A Contribution to a Discussion of
Freud's Group Psychology and
the Analysis of the Ego

Freud showed the possibility of reasoning about psychological processes by the examination of group life. I should like to consider the present-day position by looking at group behavior in the light of analytic developments since 1920 in the understanding of psychotic areas in neurotic and normal personalities as well as in psychotics.

Let me start by inquiring why it is that psychotics cannot form groups? For example, if you try to get them to play football or otherwise cooperate in groups, they tend to wander aimlessly about. Severely disturbed neurotics do form groups, but the tendency is to form groups that are rather unstable or inflexibly rigid, in such a way that the individuals become embedded in the group. The more normal the personalities in individuals, the more effective the groups that they can form. Why should this be so?

Freud recognized that groups can have both a constructive effect and an inhibiting effect on the individuals who compose them. He tended to confine his considerations, however, to the inhibiting effect of groups. I would like to reverse the process and look first of all at the constructive side.

Life, in fact, begins and goes on in a group situation, despite the fact that the infant has only rudimentary ego-function and cannot consciously differentiate itself into self and other.

With individual development, however, and the independence which goes along with more mature ego development and formation which allows for symbol formation, and the recognition of the difference between self and others, constructive group relationships become possible.

Thus, for example, in committee work, and in work groups and work organizations, individuals are able to work cooperatively in such a manner as to reinforce each other's effectiveness. Group decisions become possible that are better decisions than those that might have been taken by any of the individuals concerned. Or there is the spontaneous structuring of leaderless groups in such a way that different individuals take up the lead depending upon the problem being tackled and their own individual skills for tackling them. Or again, in what Freud calls artificial groups, a hierarchy of decision taking becomes possible, calling for greater capacity the higher in the system one goes, with individuals opting into roles in these systems at a level consistent with their capacity.

These examples show that under certain group conditions, individuals are capable of publicly manifesting their own capacity level as a matter of social reality.

The constructive role-taking described requires that relationships are to some extent inhibited; in order for such inhibition and sublimation to occur, the individuals must be operating under the dominance of libido with fusion of hate transformed to constructive aggression. These psychic conditions are the same as those required for the acceptance of the reality principle and reality-testing, as against the pleasure principle.

In this connection it can be noted that it is by membership of the group that the individual achieves an important aspect of his reality-testing, for it is the group which records the socially verified results of reality-testing and transmits these results from one person to another and from one generation to another. Thus, it is the group which communicates the conceptualization of reality, that is to say, reality expressed in symbolic form.

But why is it that groups do not always function in this constructive manner?

Freud sets the stage for analyzing this problem by establishing the identification processes by which group formation occurs. In *Group Psychology and the Analysis of the Ego* (1921), he establishes both processes of identification; that is to say, identification by introjection of the object, and identification by projection into the object. Indeed it is in that book that the process later called "projective identification" by Melanie Klein (1945) is first described.

If now we look at Melanie Klein's development of these concepts, she makes a distinction which is germane to an understanding of group processes. That is the distinction between normal and pathological projection and introjection.

Her view is that when anxiety is strong then a great deal of splitting and possibly fragmentation takes place in the ego, with the result that projective and introjective identifications take on a fixed or psychotic quality; that is to say, the introjected object is felt concretely as inside in either split or fragmented form. Equally, when parts of the self, impulses and objects, are projected into the external object, the external object is concretely experienced as controlled or dominated by the bits that have been projected into it.

When pathological projective and introjective identifications are being made, then the experience tends to be that of the ghostly or the uncanny in the sense of being penetrated or controlled by objects or having omnipotent control over them. I think it is this quality which Freud remarks on when he points out that one of the outstanding characteristics of hypnosis is its uncanny quality.

Practical experience suggests that in ordinary social life or group processes, normal processes tend to exist side by side with processes that give the appearance of being psychotic and which I think are most accurately identified as being psychotic in fact. Let me give an example from industry. It has to do with setting prices.

What commonly happens is that the cost per unit is estimated, and a percentage profit added. This estimating procedure is complex and costly and the results are not really used. For if sales say the estimated price is too high, the job is usually reestimated. Or if too low, then a higher price is set; that is, the price is set in relation to what it is known the market will pay—and this fact is known before the estimate is drawn up.

Moreover, the estimating procedures are based upon unrealistic costing procedures, which I do not propose to go into here (Brown and Jaques, 1964).

The point I want to illustrate is that the price is fixed by means of the reality-based procedure of assessing the market. But not without going through the costly and troublesome unreality-based estimating procedure.

The striking thing is the way in which the unreal procedure is embedded in and coexists with the realistic perception, and is corrected by it.

The unreality-based perceptions I think are dependent mainly upon the play of unconscious omnipotence—the fantasy that whatever one creates must be good and must be valuable. There is a denial, indulged in by all the group, of the fact that it is quite possible to create valueless goods unwanted by others.

Another example is that given by Freud of the girls and their movie idol, in which there is a denial of jealousy and they become the equals of each other. There is a group-supported denial of the reality of differences among them.

There are dozens of examples that one can give all the way from the mixed picture which tends to be characteristic of reality-based work groups, through to group formations whose sole purpose seems to be to act as vehicles for the expression of psychotic processes in the individuals.

Or to take another example, although in hierarchically structured groups the reality principle requires the recognition of differences in status and capacity, and individuals are able to work to some extent on this basis, there exists side by side with reality the expression of unconscious pride or arrogance and omnipotence in these groups. These occur in the endowment of "higher-ups" with magical power and the resentment and fear of that power; and in the split between the idealization of those at the top and the disparagement of those in intermediate groups.

Now what purpose does this participation in group psychotic processes play in the psychic economy of the individual? I would suggest that we are dealing with a fundamental defense against anxiety in the so-called normal individual; I say "so-called normal" because if any of us were in fact genuinely and deeply normal in the sense of having full insight into the psychotic content of our anxieties, then this kind of group formation would no longer serve any purpose.

By unconscious collusive relations with other individuals, it is possible for us to play out and externalize—get outside of ourselves—conflicts and anxieties which would otherwise be experienced at the deeper levels of the mind in terms of overwhelming anxiety or unendurable psychic pain and torment.

By anxiety and psychic pain I am referring to the unconscious fantasies of persecution internally by objects experienced as hostile and destructive, and to the intense unendurable psychic pain for good objects which have been experienced as damaged or injured and which may be the source of the most horrific guilt and remorse.

We can deal with these conflicts and impulses to some extent by collusive interplay in groups. Manic denial of envy and jealousy, for example, can be reinforced in the group as in Freud's example of the girls and the movie idol. Destructive impulses, hate, death wishes, can be split off and projected into members of the out-group: with the attendant development of idealization and of whitewashing of the good in-group, and paranoid attitude toward the bad out-group. Destructive impulses and paranoid impulses can then be coped with externally, to some extent by active public hate and paranoia and by psychological and, in the final analysis physical, violence. These forms are vividly observable, for example, in political debate, where the most violent slanging of the opposite camp is used as a means of exposing concealed anxieties.

One of the features about the group which is both consoling and provocative of anxiety is the fact that groups—especially corporate groups—are in fact immortal; individuals may die but the group goes on. Thus it is that by achieving his individuality within a group an individual also becomes aware of the fact of his own personal death.

As a result of the play of psychotic processes, he seeks

immortality by identification with the group which is idealized; by being a member of a powerful and ideal group, he becomes powerful and ideal as well as immortal. The most effective of such groups from the point of view of allaying anxiety, but in a pathological way, are groups which establish deities representing in a concrete way the group's sense of its own immortality.

These projections into group life cause diminution of effectiveness in individuals and are a noteworthy characteristic of many groups.

In short, since our knowledge of reality is limited at any given time, group relationships allow for the collusive avowal of a wide range of psychotic or unreal fantasies. These fantasies then become highly structured, they allow for a variety of idealization processes: splitting and fragmentation; paranoid denigration and a cutting of the existence of omnipotent external persons and deities; denial of envy, hate, jealousy, rage, murderousness, all expressed in socially sanctioned and therefore concealed and denied ways, side by side with, and fused with, reality-based processes.

The fact that these impulses and conflicts are externally projected and built into social structures becomes clear when they are challenged by observations of reality. Resentment and fury are engendered and intense denial occurs.

In other words, resistance to new ideas is directly dependent upon how far the ideas which they would replace are the subject of unconscious collusive processes in which the individuals are involved in order to avoid anxiety and psychic pain.

The behavior of the townsfolk in the story of the Emperor's new clothes is the myth which best embodies the psychic processes which I am trying to describe.

Coming back now to the individual, the following conclusions present themselves.

The way in which psychotic and nonpsychotic processes appear side by side in a quasi-integrated manner in groups suggests that in the so-called normal personality these psychic processes are integrated in the same way.

Following the kind of sequence described by Freud in the postscript in which he tries to discriminate between the states of being in love, hypnosis, and neurosis, the following list suggests itself:

1. The psychotic individual is one in whom the psychotic parts of personality are overwhelmingly strong, split off from the rest of the personality, unmitigated by normal processes, and with independence of action for longer or shorter periods of time; psychotic individuals are unable to form groups because their projections and introjections are so overwhelmingly concrete and intense that relationships with others are experienced as too persecuting and painful; they aimlessly wander about if presented with group tasks or games;

2. Neurosis is a process in which the psychotic and the reality-based processes are more evenly balanced and intermingled, with psychotic processes from time to time gaining the upper hand;

3. The so-called normal individual is one in whom psychotic processes are fused with reality-based psychic processes and mitigated by them, making it possible to take part in reality-based group activities, but still using group life to play out in a psychotic way his deeper-lying conflicts;

4. The model of the genuinely normal individual is that of a person with conscious and unconscious

insight into the psychotic contents of his mental processes, so that a more complete mitigation of these by reality-based processes is achieved, with reduced necessity to play out psychotic contents in unconscious collusive behavior with other individuals in group life. He can form effective working relationships without unconscious group collusion because of the tolerance and resignation made possible by insight.

As a side issue, it may be of interest to note that with the development of society the independent individual comes more prominently to the fore. In primitive society the group is dominated by the family, and the individual tends to remain embedded in his family throughout his life. Primitive law is based on this fact and tends to be the law of the family rather than a law of the individual in his society. Modern industrial society requires a greater independence in the individual in the sense that it requires the individual to relate himself more to the large social unit unprotected by the family group in which he has grown up.

The observation of group processes and the interplay between individual and group life can give a particular perspective on primitive preverbal infant impulses and conflicts, and relationships; it gives a kind of magnified picture of these processes, and as such can complement both analysis and infant observation.

REFERENCES

Brown, W., & Jaques, E. (1964), *Product Analysis Pricing*. London: Heinemann Educational Books Ltd.

Freud, S. (1921), Group psychology and the analysis of the ego. *Standard Edition*, 18:69–142. London: Hogarth Press, 1961.

Klein, M. (1945), The Oedipus complex in the light of early anxieties. *Internat. J. Psycho-Anal.*, 26:370–419.

Chapter 16

Psychotic Anxieties and the Sense of Justice

I

The aspiration toward the discovery of inherent norms of justice in mankind has been a recurring theme in the theories of law propounded by jurists for the past two thousand years—through Aristotle, Cicero, St. Augustine, Aquinas, Locke, Hume, and Kant. It is the theme of natural law. Because, however, the concept of natural law has been founded upon moral, ethical, political, and religious imperatives, it has fallen into lesser repute among present-day thinkers.

Psychoanalytical experience and theory strongly support the intuitive basis of the theory of natural law, even if they differ radically from any of the philosophically derived arguments propounded to establish the theory. This comes especially from Freud's conception of superego development and function. The sense of what is right and wrong, just and unjust, fair and unfair develops in early childhood, and sets the groundwork for what appear later as the more sophisticated judgments of justice and of culpability.

The further developments of Freud's work which are associated with Melanie Klein have served to strengthen the bond between psychoanalytical theory and the conception of natural law. I refer particularly to her concepts of the early infantile development of the experience or sense of good and bad objects, good and bad impulses, and of the primordial superego and primal guilt; and her discovery of the unconscious psychotic anxieties and processes, deriving from early infancy, which disturb and distort normal adult behavior. These conceptions reinforce the implication of Freud's theories that there is a normal sense of morality and justice which would emerge and express itself were human behavior not so commonly and intensely influenced by personality disorders stemming from the force of those psychotic anxieties. The possibility thus emerges of laying a basis for making objective judgments about human values and norms of justice.

I propose to combine these leading notions from psychoanalysis with certain data from my social-analytic work to establish that in fact an empirical science of human law may be a practical endeavor. In order to preclude any possible confusion between this scientific approach to human behavior, and the moral, ethical, religious, or political approach of the natural law theorists and philosophers, I shall use the concept of requisite law rather than that of natural law. By requisite, I mean reality-determined, required by the real properties of the situation, or, as the dictionary has it, required by the nature of things. By the phrase requisite law, I shall refer to law which is required to facilitate psychic equilibrium in the individual members of a society and social equilibrium within the society as a whole. I shall hope to show that the establishment of such equilibrium in individuals and in the social groups they compose is entirely possible, so long as their behavior is not too much under the domination of unconscious psychotic anxieties and processes.

II

We each have a sense of when we are being treated fairly or unfairly. Equally, we know, or feel, when we are behaving fairly or unfairly toward others. How we come to have these feelings, or make our judgments on these questions of the justice or injustice of others or of ourselves may not be immediately apparent. Our sense of right or wrong, of grievance or gratitude, of self-righteousness or guilt, is not usually a thought-out reaction. It is a spontaneous response. And if the issue is one which seems important to us, our response is not only spontaneous but very strong.

Thus when a person does something which he considers to be deserving of some reward or recognition, he has a strong and definite sense of whether the reward he receives is an appropriate one. He is aggrieved if it is less than he deems fair. I will suggest that he is also chagrined or uneasy in some part of his mind if it is more than he feels is fair. Similarly, he has an aggrieved sense if he receives too great a punishment for a misdemeanor; and, I will suggest, he will somehow feel overindulged and guilty if he gets off too lightly.

When we ourselves do the rewarding or punishing, we equally have an intuitive sense of whether we are being mean or overgenerous with our praise or other reward, and of whether we are being cruel and sadistic or fainthearted and indulgent in taking someone to task.

In considering these questions of right and wrong, fair and unfair, just and unjust, there are two points worth noting. First, we are dealing with relationships between people—with the differential entitlements of people under given circumstances. It is a question of what is fair, or right, or just, relative to someone else or to some others. What is fair for A depends on the entitlements of B, C,

and D. Whether it is a case of children assessing the
fairness of parents or teachers, or employees assessing
the fairness of their pay, or a citizen evaluating the fairness of his treatment by a magistrate or by the tax
laws—there is a common thread: "Why should I get only
this much, when he got that?" or "Why should he have
forefeited only that, when I suffered so heavily?"

The second point is that we are dealing not only with
differential entitlements—with comparative treatment
—but with a sense of balance or equilibrium. For something to be fair or just connotes that it is just right; neither
too much nor yet too little. There is a point at which the
amount of gratification, or obligation of reward or punishment, just balances the act to which it is connected.
If the amount is any more or less then there is an imbalance, a disequilibrium. It is this disequilibrium which
is experienced as a grievance or a feeling of persecution
if the punishment is too great or the reward too small;
and as guilt or fear of the envy of others if the punishment
is too little or the reward too great.

III

It is a matter of common experience and common expectation that the expressed judgment of individuals on what
is fair or unfair tend to be pretty unreliable—especially
when their own interests are at stake. Two persons in
conflict with each other over a question of their respective
rights are hardly likely to be good judges of the merits
of their own argument on the matter at issue. It would
appear that we simply do not have any common individual standards or norms of justice which can be relied
upon. We each apparently differ in our standards—our
judgment being distorted by the operation of such mental
processes as jealousy or envy, pride or vanity, omnipotent
self-justification and aggrandizement or masochistic self-

punishment. More, our needs and desires differ, as do our backgrounds, our experiences, our outlook on life. It would hardly be surprising, therefore, if we had widely varying notions about what constitutes justice.

And yet, our views cannot be all that fortuitous and individually determined. We do have laws to which we all conform, many of which are pretty universally held to be fair and just. The fact that law based on equity is possible as well as common law suggests that deep inside us there are at least some common standards of justice. Both consciously and unconsciously we have a strong desire for law and order in our social relations, and we shun chaos and disorder, whatever unconscious impulses there may be to the contrary. However much the play of the pleasure principle may distort our desires and judgment, the reality principle demands that we bring reason into our relationships with one another.

The possibility that in the reality-bound conscious and unconscious areas of the mind we may have standards of equity which are the product of our psychological makeup, and which we share in common with each other, was brought home to me in the course of studying the reactions of employed people to the wage or salary they received for their work. This subject of payment is an explosive one. The levels of payment appear to be determined pretty exclusively by power bargaining. Actions based on principle do not appear to have much of a part in the process. Employers are assumed solely to want to buy labor at the lowest possible rate; and every employed person is assumed solely to be out to get for himself just as much as he can. The balance is thought to be held by the labor supply and demand situation, which strongly influences the power positions and thereby affects the precise level at which the bargain will finally be struck.

That these competitive and self-seeking motives operate there is little reason to doubt. They are revealed in the actual conduct of negotiations. And they are to be expected from the destructive impulses—the unconscious hate, greed, envy, omnipotence—which influence human behavior. The question is whether there are not other motives and judgments which play a part as well. In particular, what part do the loving impulses—reflecting the operation of the life instinct—play? My evidence is that they have a most important influence, which is usually unrecognized.

I have had considerable opportunity to collect information about people's reactions to their pay. This information was gathered under the special conditions of a method of measuring the level of responsibility in individual jobs, so that each person's feelings about his payment for his work could be matched against the size of responsibility he was carrying in his job. What may at first sight seem a very surprising result was obtained. People carrying the same level of responsibility in their jobs stated the same level of payment as fair for the work they were being given to do. Regardless of their occupation—manual worker, clerk, engineer, chemist, factory manager, accountant, managing director—regardless of what they were actually getting paid, and regardless of their income tax levels, each person carries a private opinion of what his job is worth. These private opinions of individuals match, as though each person, without knowing it, is using precisely the same standards in judging what he considers to be fair pay for this work.

This pattern of felt-fair payment I have termed the *equitable work–payment scale*. I have data from persons with incomes of $7.00 an hour at the bottom level, to $80,000 per annum at the top.[1]

[1] These figures are as of 1968. My current data (1988) range from $35,000 to $450,000 per annum.

IV

When reactions of individuals to their actual payment are considered in the light of their level of work, a characteristic pattern of responses can be found. Payment at the equitable level is intuitively experienced as fair relative to others, although there may be a simultaneously held view that the economy as a whole ought to provide a generally higher standard of living for all. Deviations in payment below the equitable level are accompanied by feelings of dissatisfaction which become stronger the greater the deviation. Deviations at the 10 percent level lead to an active sense of grievance, complaints or the desire to complain, and, if no redress is given, an active desire to change jobs, or to take collective action if an organized group is involved; these reactions become very strong at the 15 to 20 percent level of deviation.

Deviations above the equitable level (rare in the recent inflationary situation) are accompanied by feelings of being *relatively* well off as compared with others; at the 10 to 15 percent level of deviation there is a strong sense of receiving preferential treatment, which may harden into bravado. There is an underlying feeling of unease about the arousal of jealous resentment and envy in others and therefore uncertainty about how long the relatively advantageous position can be maintained.

The results suggest that it is not necessarily the case that each one is solely out to get as much as he can for himself for his work. There appear to be equally strong desires that each one should earn the right amount—a fair and reasonable amount relative to others.

At the same time, results were obtained which indicate that each person has an intuitive judgment both of his level of capacity and of the rate of progress of his capacity. Without presenting the results in detail, I can

say that they show that we have a sharp intuitive judgment not only of whether our work is above or below our
capacity, but also of just what the equitable level of payment is for work that would be consistent with our capacity.

In short, the upshot of these findings is that we each
have an accurate intuitive judgment of:

1. the level of work we are capable of doing;
2. the actual level of work in our job;
3. the payment that would be equitable for our job;
4. the payment that would be equitable for work con-
    sistent with our capacity.

Most striking of all, however, were those findings connected with our intuitive comparisons of differentials. In
the first place, the differential distribution of the equitable work–payment scale was felt to be fair. Suppose for
example, $33,000 a year is the equitable rate for the level
of work A, and $155,000 a year is the equitable rate for
level of work B. And suppose that one person is working,
say, as a designer in a job with level of work A, while
another person is working in a job as a factory manager,
with a level of work B. Then they will each feel they are
being paid fairly relative to each other, if in fact the first
is receiving $33,000 and the second $155,000. We feel
that differential reward should go with differential responsibility carried.

Second, we have a strong intuitive sense of how we
are faring relative to each other with respect to the equity
of our pay. If our own payment is equitable, and others
also are in receipt of equitable payment and not overequity, then ferment over payment dies down to a low
level. If, in addition, the conditions are such that there

is opportunity for individuals to be employed at a level consistent with their capacity and to be progressed in work and payment at a rate consistent with their rate of progress in capacity, a state of equilibrium is created, with the induction of feelings of incentive toward work.

V

These findings and conclusions about our unconscious awareness of the degree of consistency between our capacity, work, earnings, and consumption, and of the sense of balance and peace of mind which we tend to experience when we judge all to be in line with each other, may be at variance with everyday notions and with customary ways of talking about these matters. Work and money are so commonly the source of fantasies and daydreams of wealth and creativity, comfort and security, greatness and power—or, in contrast, of masochistic fantasies of failure, impotence, and destructiveness. Our conscious self-evaluation and ambitions may be subject to gross fluctuation from depressed self-contempt to omnipotent aggrandizement, according to our mood as affected by our unconscious fantasies.

There is an apparent paradox in our outlook. Our unconscious awareness appears on the one hand to be unexpectedly realistic, and on the other hand and at the same time, to be irrational and emotionally unstable. This paradox is resolved once it is recognized that both processes—reality-tested awareness, and fantasy-dominated wish fulfillment—may go on simultaneously in different parts of the unconscious mind. In the neurotic parts of our unconscious minds—and indeed in the psychotic-dominated pockets which are a part of the mental makeup of even the most normal persons—the picture we

may have of ourselves and our economic condition may
be totally at variance with that outlined in the foregoing
assumptions.

It is likely that anyone who is capable of earning his
own living has developed a sufficient degree of inner reality to be able to make the unconscious judgments about
himself and his work of which I am speaking. But the
existence of an unconscious assessment of our real capacity does not necessarily mean that this assessment is
consciously accepted. Quite the contrary. Very few of us
are capable of tolerating consciously an accurate and stable self-appraisal of our capacities and limitations. Some
of our deepest unconscious defenses against anxiety
would be threatened—fantasy gratification and omnipotence, or by contrast, self-effacement. We repress our
knowledge of our true capacity, and retain it repressed
and split-off in our unconscious mind. This splitting and
repression makes for emotional oscillations in our conscious self-evaluation, while at the same time we may
maintain our unconscious awareness of our adjustment
to work reality. It is only in the exceptional mature and
integrated person that the unconscious awareness of
work and capacity becomes the sole or even the major
determinant of conscious self-appraisal.

At the same time, just because our conscious picture
of ourselves and our capacities may be heavily influenced
by unrealistic unconscious fantasies, this does not necessarily imply that we will behave unrealistically in our
work and economic life. The unconscious reality sense
has an extremely powerful influence on behavior in the
real world, particularly in that area of the real world
where behavior is reality-tested by economic satisfaction
or dissatisfaction, and, in the final analysis, by economic
survival. We are always dealing, therefore, with a typically human situation of conflict in each person between

the demands of fantasy satisfaction and the demands of reality.

VI

The existence of such powerful and consistently experienced norms as I have described may seem to make it difficult to explain why there is so much trouble about payment differentials and wage negotiations. How is it that the norms do not simply dominate the social scene and impose a pattern on the economic relationships between individuals such that the demands of equity are met? This question raises the fundamental issue of the difference in the effect on behavior between unconscious intuitively comprehended norms and comparisons, and those norms when they are made explicit and consciously recognized and applied by appropriate objective social mechanisms.

In fact, the unconscious norms of equity play a larger part in wage and salary negotiations than is usually recognized or assumed. Notions of what is fair figure very prominently in these discussions and negotiations, and in the feelings of unrest which stimulate demands for increase. It is not possible for one group to get too great an increase without stimulating demands all round precisely on grounds of fairness and justice, mixed with jealousy, envy, and hostility, which are also aroused. Thus considerations of what is fair and equitable play a considerable part in determining the general pattern of differentials in distribution of incomes in the country at large. But, in the absence of explicit and conscious control, there is room for sufficient uncertainty and unclarity to allow for trouble, but without the whole system necessarily breaking down.

The extent to which unconscious motivations enter

into the continuing troubles over payment differentials
may be observed if we consider for a moment what the
situation would be if there existed requisite procedures
for regulating payment in an equitable way.

Given requisite law controlling the actual relations
between individuals, each one is more exposed in himself
to his own unconscious destructive impulses and the anxieties which arise from them. The opportunity to express
greed, envy, hate, jealousy, and dissatisfaction, by unconscious participation in social relations which in reality
contain some economic inequity, is lost. To the extent,
therefore, that we are influenced in our behavior by unconscious psychotic processes, requisitely controlled social relations externally appear to threaten our inner
psychic equilibrium. To demonstrate this point, I shall
turn for a moment to consider the general question of
psychic gratification and equilibrium.

VII

The gratifications we receive, and frustrations to which
we are subjected, have two main aspects: the requisite,
and the psychotic. The requisite gratifications are both
physiological and symbolic. They include sexual gratification and the taking in and putting out of water, food,
and air necessary for the material maintenance of life.
The symbolic gratifications include the intake and output
of love and affection, the emotional aspect of material
things, language and ideas, arts, competition, and recognition—and all the activities which we think of as human activities, concerned with the psychological
satisfaction of the individual and the carrying on of social
relations.

As against the requisite content of gratification, the
psychotic content of gratification and frustration is that

which is based upon unconscious psychotic processes—upon unconscious magical fantasies—in which the gratification is disconnected from the reality of either the material or the symbolic content of the object which is taken in or given out.

The distinction I am making is one aspect of the distinction made by Freud in terms of the operation of the pleasure principle and the reality principle. In the deep unconscious mind, instinctual gratification gained under the dominance of the pleasure principle is connected with the hallucinatory gratification of the young infant.

It is to the work of Melanie Klein that we owe a much clearer understanding of these psychotic processes in the normal personality. According to her theories derived from her clinical experiences, unresolved psychotic anxieties—both persecutory and depressive—from earliest infancy persist into adult life. The operation of these anxieties, and of the defenses against them, influence our behavior in a decisive manner. The most fundamental of these influences is the use unconsciously of violent splitting and fragmentation of objects, impulses, and parts of the self as a defense against persecutory anxiety and internal persecutors. This violent splitting is accompanied by a type of projective and introjective identification which gives an unconscious hallucinoid aspect to all of our perceptions and experiences. That is to say, in addition to the normal requisite and symbolic content of our perceptions, in the deepest layers of our unconscious minds we deal with our objects in a quasi-psychotic manner. We concretely expel the products of our internal violent splitting and fragmentation into external objects, and partially behave toward those objects as though they really are the projected bits with which we are identified. Simultaneously, we violently introject the projectively modified object, and experience it inside as though it were concretely there.

These processes of violent projective and introjective identification based on unconscious splitting and fragmentation, must be distinguished from the normal processes of projection and introjection which lead to symbol formation and symbolic relationships. In symbolism, the external objects are perceived in their own right, the split-off and projected objects being experienced as in the external object, but not engulfing it.

According to the view outlined, every experience of gratification—material and symbolic—always contains an element of unconscious giving out and taking in of parts of our selves, our impulses and our internal objects. And we unconsciously experience similar processes of projection and introjection on the part of those to whom we are related in connection with the gratification. The hallucinoid content of the process, however, distorts our relation to the event, so that unconscious elements enter into our response based on our identification of the gratification or frustration with our own unconscious psychotic projections. It is these last elements which are responsible for the most intractable forms of personal disequilibrium, and which contribute heavily to the persistence of motivated injustice in human affairs.

VIII

If we were motivated only by loving impulses, our psychological processes would by implication be requisite ones, and there would be a certain balance or equilibrium in our material and symbolic gratifications and frustrations. Thus, for example, the intuitively equitable norms and standards which I have described would be free to operate unhampered. We would be in a state of quasi-stable equilibrium—that is to say, a state not of perfect equilibrium, but of ups and downs, in which we would seek requisite gratification, and accept requisite obligations, and experience satisfaction when we had had enough. Moreover, frustrations would be more effectively withstood. Frustration, indeed severe frustration, arising from real external difficulties or catastrophe, can be tolerated so long as it can be felt that everyone is suffering to the same relative degree; that is, so long as it is experienced as equitably shared.

From the very earliest days, genuine gratification is derived from the experience and taking in of feeding and maternal care, and the putting out of excreta and love under the dominance of loving impulses. There is a minimum of greed and demandingness. The healthy ego knows when it has had enough. Sucking is followed by loving play and reparation, followed by sleep. Under these conditions the groundwork of the healthy superego is constructed—and the basis for healthy self-restraint and due regard for the needs of others is laid—through the introjection of the satisfying breast and mother, and identification with these objects and loving impulses.

But we are not simply under the influence of libidinal impulses. The death instinct, and its reflections in our destructiveness—in hate, greed, envy, jealousy, omnipotence—powerfully influences our behavior. In the infant in the paranoid–schizoid position, it distorts gratification by threatening to destroy good objects and the self. Violent splitting and fragmentation, and projective and introjective identification, are used as defense against the resulting unconscious threat of annihilation. These defenses lead to the establishment in the deep layers of the unconscious mind of primordial persecuting objects split off from primordial idealized objects. These objects disturb the formation of the superego, and adversely distort its functioning. In the depressive position, when whole objects are created, under the impact of greater integration and capacity for reparation, the ability to achieve symbolic along with material gratification is strengthened. But the deeper-lying unconscious relationship with the primordial idealized and persecuting objects remains. Gratification is always tinged with a degree of disappointment, either through shortcomings in the idealized content of the object, or unconscious fantasies of annihilation by its persecuting contents. Both frustration and punishment are experienced as intensely persecuting. At this level of mental functioning there is no differential justice. There is either persecutory injustice threatening the self, or guilt-provoking favoritism depriving one's good objects of their due share, and stimulating their hatred and envy.

The strength of these psychotic processes determines how much we fall short of a genuine quasi-stable equilibrium in our psychic life and limits our capacity to tolerate justice and law and order. Superimposed upon the requisite and genuine quasi-stable equilibrium is the pseudo-equilibrium of successful defenses against psychotic anxiety. This equilibrium is a pseudo-equilibrium because it is not based upon positive satisfaction. It arises rather from schizoid and manic defenses which wall off and segregate persecutory and depressive anxiety, but do not resolve them. The individual is therefore constantly threatened by recrudescence of anxiety, and the pseudo-equilibrium likely to be broken.

Our defenses against psychotic anxiety—other than by retreat into psychosis—are markedly enhanced by evidence of the existence of external injustice, and by internal evidence of resulting unfair frustration produced by the greed, cunning, dishonesty, selfishness, and deceit of others. Such external conditions constitute a projection screen which support splitting and denial mechanisms. The basic psychological mechanism is that of nursing a grievance.

Nursing a grievance for purposes of self-justification is an everyday phenomenon. Children often refuse to be humored when they feel persecuted or guilty. Adults harbor grievances against each other. In the clinical situation, patients frequently develop and harbor grievances, in the transference relationship, as for example in the following case of Mrs. X, a forty-five-year-old divorced woman. She reexperienced her oedipal conflicts in her resentment of my being married. She envied my wife for enjoying what the patient perceived as an ideally good marriage, and was jealous of me for giving my wife such ideally good care and attention. She was equally grudging of the analysis she received from me. On one occasion, for example, when she consciously thought my interpretations were especially accurate and good, she became hostile and spiteful. She hated everyone, she said, and felt I was trying to get her to be nice, and to like everyone.

From previous sessions, I was able to analyze this material in terms of her nursing a grievance against me representing her mother, and particularly against the feeding breast. She felt she had destroyed her mother's peace of mind and sanity, and at a deeper level, the creativeness and goodness of the breast. She, therefore, projected her destructive impulses, her envy, her greed, her unfairness, into me representing her mother and the breast. I was then unfair and mad, and good to my wife in order to make the patient jealous and envious. She in turn was therefore justifiably aggrieved. But if I appeared to give her good analysis, much of the justification for her grievance was removed. She was then more exposed to her own guilt-ridden anxieties, and thus begrudged and resisted her analysis—a typical negative therapeutic reaction.

She then recalled occasions when she was a very small child, when her mother would tickle her tummy in order to get her out of severe temper tantrums. She responded to this treatment overtly with glowering rejection, but inwardly with delight. From this and subsequent material, we were able to explore how she introjected her good mother and good breast, and tried to get rid of her own bad impulses, parts of herself, and persecuting objects, by projection into external objects. Being aggrieved and nursing the grievance thereby took on a double function, which I think is probably present to some extent in all grievances. She was aggrieved, in the sense of *having a grievance against* the split-off and projected bad objects; and she was aggrieved, in the sense of being *grief-stricken about* her destroyed good objects, toward which she tried to make reparation by internally nursing them.

When anxiety, guilt, and despair became unbearable, she would become confused, resort to drugs and alcohol, and precipitate her affairs into a chaotic state. She blamed all the people she attacked, for her troubles, and was aggrieved by her unconsciously motivated perception of their hostility. She had little capacity to enjoy gratification, and accept obligations, without feeling guilty and persecuted. A certain amount of external chaos was essential to her defenses against her anxieties. Without this chaos, her self-justification was weakened. To the extent that ideas of justice entered into her world, it was the obsession of a harsh and severe superego. Real ideas of justice were displaced by chronic grievance.

IX

I have illustrated the nursing of grievances, and unconscious need for external chaos, because I consider these mechanisms to be the paradigm for the psychological forces which inhibit and distort the play of equity in social life. Self-justification swamps justice. Or, contrariwise, equity and justice are unconsciously perceived as threatening to the denial by means of self-justification which is used as a defense against persecutory and depressive anxiety.

Where payment questions are concerned, the reflection can be observed in social processes of the defenses against psychotic anxiety I have mentioned in the brief case illustration. A prominent feature is the chaos and confusion, which can be blamed on "the other side." Splitting is complete. Our side is right. Their side is wrong. "They" are accused of being greedy. Everyone is seen as out for all he can get. Denial of reality is very strong, as witness the internal inconsistency of the majority of the arguments and counterarguments put forward in favor of one case or another.

Triumph and the exercise of power, and the attribution of omnipotence to one's own arguments and of omniscience to one's leaders, are prominent features. Unprincipled cunning in bargaining, and mutual vilification, are accepted as a part of the game.

This social situation gives full scope for the concealed and socially sanctioned play of greed and envy, including, on occasions, carrying chaos to the point where there is likelihood of spoiling it for everyone—the natural fruit of envy. Hostility is rife, and open aggression often occurs. Genuine exploitation is in fact carried out by the most powerful side. There is the fullest opportunity for idealization of one's cause, grievances against the exploiting persecutor, self-justification, and a general playing out of schizoid and manic defenses in mass social processes which effectively obscure the unconsciously collusive participation of each individual person composing the mass.

But all the time, balancing these psychotically dominated social processes are the reality-dominated forces, and the strong impulses in individuals toward genuine gratification and equilibrium. The effective operation of these forces is partially blocked by the fact that conscious intellectual clarification of the problem is inhibited by the psychotic anxieties and processes. The development of principle and law is therefore held back, so that the constructive strivings get little or no support from externally established requisite knowledge and social institutions.

Nevertheless, as the findings on equity in payment demonstrate, the unconscious intuitive awareness of individuals about differential entitlement and equity set a frame, a limit, to the play of psychotic anxieties in social relations.

These norms of equity are a part of healthy superego functioning. If, for example, the members of one group go too far in blackening the character of members of the opposing group, projecting into them their own malice, greed, and destructiveness, then the sense of requisite guilt, derived from the healthy areas of the superego, becomes too powerful, and inhibits further irrational behavior.

It is thus in connection with the healthy areas of the ego and the superego that social life, justice, and law have their effect. The sense of justice in the individual is most actively tapped by laws and regulations which conform to our unconscious norms of right and wrong and which thus contribute to genuine equilibrium in the individual. The explicit formulation of law allows the healthy parts of the superego to be projected into the institutions which mediate the law, and to be reintrojected and reinforced by contact with the consciously recognized and accepted social consensus. The good law symbolizes the good conscience; and the scales of justice symbolize genuine equilibrium in the individual as much as they do the act of weighing the evidence.

X

Because the concept of natural law has been founded upon moral, ethical, and political imperatives, it is not of use for our present purposes. In its place, I would substitute the concept of requisite law; that is to say, law based upon scientifically discovered and objectively demonstrable, generally occurring, human norms. It is law which springs from the inherently orderly parts of the mind of men, and which, when correctly understood, is as immutable as is our basic psychological makeup.

The discovery by Melanie Klein of the unconscious psychotic anxieties and processes in normal adult behavior makes it possible to distinguish between requisite and nonrequisite law, in terms of the extent to which these psychotic processes and unconscious collusions are involved. This discrimination between right and wrong, in terms of the intensity of psychotic gratification, is one example of what is likely to be one of her fundamental contributions—her extension of the work begun by Freud, to lay a basis for making objective judgments about human values.

One of the main tasks of law and of legal procedures and institutions is to establish in a manifest and external form the conditions governing the duties and entitlements of individuals and corporate bodies in relation to each other and to the state, when interests overlap and encroach upon each other. In its fullest sense, requisite law should not only express what we might consciously consider reasonable and just in the sorting out of conflicting needs and requirements were we not ourselves personally involved in the matter. It ought to express the deep unconscious sense of order and norms of fairness which, given unfettered outlets, would suffuse our conscious awareness with the impulse to achieve what is sane and balanced in human relations, and would provide the solid intuitive foundation for that conscious achievement.

Side by side with the unconscious constructive and balanced sense of individuals occur the psychotic processes which we have considered. It is these processes, based on anxiety and conflict, which cause such profound distortion of the way we see things in practice, and sway our judgment away from balanced and equitable conclusions toward unconscious collusive involvement in psychotic group processes designed to relieve anxiety and personal confusion and chaos, regardless of the cost in social injustice and strife. In our minds, a sense of natural law and order coexists with the impulse toward lawlessness and chaos. It is the function of the externalized statement of requisite law to reify the internal sense of law and order we possess, so that we can exert conscious effort and employ our intellect in negating the effects of the outpouring of unconscious and disruptive forces into our social relationships.

The equitable society, then, is a lawful society in the deepest sense of lawful. Its laws bolster the rational strivings of its members. And they inhibit the dumping into its social relationships of the irrational hate, envy, greed, and omnipotence which undermine those relationships and the institutions which mediate them.

To the extent that requisite laws exist, we are gripped more firmly in contact with our inner selves. These conditions are among those essential to psychological health and integration. They support the strengthening of character and the growth of moral courage. To achieve and maintain these conditions we must understand the reality of the power of our unconscious destructiveness, and equally learn to trust the power of our unconscious striving toward psychic equilibrium and to express those strivings in the form of conscious and explicit norms and requisite social institutions.

Chapter 17

Guilt, Conscience, and Social Behavior

What makes civilized social behavior possible? Here is a question that has engaged the interest of men through countless centuries. How is it that it is possible to have laws to which people on the whole will conform? Why do most conform? Why do some break the laws? And most particularly, why do most of us not break the law, even when we might gain considerably from doing so and there is no apparent risk of being caught?

It is this question that I wish to consider here. For contained within it is the intriguing question of the sense of morality, of conscience, of justice, which we all have, and which causes us to behave in accord with externally prescribed modes of conduct and behavior. To understand the nature of this inner sense of conscience is of the greatest importance. It is the key to an understanding of the process whereby we learn to live in our families, among our friends, and in society at large, the process of the socialization of the individual. In order to understand it, we should have to understand where our social awareness and conscience came from; how it develops; why it is very strong in some and weak in others; why it is sometimes felt as harsh and oppressive; and why it is sometimes accompanied by rejection and rebelliousness.

To these questions, psychoanalysis has certain solutions to offer. These solutions stem from Freud's profound and original insight into the nature of human guilt, an insight which marked a great step forward in our understanding of human behavior. It set the stage, as we shall see, for understanding that social relations, and concern for law and order, are not just imposed upon the individual, but result from active needs and strivings whose roots are established in earliest infancy.

Before proceeding further, let me first make clear the sense in which I shall be using the term *guilt*, for there are two main meanings and I wish to focus only upon one. The use with which many of you will be most familiar is that in which someone is held guilty of having done something wrong: he is pronounced guilty by a judge, or by some other authority, or by his parents, or friends, in short a judgment of guilt from outside the person. The second use is that of guilt in the sense of how someone feels, that of personal guilt. You will know that these two uses are not the same, for it is possible, and indeed not uncommon, to be held to be guilty of some misdeed but not to feel guilty about it. And, psychologically even more interesting, it is possible to feel guilty without having done anything which others would declare you to be guilty of—to feel intensely guilty for some reason or other which may be vague—perhaps for thoughts we might have—or even for reasons which may be entirely out of the reach of our conscious minds.

It is upon this latter sense of the feeling of guilt that psychoanalysis has concentrated its attention. It is this feeling of guilt, or conscience, that is so fundamental to our capacity to become social beings. It is the mental process that Freud attributed to the mental structure which he named the superego, but I shall return to that in a moment.

Everyone knows what it is like to feel guilty. In its mildest form it is that sense of having done wrong, of something inside you speaking to you and telling yourself that it was wrong. In more intense form, it is that inner voice criticizing and castigating. It can be ceaseless and unrelenting, taking over our thoughts completely, until it seems that everyone must know what is going on in our minds. Our expression may change and become suffused with the guilt we feel within. We are forced, in order to assuage the guilt, to do something about our wrongdoing; to make reparation in some way and so gain relief from inner judgment. In still more extreme form, guilt may reach pathological proportion, leaving the person abject and depressed, a prey to unconscious feelings of having harmed or damaged or destroyed others, of being worthless and of meriting only the severest punishment and retribution.

II

Freud's first big breakthrough to an understanding of the norms which control our behavior from inside came from his analysis of the Oedipus complex. The theme is well known. The young child, between the ages of four and six, deeply attached to his mother with a strong unconscious sexual bond, finds himself in an unconscious rivalry situation with his father. Jealous of his mother, envious of his father, he unconsciously wishes his father dead. Overwhelmed by anxiety, and seized by guilt, he suffers acute disturbance. How is the conflict to be resolved? In Freud's terms the boy suffering severely from the threat of being castrated turns to his father and identifies with him. He takes over his father's standards for his own—in other words internalizes these standards, and takes over the responsibility for the control of his own behavior.

By this process, the resolution of the Oedipus complex results in a situation in which standards of conduct that previously existed in the form of external parental remonstrance and control, now become the boy's own internal standards, by virtue of which he tries to control his own behavior. The father's voice from without becomes the voice from within. As Freud has put it, the superego is the inheritor of the Oedipus complex.

By the superego, Freud refers to a mental organization, a structural concept, which differentiates out from the ego. Superego formation takes place as a result of identification with outer figures—or, in more general terms, with external objects. This identification occurs by means of introjection, the process of taking in and establishing the object inside. The superego thus built up acts as though above the ego, scrutinizing our thoughts and impulses, and exercising a moralistic censorship and control.

These identification processes, as Freud has shown, are fundamental to all group formations. Thus, for example in religious groups, identification takes place with the religious figure—God, or Christ, or Buddha, or Mohammed—so that all followers of the particular faith introject or contain a common set of precepts or controls and can behave in common ways through this identification. By the same means we can learn to obey common laws.

But to describe this process is to raise numberless additional questions. How is it that external standards become internalized? What does internalized mean? What kind of mental structure must be assumed when we speak of internalized parents? To put it into more technical language, what is the nature of the process by which we identify with another person and not only accept his standards but internalize or introject them; that is to say, how does introjective identification come about?

Moreover, what are the factors which determine the nature of the Oedipus complex and its resolution? Why is it more intense in some children than in others? Why does it lead to constructive identification and superego formation in some, and why to a restrictive superego in others?

The answers to some of these questions were indicated by Karl Abraham (1927). Abraham picked up Freud's formulations and considered them in terms of the earlier developmental stages in the life of the child. He differentiated out the more primitive aspects of development, and laid the foundation for our understanding of infant mental life. Three main features of his theories are of particular interest to our present theme. First, his hypothesis of an early oral phase of development followed by an anal phase; second, the emphasis he placed upon the psychological processes of expulsion and incorporation, or projection and introjection; and third, his recognition of the great importance of Freud's double instinct theory—the interaction between love and hate.

In short, Abraham, before his untimely death in the mid-1920s, was actively concerned with unfolding the picture of development in infancy and the first few years of life. In that period he sought the sources of character formation and of psychological disturbance. The infant he perceived as torn by conflict between its loving impulses and powerful forces of hate and sadism. Its earliest relations were lived in terms of active fantasies of taking into itself the mother and breast upon which it suckled, either lovingly establishing them inside or sadistically biting and attacking them. This phase he saw as suc-

ceeded by one in which the primary emotional zone moved
from the mouth to the anus, with the infant's external
objects related to in terms of loving or sadistic incorporation or expulsion.

The significance of Abraham's formulations in terms
of zones need not here concern us. The important thing
is his description of the way the infant makes relations
with the people in his outside world in terms of fantasies
of taking them in and forcing them out; it is as though
psychological relationships in the primitive recesses of
the mind are carried out in terms of digestive processes—a
process not unfamiliar to those who work with the problems of psychosis.

III

Upon these foundations has been constructed the particular picture of infant and early child development with
which many British psychoanalysts have been associated,
and which has come to be identified as the British School.
The central figure in these developments has been Melanie Klein, and certain of her formulations may help to
throw some further light upon the question of how moral
standards and social behavior come about.

Taking as her starting point Freud's formulation of
the Oedipus complex and its significance for the child's
social relationships, Klein, through her direct analysis
of children from the age of three, observed the existence
of much earlier processes akin to those hypothesized by
Abraham. She noted especially the way in which these
very young children, and infants, are in fact tied up in
social relationships from the very beginning. The infant
is actively concerned about its objects. It loves, and its
love is intensified and supported when it is satisfied. It
hates, and its hate is aroused and expressed when it feels

frustrated. It responds in the very early months not only to parental handling and fondling and feeding, but also to parental expression.

The central point, however, is that the infant is an active agent. It feels and reacts. This active mental life of the infant is carried out in terms of very primitive fantasies akin to those suggested by Freud and elaborated by Abraham. I should like to try to outline these, so that those who have not had the good fortune to have direct experience of working with small children may get some feeling for what I am talking about. When I say that the infant is active, I mean that its reactions are not just the project of stimuli from its environment. It is not limited in its behavior simply to responding to whatever happens to it—feeling satiated and content when fed, angry when frustrated, disturbed when ill. On the contrary, the infant (and certainly the young child) reaches out to its environment. It colors its environment with its own feelings. It makes assumptions about its environment, and its responses are duly influenced by those assumptions.

One of the infant's earliest tasks is to learn to sort out the difference between what is going on in reality in its environment, in itself, and in its relationship with its environment, and what the infant unconsciously supposes to be going on as a result of its own fantasies and impulses. This task, described by Freud in terms of the process of reality-testing, is one that is never completed. Is there any one of us who can lay claim to that perfection of understanding of himself and his world that allows him to say that his perceptions and his judgments are unclouded by his own unconscious prejudices or by his impulses, wishes, or desires? There is always the struggle, and reality is not always the victor, between the command of the reality principle on the one hand, and on the other hand, the pleasure principle dictating that we treat the world as though it is in fact taken up with nothing other than meeting our own needs, or at least ought to be.

It is out of this struggle to get through to reality that the early foundation of the superego, and thus of our capacity for social behavior, is laid down. For, let us note, there is a very real sense in which ideas of good and bad exist from the very beginning. I say "ideas" of good and bad, where perhaps I really mean feelings. It is that sense of satisfaction and love, or of frustration and hate and rage, that constitutes the primitive emotional substrate of the idea of goodness and badness.

It is in finding a formulation of how the mental life of the infant goes on that one of the greatest difficulties arises. How are we to describe in words that which occurs in feeling and behavior but is not expressed in words? Moreover, the moment we try to put into words how an infant thinks and feels, it is all too easy to assume that we are attributing to the infant the self-same words and ideas. With this difficulty in mind, let us attempt the task of outlining what in Melanie Klein's theory is the critical stage in child development prior to the Oedipus complex—that stage occurring during the second six months of life.

The infant is in a situation in which maturation has occurred to the point where conscious experience is becoming a significant part of total experience. The infant is aware of his relationship with his mother as a whole intact object, a person with continuity. The use of language is looming on the horizon. Under these circumstances, there is a problem of a special kind encountered, head-on and unavoidable—the problem of mixed feelings, of conflict, of ambivalence. The difficulty of this problem for human beings of all ages cannot be overestimated. It is the problem of enduring shortcomings in those we love, of recognizing good features in those we dislike or oppose, of being capable of experiencing conflict, that simultaneity of positive and negative feelings, without turning away from conflict by emphasizing the good and denying the bad, or vice versa.

In the infant, the problem of handling conflict is a major one. To hate the one you love, because you are frustrated, can be a catastrophically frightening feeling when you are so dependent; to love the one you hate can be exceedingly difficult when explosive fits of rage have taken over the whole of experience for the time being. But the main difficulty centers on the problems attendant upon ambivalence itself. Love and hate, simultaneously, for the same person, are the prime producer of feelings of guilt. Most of us can recall situations in which this kind of conflict resulted in guilt. In the infant, much more is at the mercy of feeling, because feelings are so much less controlled, the conflict and the guilt are incomparably greater.

In order to appreciate the problem of the infant in its first encounter with the exigencies of the *depressive position* (the term used by Klein [1940] to refer to the complex of impulses, conflicts, anxieties, and defenses in the period under consideration) we must consider, however briefly, the situation that existed before, in the very earliest stages of development. Here evidence from child analysis, child observation, and the treatment of psychosis, and of psychotic phenomena in the neurotic and the so-called normal, suggests the following picture.

The infant is from birth impelled by very strong impulses of love and hate, the hating or destructive impulses being at the high point of the whole of the individual's life. Ambivalence, conflict, and guilt are avoided by splitting mechanisms. That is to say, the infant experiences either his good or bad impulses, his good or bad objects,

separately and not together. He hates the bad, and loves
the good, and deals with the opposite feelings in each case
by denial and by projection. In essence when enraged, he
puts his love and the parts of himself he loves into his
good objects (in the earliest phases into his mother and
the feeding breast), and is able to hate the bad or frustrating mother and breast in an uncomplicated and ful-
some manner. Or, vice versa, he splits off his hate and
the parts of himself that he hates, and projects them into
his bad objects, leaving himself free to love without re-
servation or conflict.

The price to be paid for this freedom from conflict is
considerable. The good objects become idealized: and as
such they are demanding of care. The bad objects become
persecuting: they threaten and harass, and the persecution cannot be mitigated by love and reassurance, because
of the splitting that has occurred.

Under these conditions, our first relationships with
the world are established, and the precursors of the superego and of social relationships are formed. For along
with the projection of its own impulses, the infant identifies with its objects, and introjects and incorporates
them. With the concrete fantasies characteristic of this
stage of development, the idealized objects in the surrounding world, with all their bountiful but demanding
characteristics, are experienced as being inside as well
as outside the infant. So too are the bad frightening objects into which the infant has projected his hate and
destructiveness, and which are then experienced as internal persecuting and terrifying things.

So an internal world is built up in which good is good
and bad is bad, and the groundwork of morality, the primitive sense of good and bad, is fixed. The very earliest
superego precursors are thus built up from a mixture of
threatening internal bad objects, and of idealized de-

manding objects. The nature and strength of these processes will be much influenced by the infant's experiences,
and by the strength of his own impulses. If he experiences
normally good care and love, and if his own loving impulses are sufficiently strong and his hate of manageable
proportion, these primitive social processes will not be
too difficult. If, however, hate is strong, and frustration
high, then the external and the internal world will be
deeply split into highly idealized objects making strong
demands, and very frightening persecutors. The resulting
internal situation is nightmarish; and a foundation is
laid for social relationships being experienced as harsh,
and persecuting. This latter condition is important in
criminality, where one of the main features is the failure
to advance significantly past this state of splitting and
projection mechanisms. The lovelessness so characteristic
of the psychopathic criminal is not so much a matter of
lovelessness, as the inability to bring loving impulses to
bear upon the criminal's hostility and destructiveness.
By maintaining the separation, the capacity for guilt does
not develop, for he remains totally unconcerned about the
objects of his hate. His love is split off and denied, or
directed elsewhere.

IV

Given an adequate balance between love and hate, the
infant is able to advance toward the depressive position.
His growing capacities and skills strengthen the reality
sense, and make him more aware of the wholeness of his
objects. Splitting mechanisms are weakened; and he begins to recognize that the objects he hates and those he
loves are the same. As ambivalence and conflict enter the
mental scene, extremes of pain are experienced. For under the influence of the primitive processes we have de-

scribed, the infant's hate is experienced as destructive of the very things he loves. When hate takes over, the infant has fantasies of having injured and damaged his loved objects. The depressive reaction encountered is to set the scene for every subsequent experience of loss. Where the experience of the infant has been such that the internal situation is not too threatening, then love and sadness can be felt when conflict occurs. The sense of guilt can develop, not too harshly, but enough to help the infant to want to make reparation to the object he has in fantasy so miserably treated and damaged. The function of guilt expressed by the emerging superego is to allow of concern for the object, without having to deny love, and the reassurance that the infant's own hate and destructiveness can be mitigated by love.

If the conditions are not so good, then refuge is sought in various defenses. Reality is denied, and manic activity and playfulness take the place of guilt and concern. Or depression takes over, with inaction and immobility. Or there is a retreat, a regression, to the more primitive processes that I have described—with a return to splitting, projection, and denial mechanisms, and the elimination once again of ambivalent feelings and conflict.

This kind of regression to primitive splitting mechanisms may occur at any time in life when a person is threatened by conflict and guilt, and does occur, at least to some extent, every time we experience loss and mourning. In the previous chapter, I illustrated this kind of situation in the adult, with childhood memories to show how feelings of guilt are avoided by denying love and insisting that persecution is the order of the day. The basic psychological mechanism was that of nursing a grievance, and the clinical material showed how extremely damaging it could be to social relationships.

V

One point about the clinical material described in the previous chapter is that it may demonstrate how much a retreat from guilt and anxiety carries with it a retreat from reality. For the infant to move forward, to make progress toward an enhanced sense of reality, it must learn to cope with conflict and guilt. In order to do that, it must have sufficient confidence in its capacity to love to enable it to tolerate the pain of guilt or depressive anxiety. This pain reaches its peak at the time of weaning. The feeding breast is lost. Its loss is mourned—a process in which, as Freud has described, the fullness of love is gradually detached from the lost object, and life can go on. To the extent that the loss is experienced in unconscious fantasy as the result of the infant's own sadistic aggressiveness, mourning is warded off and inhibited, because to that extent the pain is too unbearable. "I have destroyed what I love, I have lost it through my own hate" is the emotional experience. It is an experience that in later life when once we can talk, we express poignantly in terms of "if only—if only I hadn't . . . if only I could have another chance."

But time goes on. The infant becomes the young child. It can walk, and talk, and get about. The early stages of the oedipal situation begin. We can pick up the thread of our earlier theme and ask once again, what are the conditions under which conscious norms of conduct are established.

If the earlier depressive position has been successfully worked through, then the oedipal situation will be experienced as less threatening than it would otherwise be. For the child is less persecuted by its superego, and therefore is not subjected to such harsh treatment internally for its jealousy, and rivalry and hatred. At the same time, it has less need to project into its parents its own destructiveness and hate, and thus they are not experienced as persecuting disciplinarians, however firm or rigorous their handling. Under such conditions, parental admonition can be perceived in perspective, in proportion, for what it is, without too much of a persecutory increment from the child; that is, without the child unconsciously perceiving them as frightening and hostile.

If, however, there has been a less successful working through of the depressive position, the child through its own projections of hate and badness into its parents will be subject to an oedipal situation which will be experienced as more harsh and persecuting than it would otherwise be.

Thus, in short, under moderately good conditions, the full-scale superego, with its norms of behavior, will precipitate out, and parental norms identified with and internalized in a constructive way. Codes of conduct can be accepted and conformed to, in an understanding way. Under unconscious persecuting conditions, the parental norms become yet a further harsh admonishing voice added to the superego.

VI

From these considerations it would appear that our ability to conform to the norms and codes and laws that make human relationships possible is not just something forced upon us from outside. We start out in a situation of primitive object relations—social relations—and with an endowment of conflicting love and hate that takes us into active relationships with our objects. As a result of ambivalence and conflict, we develop early on a primitive sense of concern for our objects, and for what we do to them. In short, the live human being *is* concerned about others, and does not have to wait to be taught through outside pressure to be concerned about them.

To take but one example, I cite the inability of our society to control inflation without unemployment, and our growing acceptance of the notion that 5 percent unemployment may have to be tolerated. We cannot afford to tolerate this notion for there is nothing that society can arrange that is so calculated to bring the primitive anxieties we have described so forcibly into play. And these primitive anxieties are not allayed by unemployment benefits, for in addition to the threat of financial deprivation, there is also the threat of role-deprivation; that is, deprivation of the right to participate in a social relationship with others, in creating our economic security. And unconsciously the full impact is felt in terms of deprivation of an effective social relationship in the early care and feeding situation. Paranoid anxieties are added to objective economic fears, and the mixture is intensely disruptive for the mental health of the individual.

The basis of social concern lies in the capacity for guilt which results from internal conflict. By virtue of guilt and concern we seek for external support for our good and constructive social impulses. Such support, to be found initially in early maternal care, is later sought from both parents, and then from teachers, the law, and other parental surrogates.

The existence of deeply rooted norms of justice and social cohesion has been borne in upon me by my experience in research in social and industrial relations. Here, underneath the turmoil and conflict on the surface, one finds underlying norms of equity, justice and fairness, even, for example, in such conflict areas as payment. The problem is to formulate policies that express these deep and primitive norms, so that justice can be seen to be done. Indeed, one of the conclusions to which we are led is that if a sound mental health program must include not only treatment but prevention, then prevention must include attention to our modes of social organization and our laws—the way we organize and run our schools, our industries, and our government; the way we construct our laws; the way in which every institution which mediates social relations is established.

Sound social relationships and soundly constructed law are thus immensely important for the psychological health and well-being of the members of society. They support the constructive impulses in individuals and reduce the amount of projection of hate and destructiveness. For when our laws and codes are not soundly based (as, for example, they are not where differential payment and reward are concerned) not only are they perceived as manifestly unfair, but they attract masses of projected guilt and persecution. The effect is that society itself, or its leaders, is experienced not just as bad or inadequate, but as persecuting and beyond repair. Paranoid attitudes are reinforced and expressed in such ways as political splits, prejudices, xenophobia, and in social withdrawal, strife, and chaos.

One point, however, perhaps needs mentioning before I finish. In all that I have described, I have assumed that in the connections between the adult and his laws and social behavior, there are also still in play the more primitive processes which so markedly color the quality of an individual's perception of and relation to his society. I tried to illustrate this process in showing how the child's development in the depressive position, and in the oedipal situation, could readily regress or throw back to the earlier and more primitive processes of splitting and projection. It would appear that I am suggesting that the adult carries with him the whole of his past. And, of course, that is what I am suggesting. For that is one of the basic tenets of the psychoanalytic model of human behavior. The accretions of experience are piled on layer after layer, and, as Freud has described, can be observed in the same way that archaeological findings are exposed layer after layer, deeper and deeper into the past.

Unlike archaeological remains, however, the earlier psychological layers remain active. They are dynamic, and affect the ongoing psychological field. As we work out our current social relationships, we are influenced by the extent to which our more primitive conflicts and reactions are aroused and come unconsciously into our perceptions and responses.

Thus it is that a healthy society, like good psychotherapy, helps to support the healthy side of human behavior. As we work out our social relationships, so too do we work through, again and again, the more primitive conflicts, anxieties, and guilt that we carry with us from our infant and our childhood days. And most important, our reality sense, as well as our concern for others, which we ought never to take for granted, is thereby reinforced and extended.

REFERENCES

Abraham, K. (1927), *Selected Papers on Psychoanalysis*. London: Hogarth Press.
Klein, M. (1940), Mourning and its relation to manic-depressive states. *Internat. J. Psycho-Anal.*, 21:71–93.

Name Index

Abercrombie, M. L. J., 154–155
Abraham, K., 399–400, 401
Aeneas, 184
Aristotle, 38

Bach, J. S., 298–299
Bacon, F., 3
Bagehot, W., 9
Bergson, H., 225, 226
Billis, D., 45
Bion, W. R., 157, 193n, 322, 325, 335, 345
Bonaparte, M., 239–240
Bridgman, 12, 250
Brown, W., 12, 40, 272, 364
Bruner, J. S., 109

Campbell, N. R., 260–261, 274n, 279n, 280n, 284–285n, 290n
Church, R., 298
Constable, J., 299
Coombs, C., 262, 263
Couchman, T., 62–63, 111
Croce, B., 308

Dante, 306–308, 328–329
Davidson, S. S., 336
Dawes, R., 262, 287–288n
Democritus, 226
Dickens, C., 304
Donatello, 299
Dummett, M., 214

Edwards, W., 286n
Einstein, A., 226
Erikson, E., 116
Evans, J. S., 45, 102–103

Freud, S., 3, 114–116, 167–168, 194n, 215, 217n, 217–218, 218n, 222–223, 224, 233, 239–240, 302–303, 309–310, 312, 324, 331, 345, 361, 363–366, 368–369, 371–372, 391, 396–398, 399, 401–402, 407, 411

Galileo, 248, 270
Gauguin, P., 299
Gibson, R. O., 45, 109
Gittings, R., 301
Goethe, J. W. von, 299
Goldsmith, O., 299
Goldstein, K., 334–335n
Goya, F. J. de, 299
Greenfield, P. M., 109
Guttentag, M., 286n

Hartmann, H., 336
Hays, W. L., 261–262, 264
Hegel, G., 226
Hendrick, I., 331n
Heraclitus, 225, 226
Humphreys, P. C., 241
Husserl, E., 216

413

Vesalius, 9
Virgil, 326

Weber, M., 21
Wilcox, H. J., 290n

Wishuda, A., 241

Yeats, W. B., 177

Zeno, 222

Subject Index

Absolute zero, 275–276
Absolute zero-based concatenation, 274–278
Abstraction levels, 45
    higher, 96
Academic freedom, 15
Action, with decision making, 345–347
Additive concatenation, 275
Administration, definition of, 1
Aggression, against work, 185
Aging, sense of, 321
Ambition, excessive, 186
Ambivalence
    capacity to tolerate, 327
    difficulty coping with, 314
    in infant, 403–404
    resolution of, 32
    in work process, 338
Anatomy, discoveries in, 9
Annihilation, threat of, 385
Anxiety
    with assessment, 165–166
    capacity to tolerate, 347
    and capacity to work, 353–354
    decision and, 178
    defenses against, 186, 189, 193–194; manic, 186–187; obsessional, 187; paranoid-schizoid regression, 188
    depressive, 185

    increase in, with bad management, 188–189
    Oedipus complex and, 397–400
    paranoid, 409
    psychotic, 383–384, 391–393; defenses against, 386–387; and sense of justice, 371–393
    sources of, in intermediate zone, 30–31
    splitting and fragmentation with, 363–364
    with symbol formation, 183–184
    with symbolic work, 178–179
    with use of discretion and decision, 332
    work and, 181–182
Assessment
    anxieties connected with, 165–166
    difficulty of, 161–163
    in human relationships, 163–164
Asset values, 58–60
Authority-accountability relationships, 28, 39

Balance. *See also* Equilibrium
    achievement of, 179
    sense of justice and, 374

417